Active
Visual J++™

Scott Robert Ladd

Microsoft *Press*

PUBLISHED BY
Microsoft Press
A Division of Microsoft Corporation
One Microsoft Way
Redmond, Washington 98052-6399

Library of Congress Cataloging-in-Publication Data
Ladd, Scott.
    Active Visual J++ / Scott Robert Ladd.
       p.   cm.
    Includes index.
    ISBN 1-57231-609-8
    1. Java (Computer program language)   2. Microsoft Visual J++.
  I. Title.
  QA76.76.J38L33   1997
  005.13'3—dc21   97-20719
                                               CIP

Printed and bound in the United States of America.

1 2 3 4 5 6 7 8 9 QMQM 2 1 0 9 8 7

Distributed to the book trade in Canada by Macmillan of Canada, a division of Canada Publishing Corporation.

A CIP catalogue record for this book is available from the British Library.

Microsoft Press books are available through booksellers and distributors worldwide. For further information about international editions, contact your local Microsoft Corporation office. Or contact Microsoft Press International directly at fax (206) 936-7329.

Acquisitions Editor: Eric Stroo
Project Editor: Barbara Moreland
Technical Editors: Marc Young, Jim Fuchs

Back in the mid-1970s, personal computers were scarcer than hen's teeth. But my small town high school had a connection to a nearby university, by way of what is now an ancient teletype terminal. My parents saw my fascination with technology and bought one of the first personal computers. From that foundation, I built a career. Twenty years later, I'm still banging out code, on machines that grow more sophisticated each year.

It is my parents' support—not any hardware—that made this book possible. So I dedicate this work to my mother and father. Wherever I wanted to go as a child, they provided a path. May all children be so fortunate.

Contents

Preface

This is a book about interfaces, both human and machine. There is the interface between the programmer and the Java language, which the first part of this book addresses by teaching you a philosophy of object-oriented Java programming. Another interface, one between software components, comes to the fore in the second part of the book. There I discuss the Java models for creating independent software components using Microsoft's Component Object Model (COM) and the more general Java Bean technology. The final interface is covered in the third part. That interface occurs between an application and its user—the look and feel of *your* application, as expressed by using the Abstract Window Toolkit to develop Java applets.

So far, Java has been used primarily to create nifty visual effects and fancy web-page features; if you browse the web, you'll notice a dearth of serious applications. In part, this condition stems from Java's relative youth: it has been only two years since its introduction. And since its debut, Java has evolved rapidly, with new language features and packages appearing almost daily. In such a heady environment, it's no wonder that Java programmers are still learning about the capabilities of their new tool. Contrary to pundits' complaints that Java isn't ready for the big leagues, Java is moving toward a day when it will be suited to almost any development task. This book addresses the need for examples of serious applications in Java; it's about building complex, useful programs creatively and efficiently. In the following chapters, I'll show you how to put Java to work, to get the most from a language that goes far beyond its web-based roots.

You won't learn to write Java applications by looking at snippets of code and small applets. I've always liked to teach programming by showing programs, and that's what I've done in this book. Some of the example programs are quite large—but they contain code that does something substantial. I hope these applications will be interesting, challenging, and even a bit entertaining.

Scott Robert Ladd
Silverton, Colorado
June 1997
srladd@frontier.net
http://www.frontier.net/~srladd

Part 1

Object-Oriented Programming

Capital ———

Fluted Shaft ———

Base ———

Tasting Java

Programming shouldn't be a haphazard activity; you need to understand your tools and their rationale before you can create quality software. So where does Java fit into the world of computer technology? At the most basic level, it's a new programming language, developed for the purpose of delivering software over the Internet. But Java is much more; it represents, in many ways, the current state of the art in software development. I see Java as part of a common theme that runs through the evolution of software development. In this opening chapter, I put Java into a philosophical context so that you will understand not only the *what* but also the *why* of this new development tool.

The Internet as a Communications System

Technology is the amplifier that makes human civilization possible. What we can't lift with muscles, we lift with machines; if our listeners are too far away to hear us, we use devices to transmit our voices. If anything sets humans apart from other species, it is our dependence on—and fascination with—the inventions of our imaginations.

We rarely know where a new technology will take us. The Internet began as a system for reliable communication between military, educational, and government organizations. In that first incarnation, the Internet was useful only to those who mastered its arcane interface, and most of the information was in an unexciting text form. That's why most people didn't know or care that computers all over the world were communicating with one another. What personal computer user would want to look at text files and type cryptic commands when his or her own computer had a flashy graphic interface? As late as 1992, I would talk to computer users about the Internet, only to hear questions such as, "What's in it for me?"

> *"Technology is not an image of the world but a way of operating on reality."*
>
> **Octavio Paz (1914–),
> Nobel Prize–winning Mexican poet**

Then, in the late 1980s, scientists at the European Laboratory of Particle Physics (known by its old initials as CERN) had an idea: create a universal language for describing graphic pages of information, and build a program—called a browser—to interpret that "Hypertext Markup Language" (HTML). CERN's invention allowed Internet users to create and view point-and-click documents that contained colorful images, formatted text, and more. The researchers named their Internet extension the *World Wide Web*.

Little did they imagine the popularity of the web today. You can't get people to *stop* talking about the Internet! If anything, the poor system is now overloaded with everything from recipes to images from deep space. Advertisers try to sell you new cars and new ideas. Every day the number of ways in which the web is used is increasing.

The Internet is a salient example of a technological amplifier. Here is a tool that communicates images and documents between people who otherwise would never know each other. The value of the Internet goes beyond online shopping or term paper research—the real power of the Internet is that it lets people interactively share *ideas*. Some people may feel threatened by freewheeling intellectual intercourse; others see incredible opportunity for human growth and exploration.

Programming for the Web

Like any robust organism, the World Wide Web continues to evolve. The first versions of HTML were limited to displaying text and images, which was great until some people decided that they wanted their web pages to be interactive. The web could, they reasoned, send more than fancy documents: it could distribute software. And to do that, they needed to define a way to write programs that could be executed through an Internet connection on any type of computer system.

That isn't as easy as it sounds. Although most of us use Intel-based PCs in our businesses and homes, the web is truly worldwide and diverse. Browsers run on Macintoshes, workstations, UNIX systems, and even some mainframes—machines that are highly incompatible when it comes to the mechanics of drawing images or displaying text. You have no way of knowing what type of equipment might be used to look at your web pages. And consider the future: today's high-tech wonder is tomorrow's obsolete junk. If you're going to be smart and plan ahead, you need to build Internet software that is universal—that is, you must not base it on a specific hardware or operating system architecture.

The design of the web itself provides an answer. Writers create HTML documents that conform to a standard; they know their work will be viewable on any machine running a browser that supports that standard. The writers don't need to know the intricacies of Windows or UNIX or whatever—they just need to know that any machine hooked up to the web is going to have a browser that displays their documents. When a new operating system or hardware architecture comes along, its programmers can provide *one* browser program to access the entire existing universe of web information. That's a lot more practical than rewriting every document on the web to fit every new computer!

Visual J++ takes these ideas a step further by letting developers build universal software, just as HTML allows the creation of universal documents.

Virtual Computing with Java

A browser is a virtual document display that reads an HTML document and interprets it according to the requirements of a specific computer. A step beyond the browser is the *virtual machine,* which you can think of as a theoretical computer inside a physical computer. The virtual machine software translates its generalized operations into the appropriate instructions for a given hardware and software environment. If you design a program for a virtual machine, it will run on any kind of computer that implements a compatible emulator. Programmers no longer need to worry about where their programs will run; they simply write code for a virtual machine.

Java is a programming language for virtual machines. After you write a Java program—usually called an *applet*—you'll compile it into a special "virtual machine language." In that form, your applet will run on any computer that implements the virtual machine correctly. As computers change, new virtual machines will let old Java programs run without modification. Again, the focus has changed: instead of writing separate programs for specific computers, programmers write one program for virtual machines and leave the hardware-specific details to the virtual machine developers. Now software is as universal as HTML documents.

The virtual machine also provides something else: a predefined library of program components. All programming languages have a standard library of functions or types; the compiled forms of these are usually linked into a program at compile time to provide services such as I/O and video control. But library components are usually system-specific and often redundant; for example, every C program I wrote for UNIX included the standard I/O package. Even with dynamic-linking technology, each type of computer requires a custom version of the standard components.

The Java application programming interface (API) is a set of functional packages implemented *inside* the virtual machine. If your Java program uses the standard I/O and file packages, your compiled code won't contain copies of those functions—instead, your applet will have links to equivalent features in the virtual machine. The concept is similar to that of dynamic-link libraries (DLLs), in which compiled code is put into modules that are called by many programs. But whereas DLL code is system-specific, the Java API is built into every virtual machine.

The design of the API makes Java eminently efficient, since only the unique applet code will travel over the Internet. If the API were linked into the applets, as library functions are in C++, people would be downloading the standard packages over and over. The API functions *belong* in the virtual machine, where they can efficiently implement system-specific functions through a generic interface.

But Why Java?

So why was it necessary to invent a new programming language when there are so many already? At last count, I've written professional software in more than a dozen languages, ranging from FORTRAN and COBOL to Smalltalk and C++. Why not use an existing programming language for web programming? Wasn't C++ supposed to be the ultimate tool for writing programs? And isn't Java just a variant of C++?

C++ has been the darling of the computer industry for several years. All of a decade old now, it is largely compatible with C, supporting many of the idiosyncrasies found in its antecedent. In turn, C traces its ancestry to even older languages, going back to the dim past of the late 1960s. Backward compatibility is a great thing as long as you don't drown in hereditary quirks. Unfortunately, C++ is loaded with odd little bits of syntax, the legacy of its history. The ANSI/ISO standard for C++ fills two very large binders on my shelf.

Java, on the other hand, rejects compatibility with C and C++, streamlining its syntax and adding some much-needed new features. Although Java's syntax is largely taken from C++, its purpose is to provide online software over the Internet. Gone are templates and other tools for creating large applications; dangerous pointers have been replaced by an extended (and very reliable) definition of references. And the Java API library is quite different from the standard library included with C++. You'll find a thorough introduction to these differences in Chapter 3.

Microsoft Visual J++ is an interactive development environment for Java that is integrated into Microsoft Developer Studio; from within Visual J++, you can create a Java application or applet. Developer Studio also provides a powerful interactive debugger and tools for managing Java classes and resources. Traditional Java tools have been modeled on the Unix command-line model, but Visual J++ lets you build Java applications in the Microsoft Windows environment, using tools first introduced in Microsoft's popular Visual C++ product.

One more thing: Java was defined with security in mind. In today's world, you can't simply trust in the reliability and safety of every program on the Internet. Because Java programs are designed to execute automatically with the loading of a web page, all sorts of security issues arise. The virtual machine prevents applets from operating outside a specific domain within a computer. For applets that go outside the virtual machine's limits—by accessing ActiveX controls, for example—Microsoft Visual J++ implements a security system using Authenticode technology. I'll be talking about Authenticode more in Chapter11.

Object-Oriented Programming

Java is called an *object-oriented* programming language. What does that mean? Is it just another trendy buzzword, or is there a reason why most new programming languages say that they're object-oriented?

Function-Oriented Programs

"Object-oriented" refers to a philosophy of computer program design. The first programs didn't really *have* a philosophy—they began at the beginning and generally ran straight through until they reached their endpoint. Their job was to complete a narrowly defined task, such as performing a calculation. As programs grew more complex, languages such as Pascal and C came into being. These languages allowed programmers to organize a piece of software into its functional components. A specific task—reading a data file, for example—could be localized in a single routine. If anything went wrong with the process of writing to the file, the source of the problem would be found within that routine, thus simplifying the debugging process. And function-oriented programming let programmers compile routines into libraries. Once a routine was working, it could be saved for use with any number of programs.

A consequence of function-oriented design was that programs tended to define complex information in terms of structures and sets of related functions. In small programs, this wasn't much of a problem, but in large applications with thousands of lines of code, it could be impossible to find every instance in which a particular piece of data was manipulated. The more sophisticated a program was, the more types of information were being processed and the easier it was to overlook side effects and unintentional corruption of data. Confusion and conflict were even more likely in an environment in which many programmers worked on the same project.

To help them build reliable software, computer scientists introduced a new design concept based on a literal interpretation of the term *data processing*. Although the process is certainly important, they felt that their real focus should be on *what is being processed and how*. In other words, programs should be designed around data objects. So data types and their related functions are the focal point of object-oriented software development.

Programming with Objects

Object-oriented programming came into vogue in the 1980s, with the advent of languages such as Smalltalk and C++. An *object* is simply something a program works with—an action or a data record type. Object-oriented programming languages allow programs to define components that describe both an internal structure and an external interface. The functions that manipulate data become a part of the data type, linked to it intimately in a technique known as *encapsulation*. When a function is part of an object, it is called a *method*. Yes, the terminology is new, but anyone who has written "structured" code will understand the philosophy behind associating functions with data. Object-oriented coding is not so much new as it is a refinement of what has always been considered good programming practice.

In essence, object-oriented programming changed the focus in program design from an emphasis on what a program was doing to an emphasis on what it was acting on. And therein lies a philosophical shift that can be difficult to grasp. Essentially, an object should be a black box: you access the object through its methods, and you should have no need to know what is actually going on "inside" the object. The term for this is *abstraction,* and you use it every time you program. For instance, how often have you needed to know the internal data structure of a floating-point number? Probably never; you just define a variable and use it according to a defined set of rules. When you code the expression 2.0 + 3.5, there's no need for you to know how to load the values into the math coprocessor—the details are handled by the compiler. And the same principle should hold true for an object you define: the object definition, known as a *class,* tells you what can and can't be done to its objects by declaring publicly accessible methods. You needn't know what is going on inside the black box; your programs simply work with the expressed definition of an object. Think of a class as the definition of a new type in your program; if you create a class named *Record*, you can use it to create objects, just as you would with an intrinsic type such as *double*.

There's another reason to use object-orientation: it facilitates another time-honored practice—code recycling. Function-oriented programs allowed programmers to write a routine and store it for later use, but if they wanted to change or augment the workings of an existing routine, they had to write it anew. Object-oriented programming languages solve this problem by incorporating the concept of *extensibility,* letting programmers build on components they've already created. Programmers can *derive* a new class from an existing one, *extending* the original by adding support for new or changed features. In this way, new classes *inherit* from and enhance existing software components.

Let's say you're building a set of classes for handling documents in different formats. You begin with a generalized *Document* class that defines the attributes of all document types. Then you derive classes for specific file formats: *TextDoc,* *WordDoc,* and so forth. If necessary, the *TextDoc* class could be the basis for *RTFDoc* and *HTMLDoc.* An *RTFDoc* object would inherit the characteristics of a *TextDoc*— and through *TextDoc, RTFDoc* inherits from *Document.*

Figure 1-1 shows how these classes relate. The lines originate from the bottom of the *base* classes and connect the base classes with derived classes, showing the class hierarchy structure and flow of inheritance. In Chapter 2, I elaborate on the creation of class hierarchies, and Chapter 4 shows the organization of the Java API packages.

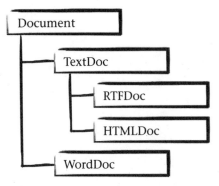

Figure 1-1. *An example of a class hierarchy.* TextDoc *and* WordDoc *extend the* Document *class; in turn,* RTFDoc *and* HTMLDoc *inherit from* TextDoc.

An Example

What follows is a complete Java program that I've written and tested with Microsoft Visual J++. I assume that you've used Java enough to understand the basic syntax, data types, and other language features. My goal is to point out the object-oriented aspects of the *Slideshow* applet, using real code.

The task that *Slideshow* performs is quite simple: it displays a sequence of six 64-by-64-pixel GIF images, changing the image according to a timer or the click of a mouse button. First take a look at the entire program. Then I'll discuss the parts of the program that relate to the topics I've introduced above.

SLIDESHOW.JAVA

```java
/*
   This program displays a sequence of images. The next image
   in the sequence is displayed when a specific number of
   seconds have passed or when the user clicks on the current
   image.
*/

// Import class packages
import java.applet.*;
import java.awt.*;

// Main Class for applet Slideshow
public class Slideshow extends Applet implements Runnable
{
    // Members for applet parameters
    //-----------------------------------------------------------
    private long m_delay = 5; // Delay in seconds

    // Members that define constants
    //-----------------------------------------------------------
    private final int NUM_IMAGES = 6; // Number of images in
                                      // set

    // Members for thread support
    //-----------------------------------------------------------
    Thread m_Slideshow = null;

    // Members for applet work
    //-----------------------------------------------------------
    private long     m_delay_ms;        // Delay in
                                        // milliseconds
    private Graphics m_Graphics;        // Applet's Graphics
                                        // context
    private Image    m_Images[];        // Array of Image
                                        // objects
    private int      m_nCurImage  = 0;  // Index of current
                                        // image
    private int      m_nImgWidth  = 0;  // Width of each
                                        // image
    private int      m_nImgHeight = 0;  // Height of each
                                        // image

    private boolean  m_fInitialized = false;

    // Parameter names. To change the name of a parameter, you
    // need only make a single change. Simply modify the
    // value of the parameter string below.
    //-----------------------------------------------------------
    private final String PARAM_delay = "delay";
```

```
// Slideshow Class Constructor
//------------------------------------------------------------
public Slideshow()
{
    // Nothing to do
}


// APPLET INFO SUPPORT:
// The getAppletInfo() method returns a string describing
// the applet's author, copyright date, or miscellaneous
// information
//------------------------------------------------------------
public String getAppletInfo()
{
    return "Name: Slideshow\r\n" +
           "Author: Scott Robert Ladd\r\n" +
           "Project: Active Visual J++\r\n" +
           "Created with Microsoft Visual J++ " +
           "Version 1.1";
}


// PARAMETER SUPPORT
// The getParameterInfo() method returns an array of
// strings describing the parameters understood by this
// applet
//
// Slideshow Parameter Information:
//  { "Name", "Type", "Description" },
//------------------------------------------------------------
public String[][] getParameterInfo()
{
    String[][] info =
    {
        {
        PARAM_delay, "long",
        "Number of seconds between slide changes"
        },
    };

    return info;
}


// The init() method is called by the AWT when an applet
// is first loaded or reloaded.  Override this method to
// perform whatever initialization your applet needs,
// such as initializing data structures, loading images
// or fonts, creating frame windows, setting the layout
// manager, or adding UI components.
//------------------------------------------------------------
```

(continued)

```java
public void init()
{
    // PARAMETER SUPPORT
    //          The following code retrieves the value of
    // each parameter specified with the <PARAM> tag and
    // stores it in a member variable
    //------------------------------------------------------
    String param;

    // delay: Number of seconds between slide changes
    //------------------------------------------------------
    param = getParameter(PARAM_delay);
    if (param != null)
        m_delay = Long.parseLong(param);

    // Set size of applet
    //------------------------------------------------------
    resize(64, 64);
}


// Place additional applet cleanup code here. destroy()
// is called when your applet is terminating and being
// unloaded.
//------------------------------------------------------------
public void destroy()
{
    // Nothing to do
}


// Slideshow image-drawing method
//------------------------------------------------------------
public void displayImage(Graphics g)
{
    // Draw current image in center of applet
    //------------------------------------------------------
    if (m_fInitialized)
    {
        g.drawImage(m_Images[m_nCurImage],
                    (size().width - m_nImgWidth)  / 2,
                    (size().height - m_nImgHeight) / 2,
                    null);
    }
}


// Slideshow draw next image in sequence
//------------------------------------------------------------
public void drawNext()
{
```

```
        // Draw next image in animation
        //----------------------------------------------------
        displayImage(m_Graphics);

        m_nCurImage++;

        if (m_nCurImage == NUM_IMAGES)
            m_nCurImage = 0;
    }

    // Slideshow Paint Handler
    //--------------------------------------------------------------
    public void paint(Graphics g)
    {

        // ANIMATION SUPPORT:
        // The following code displays a status message until
        // all the images are loaded. Then it calls
        // displayImage to display the current image.
        //----------------------------------------------------
        if (m_fInitialized)
        {
            // Clear the rectangle
            Rectangle r = g.getClipRect();
            g.clearRect(r.x, r.y, r.width, r.height);
            displayImage(g);
        }
        else
            g.drawString("Loading...", 10, 20);
    }

    // Start execution of the applet's thread
    //--------------------------------------------------------------
    public void start()
    {
        // Calculate the milliseconds of delay
        m_delay_ms = 1000 * m_delay;

        if (m_Slideshow == null)
        {
            m_Slideshow = new Thread(this);
            m_Slideshow.start();
        }
    }
```

(continued)

```java
// Stop execution of the applet's thread
//----------------------------------------------------------
public void stop()
{
    if (m_Slideshow != null)
    {
        m_Slideshow.stop();
        m_Slideshow = null;
    }
}


// The mouseDown() method is called if the mouse button
// is pressed while the mouse cursor is over the applet's
// portion of the screen
//----------------------------------------------------------
public boolean mouseDown(Event evt, int x, int y)
{
    // Skip to next image
    drawNext();
    return true;
}


// The run() method is called when the applet's thread is
// started
//----------------------------------------------------------
public void run()
{
    m_nCurImage = 0;

    // We don't need to reload the images when
    // reentering the page
    if (!m_fInitialized)
    {
        repaint();

        m_Graphics = getGraphics();
        m_Images   = new Image[NUM_IMAGES];

        // Load in all the images
        //--------------------------------------------------
        MediaTracker tracker = new MediaTracker(this);
        String imageName;

        // For each image in the sequence, this method
        // first constructs a string containing the path
        // to the image file; then it begins loading the
```

```
    // image into the m_Images array. Note that
    // the call to getImage will return before the
    // image is completely loaded.
    //------------------------------------------------------
    for (int i = 0; i < NUM_IMAGES; i++)
    {
        // Build path to next image
        //-------------------------------------------------
        imageName = "images/slide"
                + ((i < 10) ? "0" : "")
                + i + ".gif";

        m_Images[i] = getImage(getDocumentBase(),
                               imageName);

        tracker.addImage(m_Images[i], 0);
    }

    // Wait until all images are fully loaded
    //------------------------------------------------------
    try
    {
        tracker.waitForAll();
        m_fInitialized = !tracker.isErrorAny();
    }
    catch (InterruptedException e)
    {
    }
    if (!m_fInitialized)
    {
        stop();
        m_Graphics.drawString
            ("Error loading images!", 10, 40);
        return;
    }

    // Assume all images are same width and height.
    // In this case, the images are all 64-by-64
    // pixels, the same size as the applet's window.
    //------------------------------------------------------
    m_nImgWidth  = m_Images[0].getWidth(this);
    m_nImgHeight = m_Images[0].getHeight(this);
}

repaint();
```

(continued)

```
    // Draw first image
    //-------------------------------------------------------------
    displayImage(m_Graphics);

    // Timer loop, which draws next image every
    // m_delay_ms milliseconds
    //-------------------------------------------------------------
    while (true)
    {
        try
        {
            Thread.sleep(m_delay_ms);
            drawNext();
        }
        catch (InterruptedException e)
        {
            stop();
        }
    }
}
```

Visual J++ automatically wrote many of the comments in *Slideshow.java*; I added others specific to the applet. When I created the *Slideshow* project in Visual J++, the Applet Wizard generated a basic shell for my program, including the class definition with appropriate functions. Microsoft Developer Studio certainly takes some of the drudgery out of coding!

The *Slideshow* class contains the complete program. As with all Java applets, *Slideshow* derives from the API *Applet* class—so, in essence, an applet is really just another object. Within *Slideshow*, I use other objects from the API. The *Graphics* class, for example, defines objects that tell my applet about its video environment. Think of a *Graphics* object as the Java equivalent of a Microsoft Windows device context. I also define an array of *Image* objects to hold the pictures loaded from disk. *Slideshow* defines its own versions of methods inherited through *Applet* and *Runnable*, including *run*, *init*, *destroy*, *start*, and *stop*. The methods inherited from *Applet* define the general functionality of all applet classes; the *Runnable* interface declares the methods supported by a multithreaded Java program. I added the *displayImage* and *drawNext* methods, and I implemented *mouseDown* to switch images at the click of a mouse button.

By using Java's prebuilt API objects, I saved myself a lot of work. For example, the *Image* class handles all the details of working with graphic file formats; I just create an *Image* object using the *getImage* method that *Slideshow* inherited from *Applet*. The *Graphics* object "knows" how to translate an *Image* object's bits into colored pixels, so I don't have to be concerned with the type of machine *Slideshow* will be running on. *Slideshow* demonstrates two of the advantages of object-oriented programming: encapsulation of concepts in classes and the ability to extend existing code. It took me about an hour to design, write, test, and complete *Slideshow*. How long do you think it would have taken me if I had needed to write video and image-handling software from scratch?

Is the *Slideshow* applet a real piece of object-oriented programming? Yes, in the sense that it uses objects effectively. But *Slideshow* is a very small program, and it doesn't really show how to build a class hierarchy from scratch. But *Slideshow* will give you a sense of what a Java program looks and feels like. In Chapter 2, I create a set of related classes, demonstrating more of Java's object-oriented capabilities.

Onward

I've begun this book by looking at where Java—and Visual J++—fit into the worlds of programming and the Internet. In the next chapter, I'll take a detailed look at Java's object-oriented classes and interfaces and show you how object-oriented programming is done with Visual J++.

2 Java Class Design

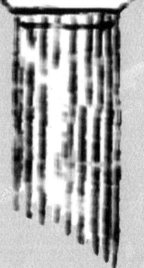

J ava provides a rich environment for object-oriented programming. Although it is based in large part on C++, Java also takes some cues from other object-oriented programming languages, such as Smalltalk. You'll find that Java is cleaner than C++; it doesn't need much of the complex syntax found in the older language because Java figures out many things that C++ programs must tell their compiler explicitly.

Although you've probably worked with Java before, you may not have thought seriously about object-oriented programming. In this chapter, I describe some things that you might already know about Java, but I focus on how they fit into the context of software components and class packages. Think of this as a refresher course in Java class development, with an emphasis on object-oriented concepts.

Classes

A class defines a set of related data and functions. Everything in a Java program is part of a class, just as it would be in a Smalltalk program. Java applets don't have global data or functions; nothing in Java is defined outside the scope of one class or another.

In C++, a class is typically defined in more than one source file. You define the class in a header file that will be included in any other source modules that use the class. The implementations of member functions and the definition of static data will then be placed in a C++ source file, to be compiled into an object module for linking. For really big classes, you may have more than one compiled module. For small classes, you might declare several classes in the same header and source files.

The biggest difference between C++ and Java is that in Java, a class is implemented entirely in a single source file. Java maintains a direct relationship between a *.java* source code file and its classes. Lacking the preprocessor found in C++, Java does not implement include or header files. Instead, a Java program imports packages, which the compiler searches for the classes that are referenced. Each *.java* source file usually defines a single class, from which the compiler generates a single *.class* file containing virtual machine code. If a program does define more than one class in a source file, a Java compiler such as Visual J++ will create a *.class* file for each individual class.

Class Syntax

Now let's look at the fundamentals of class design. The basic syntax for a Java class is

```
class Name
{
    // Field and method definitions
}
```

(Unlike C++, Java doesn't require a semicolon after the closing bracket in a class definition.)

Whereas C++ refers to data members and function members, Java uses the terms *field* and *method*. Essentially, a field is a class data item and a method is a member function. Common practice is to define fields first, and then methods, although you can mix them up if it makes your program more readable. Collectively, the fields and methods are known as the *members* of the class in which they have been defined. This code snippet shows a very simple *Temperature* class, which includes a field and two methods.

```
class Temperature
{
    // This is a field
    float m_fTemp;

    // This is a method
    float getTemp()
    {
        return m_fTemp;
    }

    // And this is a method
    void setTemp(float t)
    {
        m_fTemp = t;
    }
}
```

Remember, you must define a field before you can actually use it, even inside a class definition. Thus, the following version of *Temperature* won't compile.

```
class BadTemperature
{
    // This is a method
    float getTemp()
    {
        return m_fTemp;
    }

    // And this is a method
    void setTemp(float t)
    {
        m_fTemp = t;
    }

    // Field must be defined before it is referenced!
    float m_fTemp;
}
```

Objects

The following line of code creates a *Temperature* object.

```
Temperature t1 = new Temperature();
```

All Java objects are dynamically allocated on the heap, a reserved area of memory. Once you've created an object, you reference its elements by using the same syntax you would use in C++, combining the object's identifier and the name of the method or field you're accessing.

```
Temperature t1 = new Temperature();

float f;

f = t1.getTemp(); // Calling getTemp for the object t1
```

Note that the statement

```
Temperature tB;
```

creates a *reference* to a *Temperature* object, but it *doesn't* create an actual object. If you try to use *tB* without assigning it to an object, Java will generate an error. Java's behavior in this regard is quite different from that of C++, in which such a statement creates an object in a static data area or on the stack.

Think of a class as a formula or recipe for objects. The recipe for a cake isn't itself a cake, but it tells you how to make any number of cakes, each of which would be unique. In Java, a call to *new* creates an object according to a design specified by a class. Just as a recipe can define multiple cakes, a class can define any number of objects. Each object is a unique *instance* of the class, with its own unique fields and functions. For instance, each *Temperature* object will contain a unique field named *m_fTemp*, and the functions *setTemp* and *getTemp* will operate on the *m_fTemp* field in the object to which they are applied. For example,

```
Temperature t1 = new Temperature();
Temperature t2 = new Temperature();

t1.setTemp(10);
t2.setTemp(75);

System.out.println("t1 = ", t1.getTemp());
System.out.println("t2 = ", t2.getTemp());
```

will display

```
t1 = 10
t2 = 75
```

References tell your Java program where a particular object is so that it can be accessed. Java automatically manages the references in your program; an object will exist as long as it is attached to one or more references. It's all very existential, really, in that an object will continue to exist as long as it is actively referenced in your program. But once all references to an object are gone, Java's memory manager feels free to remove the object from memory.

Overloading

The same name can be used for two or more methods within a class. This is a technique known as overloading. Consider the following piece of code.

```
class Value
{
    double m_dNumber;

    double Add(int n)
    {
        m_dNumber += (double)n;
        return m_dNumber;
    }

    double Add(float n)
    {
        m_dNumber += (double)n;
        return m_dNumber;
    }
}

class DoThis
{
    void ThisMethod()
    {
        // Create some objects
        Value v1 = new Value();
        Value v2 = new Value();

        // Define some local variables
        int   x1 = 1;
        float x2 = 1.0F;

        // Add via overloaded methods
        v1.Add(x1); // Calls Value.Add(int n)
        v2.Add(x2); // Calls Value.Add(float n)
    }
}
```

The two *Add* methods differ in the type of parameter they accept, letting the compiler decide at compile time which one to call. You can't overload methods based on their return type, however. In the following code fragment, the compiler will complain that it can't tell the difference between the *getNumber* methods:

```
class Value
{
    double m_dNumber;

    int getNumber()
    {
```

(continued)

```
        return (int)m_dNumber;
    }

    float getNumber()
    {
        return (float)m_dNumber;
    }
}

class DoThis
{
    void ThisMethod()
    {
        // Create some objects
        Value v1 = new Value();
        Value v2 = new Value();

        // Call getNumber!
        int   x1 = v1.getNumber(); // ERROR!
        float x2 = v2.getNumber(); // ERROR!
    }
}
```

Java, like C++, lets programs call a function and ignore its return value, if any. Even when, as shown above, the compiler is explicitly told the type of value expected to be returned, it still won't accept overloaded methods that differ only in their return type.

The purpose of overloading is to make code more understandable by letting you use the same name for variations on a theme. You should never use the same name for disparate methods; that would only confuse anyone—including yourself—who might need to read the program later.

NOTE

Java does not support the overloading of operators, so you can't define your own functions for operations such as + or %.

Initializers and Constructors

By default, Java sets the fields of a new object to a zero state: *numeric* fields are set to 0, *boolean* fields are set to *false*, and references are set to null. For many objects, the default initialization works fine, but sometimes you'll want your objects to begin with some value other than the zero state. The simplest technique for accomplishing this is to include initializers in your field declarations. For example, in the following class, I've declared explicit starting values for the fields *m_field1* and *m_field2* but allowed *m_field3* to default to 0.

```
class MyClass
{
    // Explicitly initialize these fields
    int m_field1 = 100;
    boolean m_field2 = true;

    // Let this default to 0
    float m_field3;
}
```

As your objects get more complicated, you'll want to consider using constructors. These are special functions that have the same name as the class and that execute when an object is created. Here's another version of *MyClass*, in which I've defined two constructors, one with arguments and the other without.

```
class MyClass
{
    // Explicitly initialize these fields
    int m_field1 = 100;
    boolean m_field2 = true;

    // Let this default to 0
    float m_field3;

    // Constructor without arguments
    MyClass()
    {
        m_field3 = 12345.678F;
    }

    // Constructor with arguments
    MyClass(float f)
    {
        m_field3 = f;
    }
}
```

The next piece of code creates *MyClass* objects using the constructors shown in the code above:

```
MyClass mc1 = new MyClass(); // m_field3 = 12345.678
MyClass mc2 = new MyClass(999.001F); // m_field3 = 999.001
```

When you don't define a constructor, Java assumes the existence of a default constructor that sets all uninitialized fields of a new object to the zero state, as explained at the beginning of this section. The default constructor does not have any arguments. If you define even one constructor, Java does not generate a default constructor. So if you defined *MyClass* as above but with only the second, parameterized, constructor, the compiler would object to the creation of objects without constructor arguments. The first line of code in the above example would then be illegal. To allow for such a case, you must explicitly define the equivalent of a default constructor, as shown on the following page.

```
MyClass()
{
    // Nothing to do!
}
```

Now you can create *MyClass* objects without arguments, and their uninitialized fields will be set automatically to their zero state.

Java lets you do something that C++ won't: call one constructor from within another in the same class. In *MyClass*, I could define the first constructor in terms of the second, like this:

```
MyClass()
{
    this(12345.678F);
}
```

So what in the heck is *this*? It's a reference to the object for which you've called a function. In the case of the *MyClass* constructor, I've used *this* to invoke the second constructor, passing it a parameter value.

Why would you call one constructor from another? If your objects require complex initialization, you may well save a lot of code by calling from one constructor to another. And it makes sense to localize a specific initialization process in just one constructor rather than repeat code in several places.

The Finalizer

No, I'm not talking about a new Arnold Schwarzenegger movie; the *finalizer* complements constructors by providing a function that is executed when an object is removed from the heap by Java's memory manager. The *finalize* method has no parameters and returns nothing. Within *MyClass*, I can define the following method, which will be automatically invoked whenever an object is destroyed.

```
class MyClass
{
    // Various other members

    void finalize()
    {
        System.out.println
            ("The object is dead! Long live the object!");
    }
}
```

The *finalize* function seems similar to a C++ destructor, but you'll find that Java takes care of most cleanup operations for you. For example, any C++ class that allocates memory in its constructors will probably have a destructor to free that memory. Java, on the other hand, automatically releases any memory allocated to objects once they cease to be referenced. I haven't found many reasons to implement a *finalize* method in my classes; you should implement *finalize* only when you have a very clear reason for doing some cleanup work.

The *finalize* method is invoked when an object is *removed from memory*, not when the last reference to an object is gone. This is a subtle but important distinction; if Java is too busy with other tasks to clean up lost objects, your *finalize* function may not be called for some time after an object becomes eligible for disposal. Make no assumptions about when *finalize* is called.

Class and Instance Members

Classes actually define two sets of values: *class members* belong to all instances of the class, and *instance members* belong to each individual object. A field or a method is an instance member unless you define it with the *static* keyword, which declares it to be a class member. For example, I can take the *Temperature* class and add a couple of new items to adjust members shared by all *Temperature* objects.

```
class Temperature
{
    // Class field
    static float s_fMinTemp = -273.16; // Absolute zero

    // Class method
    static float getMinTemp()
    {
        return s_fMinTemp;
    }

    // Class method
    static void setMinTemp(float t)
    {
        if (t < -273.16)
            throw new InvalidArgumentException
                ("Can't get colder than -273.16");

        s_fMinTemp = t;
    }

    // Instance field
    float m_fTemp;

    // Instance method
    float getTemp()
    {
        return m_fTemp;
    }

    // Instance method
    void setTemp(float t)
    {
```

(continued)

```
        if (t < s_fMinTemp)
            throw new InvalidArgumentException
                ("Can't get colder than " + s_fMinTemp);

        m_fTemp = t;
    }
}
```

There will never be more than one *s_fMinTemp* field in any program, no matter how many *Temperature* objects you create. When you declare a field or a method static, you're saying that it's a joint feature of every object in a class; *s_fMinTemp* is shared by all instances of the *Temperature* class. The following piece of code shows how this works.

```
// Create some objects
Temperature t1 = new Temperature();
Temperature t2 = new Temperature();

t1.setTemp(-20); // Works with default s_fMinTemp of -273.16

Temperature.setMinTemp(0); // Change minimum

t2.setTemp(-20); // EXCEPTION! -20 is below the minimum.
```

A static method such as *setMinTemp* does not refer to any specific object; it refers only to the other static members of a class. When you call a class method, qualify its identifier with the name of its class instead of specifying an object reference. Also, since a static method doesn't reference an object, it will not have a *this* reference.

Java allows you to define functions to initialize class fields, just as it supports constructors that set the values of instance fields. A class can have one or more static initializers, defined by blocks of code prefaced with the *static* keyword.

```
class AnotherClass
{
    // An array of numbers
    static int[] s_nList = new int[10];

    static
    {
        for (int i = 0; i < 10; ++i)
        {
            s_nList[i] = i;
        }
    }
}
```

If you define more than one static initializer, Java executes them in the order in which they appear. A static initializer is permitted to invoke only class methods and reference only class fields.

When you are designing classes, think about what your objects have in common, and use that determination to define static members. In general, class members will define parameters and characteristics of objects; for example, the *s_fMinTemp* class field defines the lower bound of all *Temperature* objects. You must know the relationship of information in a program *before* you determine the types and interactions of classes. This requires you to thoroughly research the often-elusive program specification. If you make a wrong decision when relating your classes, the program can become difficult to understand and maintain.

Constants

When a field is declared with the *final* modifier, the field's value cannot be changed after it has been initialized. The modifiers *final* and *static* are used most often together to define class constants. In effect, this is the same as defining a *static const* data element in a C++ class. For example, in the *Temperature* class, I can define absolute zero using a *static final* member.

```
class Temperature
{
    // Constant
    static final float ABS_ZERO = -273.16;

    // Class field
    static float s_fMinTemp = ABS_ZERO;

    // Class method
    static float getMinTemp()
    {
        return s_fMinTemp;
    }

    // Instance field
    float m_fTemp;

    // Instance method
    float getTemp()
    {
        return m_fTemp;
    }

    // Instance method
    void setTemp(float t)
    {
        if (t < ABS_ZERO)
            throw new InvalidArgumentException
                ("Can't get colder than " + ABS_ZERO);

        m_fTemp = t;
    }
}
```

Declaring a method with the *final* modifier prevents a subclass (discussed in the "Inheritance" section later in this chapter) from hiding or overloading that method.

Access Modifiers

All members of a class are accessible to all other members of the same class. You control the visibility of class elements to other classes through the application of access modifiers. Java provides four levels of element access: default, public, private, protected.

◆ The **default (no modifier)** member has no access modifier and is visible to all other classes in its package. Some people call this "friendly" access.

◆ A **public** member is visible to all classes in all packages.

◆ A **private** member is invisible outside the scope of its defining class.

◆ A **protected** member is visible only inside its defining class and to subclasses.

No class should reveal any more than it has to; visibility should be strictly controlled. The general rule is that fields should be private or protected (depending on whether you want subclasses to see them), with controlled access to them through public methods. The public methods you create to update data members should validate input values, ensuring the integrity of internal data. In turn, the public methods you create to read data members can simply return the data members' current values. You'll sometimes define a protected or private method that will perform some internal operation that shouldn't be publicly available. Here's how the *Temperature* class looks after I've added the access qualifiers.

```
class Temperature
{
    // Constant
    private static final float ABS_ZERO = -273.16F;

    // Class field
    private static float s_fMinTemp = ABS_ZERO;

    // Class method
    public static float getMinTemp()
    {
        return s_fMinTemp;
    }

    // Instance field
    protected float m_fTemp;

    // Instance method
    public float getTemp()
```

```
    {
        return m_fTemp;
    }

    // Instance method
    public void setTemp(float t)
    {
        if (t < ABS_ZERO)
            throw new IllegalArgumentException
                ("Can't get colder than " + ABS_ZERO);

        m_fTemp = t;
    }
}
```

Use of access modifiers requires some thinking ahead. If I plan to create a subclass of *Temperature*, I will define fields such as *m_fTemp* as protected so that extensions can directly access them. Determining element access is often as much an art as it is a science since you need to anticipate what you'll be doing with the class in the future. I suggest that you err on the side of caution. It may be easier to eliminate the *getTemp* method and make *m_fTemp* public, but allowing direct access to that field allows direct assignment that bypasses the range checking in *setTemp*. A central focus of all object-oriented programs should be the protection of data from possible extraneous manipulation.

Inheritance

The power of object-oriented programming goes far beyond the creation of stand-alone classes. Inheritance allows new classes to use the facilities provided by existing classes. From a common *superclass*, you can derive a set of related *subclasses* with related capabilities. In C++, a superclass is usually called a *base class,* and a subclass is known as a *derived class*. You can also use the terms *parent* and *child* in reference to the relationships between classes. A set of classes related by inheritance is known as a *hierarchy*.

Inheritance Qualifiers

The syntax for defining classes is a bit more involved when you begin to consider inheritance.

```
[ abstract | final | public ]
class Name extends Superclass implements Superinterface
{
    // Field and method definitions
}
```

If your class definition includes an *extends* declaration specifying the superclass from which you intend to inherit fields and methods, you are using inheritance. The *implements* clause is another form of inheritance that I describe in the next section; for now, you can ignore it.

One or more of the following keywords can modify the definition of a class by preceding the *class* keyword: *abstract, final, public.*

- ◆ **Abstract** defines a class that cannot be instantiated; in other words, the compiler won't let you create objects of an abstract class. Abstract classes usually define superclasses that will be used only in the definition of subclasses.

- ◆ A **final** class cannot be extended. This keyword is literal: it declares that a class is complete in and of itself and that it has no subclasses.

- ◆ For now, I'll just say that a **public** class is accessible outside the package in which it is defined. If you don't declare a class as public, it can be extended only by other classes within its package.

An Example

This example requires a more sophisticated version of the *Temperature* class. My goal this time is to define two classes, *Fahrenheit* and *Celsius*, to implement temperatures on two different scales. Regardless of scale, both classes will have several features in common—and that situation calls for the creation of a superclass, *Temperature.*

```
public abstract
class Temperature
{
    // Instance field
    protected float m_fTemp;

    // Instance method
    public float getTemp()
    {
        return m_fTemp;
    }

    // Instance method
    protected float setTemp(float t)
    {
        float x = m_fTemp; // Save old value
        m_fTemp = t;       // Set new value
        return x;          // Return old value
    }

    // Abstract method declaration
    abstract String getScale();
}
```

Temperature defines the common elements for any type of temperature scale. It includes a field, *m_fTemp*, that holds the numeric temperature value. I've defined *m_fTemp* as private to prevent it from being directly manipulated. You can retrieve the value of *m_fTemp* with the public *getTemp* function. The *setTemp* function assigns its argument to *m_fTemp*; I've made this function protected because it will be used only by subclass methods that perform range checking. *Temperature* is an abstract class, and as such it cannot be instantiated. It also defines a single abstract method, *getScale*, which will be discussed in detail later.

Here are the subclasses from *Temperature*: *Celsius* and *Fahrenheit*.

```
/*
 *
 * Celsius class
 *
 */

public
class Celsius
extends Temperature
{
    // Constant
    private final static float ABS_ZERO = -273.16F;

    // Constructor
    public Celsius()
    {
        // Nothing to do
    }

    // Constructor
    public Celsius(float t)
    {
        setTemp(t);
    }

    // Instance method
    public float setTemp(float t)
    {
        if (t < ABS_ZERO)
            throw new IllegalArgumentException
                ("Can't get colder than " + ABS_ZERO +
                " C");

        return super.setTemp(t);
    }

    // Instance method
    public Fahrenheit asFahrenheit()
    {
        return new Fahrenheit(32.0F + 9.0F /
                            5.0F * m_fTemp);
    }

    // Instance method
    public float inKelvin()
    {
```

(continued)

```java
        return m_fTemp - ABS_ZERO;
    }

    // Abstract method implementation
    public String getScale()
    {
        return "C";
    }
}

/*
 *
 * Fahrenheit class
 *
 */

public
class Fahrenheit
extends Temperature
{
    // Constant
    private final static float ABS_ZERO = -459.67F;

    // Constructor
    public Fahrenheit()
    {
        // Nothing to do
    }

    // Constructor
    public Fahrenheit(float t)
    {
        setTemp(t);
    }

    // Instance method
    public float setTemp(float t)
    {
        if (t < ABS_ZERO)
            throw new IllegalArgumentException
                ("Can't get colder than " + ABS_ZERO +
                 " F");

        return super.setTemp(t);
    }

    // Instance method
    public Celsius asCelsius()
    {
        return new Celsius((m_fTemp - 32.0F) *
                        5.0F / 9.0F );
    }
```

```
    // Instance method
    public float inKelvin()
    {
        Celsius c = asCelsius();
        return c.inKelvin();
    }

    // Abstract method implementation
    public String getScale()
    {
        return "F";
    }
}
```

Celsius and *Fahrenheit* inherit the members of *Temperature*, including the *m_fTemp* field and the *getTemp* and *setTemp* methods.

OVERRIDING AND HIDING

If you look closely at *Celsius* and *Fahrenheit*, you'll notice that they both define a *setTemp* method, even though they inherit a method by that name from *Temperature*. This is a practice known as *overriding*. To override a superclass method, the subclass must define a function with the same name and parameter list. The superclass method is still there, but when the method for a subclass object is called, the subclass version of the method is invoked by default. The following piece of code shows how this works.

```
Celsius c = new Celsius();

c.setTemp(10);  // Calls setTemp defined in Celsius class
```

From within a subclass, you can call an overridden superclass method by using the *super* keyword, as I did in both subclass implementations of *setTemp*.

```
super.setTemp(t); // Calls Temperature setTemp
```

Overriding becomes most useful when you are using *polymorphism*. With polymorphism, you act upon a set of subclasses through a generic interface to their superclass. For example, because *Temperature* is an abstract class, I can't create objects from it, but I *can* create a reference to a *Temperature* object and then assign to it a reference to an object of one of its subclasses, as shown here.

```
Temperature tT = new Celsius();

tT.setTemp(-45); // It's VERY cold
```

The compiler knows to call the *setTemp* method defined for *Celsius* because the *run-time type* of *tT* is *Celsius*. However, the *compile-time type* of *tT* is *Temperature*, which prevents me from writing an additional statement such as

```
Celsius cT = tT; // Can't assign a Temperature to a Celsius
```

Java will also reject the statement at the top of the next page, since you can't create an object from an abstract class.

```
Temperature tT = new Temperature(); // Error!
```

Such power can be put to use in creating generic methods such as the following *stringTemp* method.

```
String stringTemp(Temperature t)
{
    return t.getTemp() + "° " + t.getScale();
}
```

You can then call *stringTemp* with either a *Celsius* or a *Fahrenheit* object as the argument.

```
Celsius cT = new Celsius(100);
Fahrenheit fT = new Fahrenheit(32);

String sC = stringTemp(cT);
String sF = stringTemp(fT);
```

I could redefine *stringTemp* as a method within *Temperature*, as shown here,

```
String asString()
{
return getTemp() + "° " + getScale();
}
```

and the examples above would change to

```
String sC = cT.asString();
String sF = fT.asString();
```

The *stringTemp* and *asString* methods call the abstract function *getScale*, which both subclasses override, returning strings that identify the scale they implement. But since any superclass method can be overridden by a subclass, what is the point of using the *abstract* keyword? The answer has more to do with what an abstract method *cannot* do than what it can do. Only an abstract class can define an abstract method. An abstract method does not have an implementation; it is just a description of a function common to subclasses. To implement an abstract method, a subclass must define a function with the same definition and a body but without the *abstract* keyword. Thus, an abstract method lets us define the nature of a polymorphic function without having to actually implement it. A *Temperature* object will never exist; therefore, it can't return a string from *getScale* identifying a nonexistent temperature scale. So the *abstract* keyword lets you define a characteristic of subclasses; you can think of it as a directive from a superclass to its subclasses, telling them that they must override a specific method. (There is a limitation to the *abstract* keyword's use, however: Java can instantiate only fully implemented classes, so if a subclass does not implement an inherited abstract method, it must be declared abstract itself.)

NOTE

If you're a C++ programmer, think of all Java methods as being defined with the *virtual* keyword. In other words, all Java methods are equivalent to the virtual functions of C++.

At this point, I should also mention that you can't create polymorphic fields; if a subclass defines a field with the same name as one it inherited, the superclass field is *hidden* and can be accessed only via the *super* qualifier (the same way you access an overridden superclass method). Nor can you override a static method; because a static method doesn't refer to a specific object, it cannot be polymorphic. You can, however, *hide* an inherited static method or a field.

Now back to *Celsius* and *Fahrenheit*. There isn't any need to override the *getTemp* function, but these subclasses need to check the range of values assigned to *m_fTemp* because, of course, no temperature can be lower than absolute zero. *Celsius* and *Fahrenheit* both define constants named *ABS_ZERO*, but the identifiers don't conflict because they are defined as private in separate classes. In each class, I override the base class *setTemp* function with a subclass-specific version that verifies the parameter and throws an *IllegalArgumentException* if the assigned temperature is too cold. If the argument is acceptable, *Celsius.setTemp* and *Fahrenheit.setTemp* call the superclass method *setTemp* to assign their parameter to *m_fTemp*.

To prevent code duplication, I have the parameterized constructor call *setTemp* to assign a value to a new object. Since that constructor requires an argument, I also defined a parameterless constructor for each class; this allows me to instantiate *Celsius* and *Fahrenheit* objects without providing constructor arguments in a call to *new*. The parameterless constructor doesn't do anything explicitly; it essentially allows me to use the default initialization, which sets *m_fTemp* to 0.

The *Celsius* and *Fahrenheit* classes are mutually referential in that each provides a function to convert its objects to objects of the other type. The *asCelsius* and *asFahrenheit* methods perform a calculation on *m_fTemp* and use the result to create a new object; the functions then return a reference. Thus, I can create a pair of *Celsius* and *Fahrenheit* objects and then use the conversion functions to obtain corresponding objects of the other class. Here's an example.

```
// Create temperature objects
Celsius c1 = new Celsius(-10.0F);
Fahrenheit f1 = new Fahrenheit(75.0F);

// Now create new objects by conversion
Celsius c2 = f1.asCelsius();
Fahrenheit f2 = c1.asFahrenheit();

// Display values in applet window
g.drawString("C = " + c1.getTemp() + " = F " + f2.getTemp(),
             10, 20);
g.drawString("F = " + f1.getTemp() + " = C " + c2.getTemp(),
             10, 40);
```

Finally, both classes include methods to return *m_fTemp* in terms of the Kelvin temperature scale. The Celsius and Kelvin scales use the same "size" of degree; they differ only in the location of their 0 degree mark: Celsius considers 0° to be the temperature at which water freezes, whereas the Kelvin scale counts degrees from absolute zero. That's why the *Celsius.inKelvin* method simply returns *m_fTemp* minus *ABS_ZERO*. In *Fahrenheit.inKelvin*, I use the *asCelsius* function to create a *Celsius* object named *c*; the method finishes its job by returning the result of *Celsius.inKelvin* for *c*. Such techniques for reusing and compartmentalizing code through polymorphism and inheritance lie at the heart of object-oriented programming.

Inner Classes

With the 1.1 release of the Java language specification, you can now define a class within another class. Earlier versions of Java supported only top-level classes that were defined as part of a package. Because class nesting is implemented entirely within the Java compiler, this new language feature is transparent to the Java virtual machine; in other words, inner classes will work just fine with existing browsers and applet viewers.

The following example shows an inner class definition.

```java
public class Outer
{
    // Private member
    private int m_nX;

    // Inner class
    class Inner
    {
        public void setX(int n)
        {
            m_nX = n * 2;
        }
    }

    // Constructor
    public Outer()
    {
        m_nX = 0;
    }

    // Methods
    public void setX(int n)
    {
        Inner i = new Inner();

        i.setX(n);
    }

    public int getX()
    {
        return m_nX;
    }
}
```

When compiling the *Outer* class, Visual J++ will generate two output files: *Outer.class* and *Outer$Inner.class*.

Like a method, the *Inner* class can access the members of the enclosing *Outer* class. In fact, the rules governing name visibility are quite similar for methods and inner classes. An inner class object refers to the outer class object from which it was created. I'll use the following code fragment as an example.

```
Outer obj = new Outer();
obj.setX(10);
g.drawString("Outer X = " + obj.getX(), 10, 20);
```

The call to *obj.setX* will create an *Inner* object that is "linked" to the *obj* object that created it. In other words, an inner object can use simple names to access the members of its enclosing object. If the inner class defines a member with the same name as an outer class member, the outer class name must be used to reference its overridden members. For instance, if I were to add a field named *m_nX* to *Inner*, like this,

```
// Inner class
class Inner
{
    // New field to override outer class field
    private int m_nX;

    public void setX(int n)
    {
        m_nX = n * 2;
    }
}
```

calls to *Inner.setX* would change *Inner.m_nX*, not *Outer.m_nX*. Changing the *Inner.setX* method, however, allows it to access the *m_nX* field in the enclosing class.

```
// Inner class
class Inner
{
    // New field to override outer class field
    private int m_nX;

    public void setX(int n)
    {
        Outer.this.m_nX = n * 2;
    }
}
```

In other words, you can qualify the reference with the name of an outer class to explicitly access members hidden by the inner class. You can also use the name of the inner class as a *this* qualifier, as in *Inner.this.m_nX*.

An object of an inner class can be created only within the scope of the enclosing class. The following two lines of code generate compile-time errors, since Visual J++ will not create an *Inner* object outside of *Outer*.

```
Inner inr1 = new Inner();              // Error!
Outer.Inner inr = new Outer.Inner(); // Error!
```

(continued)

If you really need to create an *Inner* object outside of its enclosing class, define a method for *Outer* that looks like this:

```
public Inner makeInner()
{
    return new Inner();
}
```

Call the *makeInner* method to create an *Inner* object connected to *obj*.

```
Outer.Inner inr = obj.makeInner();
inr.setX(6);
g.drawString("Outer X = " + obj.getX(), 10, 40);
```

The *drawString* statement will display the object's *X* value as 12 because the call to *inr.setX* referenced *obj*. Automatic garbage collection will treat the *inr* object as a reference to *obj*, preventing *obj* from being removed from memory while *inr* is still in use.

You can declare an inner class as public, private, or protected; the qualifiers have the same effect on inner class names that they do on methods and fields. Use of access qualifiers will *not* affect the ability of an inner class to reference the members of its outer class.

Interfaces

An interface is a specialized type of class. The purpose of an interface is twofold: to define constants and to declare a set of methods that must be implemented by a class. The syntax for interfaces is similar to that for classes.

```
interface [implements superinterface]
{
    // Member declarations
}
```

Like classes, interfaces can implement other interfaces, in a hierarchy of *superinterfaces* and *subinterfaces*. All interfaces are automatically abstract, and Java treats all interface members as explicitly public. You cannot define a protected or private interface member; use of the public modifier is redundant and unnecessary. Every field defined by an interface is static and final; every method is abstract. In other words, all fields in an interface can be treated as constants. If you don't provide an explicit initialization for an interface field, it will be a constant of the zero state.

I can define an interface such as the following to define the characteristics of all persistent objects.

```
interface Persistent
{
    int Factor = 10;

    void Write(String filename);
    void Read(String filename);
}
```

Then I declare a class that implements the *Persistent* interface.

```
class DataThing implements Persistent;
{
    void getFactor()
    {
        return Factor; // Inherited from Persistent
    }

    // Must define both of these methods!
    void Write(String filename)
    {
        // Write a DataThing to filename
    }

    void Read(String filename)
    {
        // Read a DataThing from filename
    }
}
```

For Java to be able to compile *DataThing*, the class either must implement the *Write* and *Read* methods or must itself be declared abstract.

I often use an interface to encapsulate a set of constants. I use the following interface later in this chapter, when I provide a complete example of an object-oriented class hierarchy. Any class that implements *NumericConstants* will have access to the six constant values I define therein.

```
// An interface of numeric constants
interface NumericConstants
{
    // Epsilon is the smallest possible difference between
    // two values of the same type

    float FLT_EPS = 1.192092896e-07F;
    float FLT_PI  = 3.141593F;
    float FLT_E   = 2.718282F;

    double DBL_EPS = 2.2204460492503131e-016D;
    double DBL_PI  = 3.14159265358979D;
    double DBL_E   = 2.71828182845905D;
}
```

C++ supports multiple inheritance, which allows a subclass to have more than one superclass. Java does not support multiple inheritance, but you can use interfaces for many of the same purposes. In fact, Java allows a class to implement any number of interfaces, even though it allows extension from only one superclass.

Class Collections

When one class is defined within another, the enclosed class can be qualified with the *static* keyword, changing it from an inner class to a top-level class qualified by the name of its enclosing class. This is similar to declaring a field or method with the *static* keyword, thus creating a global value qualified by a class name. Static member classes have complete access to other static members within the enclosing class; an object created from a static member class has a *this* pointer to its own instance but does not have a *this* pointer for its enclosing class.

Here I've created a *ClassCollection* class, which contains a static field (a constant) and two static member classes.

```
public class ClassCollection
{
    private static final float someX = 1.23456F;
    private       final float someY = 9.87654F;

    static public class ClassA
    {
        public float getX()
        {
            return someX;
        }
    }

    static public class ClassB
    {
        public float getX()
        {
            return someX;
        }

        /*
        public float getY()
        {
            return someY;
        }
        */
    }

}
```

I create *ClassA* and *ClassB* objects by qualifying the class names with the name of their enclosing class.

```
ClassCollection.ClassA cA = new ClassCollection.ClassA();
ClassCollection.ClassB cB = new ClassCollection.ClassB();

g.drawString("ClassA.getX() = " + cA.getX(), 10, 60);
g.drawString("ClassB.getX() = " + cB.getX(), 10, 80);
```

The function *ClassB.getY* is commented out in the class definition for very good reason: it won't compile because it references *someY*, a nonstatic member of *ClassCollection*. A static member class cannot reference any nonstatic members of its enclosing class.

Static member classes provide an additional mechanism for encapsulating related functions. You could use Java's packages to replace *ClassCollection* with a package-local class that defines the constant value *someX*. But by using a static member class, you can define the constant within the same source file as the classes that use it, providing a clearer association between related elements of your program.

Microsoft Visual J++ and Classes

Microsoft Visual J++ comes with Microsoft Developer Studio, a programming environment that helps you write object-oriented software by providing tools that track and construct classes. If you've used Developer Studio to create C++ programs, you may be familiar with some of this material.

On the left side of the Developer Studio display is a set of panels that let you view project files, component classes, and help information. When you load a Java project and click on the ClassView tab, you'll see a list of classes included in your applet or application. Clicking one of the small plus signs allows you to view the fields and methods in a class. Figure 2-1 shows what Developer Studio displayed for one of my projects.

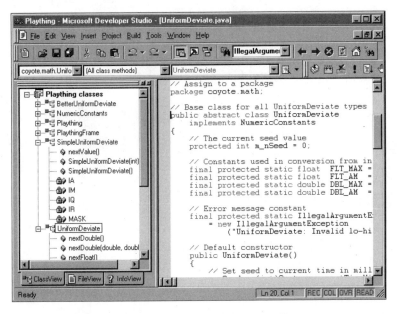

Figure 2-1. *A typical class display in Developer Studio.*

In the ClassView panel shown in Figure 2-1, you can see the fields and methods defined by the *SimpleUniformDeviate* class. If you double-click on the class name or any of its components, Developer Studio will automatically display the related source file in the edit window. If you're working on a big project, this can be a tremendously valuable tool, letting you find definitions and view class structures with ease.

Developer Studio provides an automated tool that helps you add a new class to your project. From the Insert menu, select the New Class menu item. A dialog box will appear, asking you for the name, superclass, package, and qualifiers for your new class. Figure 2-2 shows the Create New Class dialog box.

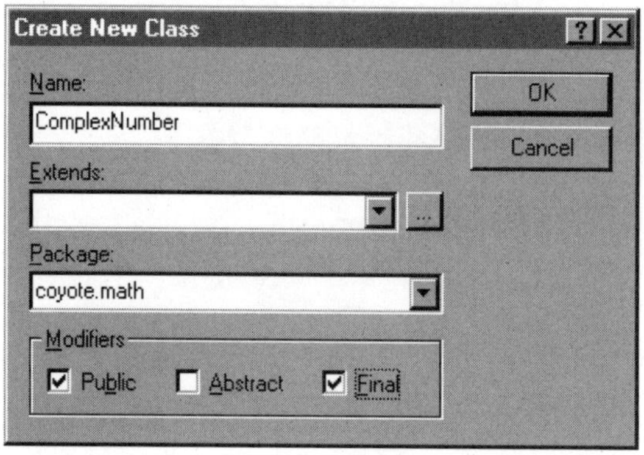

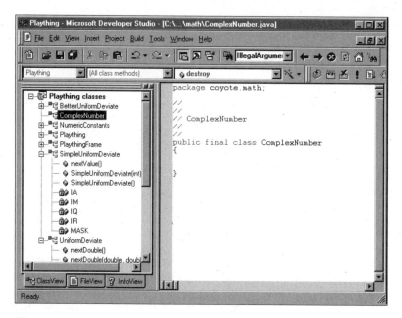

Figure 2-2. *The Create New Class dialog box.*

When you click OK, Developer Studio will generate a source file for your new class, using the parameters you have defined. The new *.java* file will be created in the directory specified by the package you selected. Suppose my project is in the C:\Dev\Plaything directory, the example in Figure 2-2 will place the *ComplexNumber.java* file in a directory named C:\Dev\Plaything\coyote\math. You can see what the generated *.java* file looks like in Figure 2-3.

Figure 2-3. *A Java source file generated by Developer Studio.*

Local Classes

Java 1.1 supports the definition of classes within block statements, methods, and expressions. This feature allows you to use classes to encapsulate local program phenomena, such as processes that have no meaning outside of a limited local context.

The following function, for example, includes a local class.

```
public void hasLocal()
{
    final int x;
    int y;

    class MethodLocal
    {
        public int squareX()
        {
            return x * x;
        }

        /*
        public int squareY()
        {
            return y * y;
        }
        */
    }
}
```

A local class can reference only those final (constant) identifiers local to its enclosing method or block. I've commented out the method *MethodLocal.squareY* because of this restriction. Also, local classes cannot be declared static, because static implies global visibility and a locally declared class is, by definition, visible only within the scope of its enclosing block. Although no members of a local class can be static, other qualifiers, including *private* and *public*, have their usual meanings.

As you can see, Visual J++ is a helpful environment for the Java programmer. Now I'll describe the design and implementation of a component I use later in this book.

Uniform Deviates: An Example

In recent years, computer science has discovered the efficacy of stochastic algorithms. Genetic algorithms, simulated annealing, and cellular automata have all found a place in software. But unlike deterministic algorithms, stochastic algorithms must rely on the generation of random numbers. Often a stochastic algorithm can use thousands—or even millions—of random numbers. So you need a reliable tool for generating *lots* of random numbers efficiently. And while the human mind has been known to be unpredictable, it isn't very good at generating a completely unrelated set of numbers. Sit down and write a list of twenty random integers selected from the range 1 through 100, inclusive. Now consider your list. Are those numbers *really* random? Even if they are, wouldn't it be tedious if you had to generate a thousand or a million random numbers?

Computers are supposed to be good at performing tedious numeric operations, but they perform calculations by using algorithms, and truly random numbers cannot be generated by an algorithm. By definition, an algorithm is a specific sequence of operations that produces a predictable output for a given set of parameters. In the case of random numbers, the last thing we want is something predictable. The best you can do with a computer is create an algorithm that *appears* to generate a random sequence of numbers. The numbers aren't really random— a human with a calculator could predict the numbers in the sequence by following the algorithm. But the sequence of numbers on its own is very difficult to follow, and a human looking at the values will not be able to see any algorithmic pattern to them. For practical applications, *pseudorandom numbers* must suffice.

Pseudorandom Number Generators

A pseudorandom number generator begins with a *seed* value, which determines the initial state of the algorithm. To produce the next number in sequence, the algorithm operates on the seed, generating a number that is reported as a pseudorandom number. That result becomes the next seed value. Every time you run a given generator with the same seed, it should produce the same set of pseudorandom values.

Researchers have devoted copious amounts of time to inventing and analyzing pseudorandom number generators. The goal of this research has been to produce the most unpredictable sequence of values, according to a series of statistical tests. Designing a good pseudorandom number generator involves solving two problems: First, the algorithm should avoid predictability in the sequence of numbers it generates. A poor pseudorandom number generator might return values with the same last digit, or that alternate between even and odd values. Second, the algorithm should maximize the size of the repetition cycle. As an iterative algorithm is applied, the seed will eventually return to its starting value, and the numbers generated will start repeating their sequence. An algorithm that repeats after generating a million numbers is more useful than a generator that repeats itself after a hundred numbers.

Although there are many fancy and complicated algorithms that generate pseudorandom numbers, one of the most commonly used algorithms is also one of the simplest. First introduced by D. Lehmer in 1951, the *linear congruential* method involves only two mathematical operations. The *java.util.Random* package defines a "random number generator" using a linear congruential algorithm. The following code is the public interface to the *Random* class.

```
public class Random
{
    public Random();
    public Random(long seed);
    public void setSeed(long seed);
    public int nextInt();
    public long nextLong();
    public float nextFloat();
    public double nextDouble();
    public double nextGaussian();
}
```

Compared to the C++ *srand* and *rand* functions, the *Random* class is a dramatic improvement, in that it allows the return of values outside the range of a 16-bit signed integer. In fact, internally, the *Random* algorithm operates on a 48-bit key, returning 32-bit *int*s, 64-bit *long*s, or floating-point values. Java even implements a function to return a double value between 0.0 and 1.0, based on a Gaussian distribution.

But I've chosen not to use the *Random* class function defined by Java because it is inadequate for many applications. What's wrong with a simple pseudo-random number generator? It works well for simple applications or games, but for scientific work, you need a robust algorithm. The linear congruential algorithm is fast, and it works well for generating short sequences, but it also tends to "bunch" numbers into groups based on the selection of factors. Even the best linear congruential algorithms fail some of the higher-level statistical tests. If you're in need of pseudorandom numbers that evenly cover a broad range of values, you'll have to use another algorithm.

THE *UniformDeviate* CLASS

I also need a generator that produces *uniform deviates*, which are numbers that fall within a specified range. Using *Random*, I could get a number between –100 and 100, for instance, by using the following piece of code.

```
Random r = new Random();
int n = (int)(200.0F * r.nextFloat() - 100.0F);
```

In fact, I could even derive a class from *Random* to implement a method that returns numbers within a specified range. But I have decided to implement a more powerful uniform deviate generator, based on some earlier code written in C++. And I have decided to implement two different generators based on different algorithms. I begin by defining an abstract base class, *UniformDeviate*, to implement features common to the two algorithms.

```
// Assign to a package
package coyote.math;

// Base class for all UniformDeviate types
public abstract class UniformDeviate
          implements NumericConstants
{
    // The current seed value
    protected int m_nSeed;

    // Constants used in conversion from int to float
    final protected static float  FLT_MAX = 1.0F - FLT_EPS;
    final protected static float  FLT_AM  = 1.0F /
                                            2147483563.0F;
    final protected static double DBL_MAX = 1.0D - DBL_EPS;
    final protected static double DBL_AM  = 1.0D /
                                            2147483563.0D;
```

(continued)

```java
// Error message constant
final protected static IllegalArgumentException ERR_HILO
    = new IllegalArgumentException
        ("UniformDeviate: Invalid lo-hi range");

// Default constructor
public UniformDeviate()
{
    // Set seed to current time in milliseconds
    m_nSeed = (int)System.currentTimeMillis();
}

// Constructor with seed value
public UniformDeviate(int seed)
{
    m_nSeed = seed;
}

// Get next value in sequence
public abstract int nextValue();

// Get next uniform deviate as a float
final public float nextFloat()
{
    // Get next value
    nextValue();

    // Convert
    float temp = FLT_AM * m_nSeed;

    if (temp > FLT_MAX)
        return FLT_MAX;
    else
        return temp;
}

// Get next uniform deviate as a double
final public double nextDouble()
{
    // Get next value
    nextValue();

    // Convert
    double temp = DBL_AM * m_nSeed;

    if (temp > DBL_MAX)
        return DBL_MAX;
    else
        return temp;
}
```

```
// Get next value between high and low extremes
final public int nextValue(int lo, int hi)
    throws IllegalArgumentException
{
    // Verify parameters
    if (lo >= hi)
        throw ERR_HILO;

    // Return ranged value
    return (int)((long)lo +
            ((long)hi - (long)lo) * nextFloat());
}

// Get next uniform deviate as a float within a range
final public float nextFloat(float lo, float hi)
    throws IllegalArgumentException
{
    // Verify parameters
    if (lo >= hi)
        throw ERR_HILO;

    // Return ranged value
    return lo + (hi - lo) * nextFloat();
}

// Get next uniform deviate as a double within a range
final public double nextDouble(double lo, double hi)
    throws IllegalArgumentException
{
    // Verify parameters
    if (lo >= hi)
        throw ERR_HILO;

    // Return ranged value
    return lo + (hi - lo) * nextDouble();
}
}
```

UniformDeviate belongs to my *coyote.math* package, and it is defined in the single source file *UniformDeviate.java*. The class implements the *NumericConstants* interface developed earlier in this chapter, so it has access to the constants *FLT_EPS* and *DBL_EPS*. *UniformDeviate* defines four constants of its own, which I use to convert 32-bit numeric values to *float* and *double* types. I defined *int m_nSeed* as a protected value to make it accessible only by *UniformDeviate* and its derived classes.

The default constructor assigns *m_nSeed* a value based on the system time; the second constructor sets *m_nSeed* to an explicit argument. When you're testing a program, it's often useful to generate the same set of pseudorandom numbers. To do that, use the second constructor with a constant seed to create your generator object.

I didn't need to specify that the ranged methods can throw an *InvalidArgumentException*, since that is one of the "unchecked" exceptions that are part of Java's standard packages. Even though the *throws* declaration isn't necessary, I still included it to clearly document the exceptions being thrown by my methods. If these methods were throwing several exceptions, I might try to avoid clutter by not listing *InvalidArgumentException*.

Subclasses will implement the abstract *nextValue* method; all other *UniformDeviate* methods output values based on the updated seed generated by *nextValue*. Calling *nextValue* itself returns *m_nSeed* after it has passed through the algorithm; the *nextFloat* and *nextDouble* methods each return a floating-point number between 0 and 1. I've also overloaded the *next* methods with versions that take arguments defining a low and high value range. The "ranged" functions throw an *IllegalArgumentException* if the low argument is greater than or equal to the high one. Since all three functions throw the same exception, I created a constant static *IllegalArgumentException* object as a field of *UniformDeviate*.

THE *SimpleUniformDeviate* CLASS

In 1988, S. K. Park and L. W. Miller studied a variety of pseudorandom number generators before suggesting what they termed to be the "minimum standard." They selected a multiplicative congruential algorithm as the best. Essentially, the algorithm updates the seed with the following formula.

$$S_{new} = (a*S) \bmod m$$

The two factors a and m must be picked with great care; Park and Miller decided that $a = 16,807$ and $m = 2,147,483,647$ were the best possible choices. Their algorithm is a solid performer, a good tool for many applications. I've implemented their algorithm in the *SimpleUniformDeviate* class.

```
// Assign to package
package coyote.math;

// Class SimpleUniformDeviate
final public class SimpleUniformDeviate
    extends UniformDeviate
{
    // Constants used in algorithm
    final private static int IA   = 16807;
    final private static int IM   = 2147483647;
    final private static int IQ   = 127773;
    final private static int IR   = 2836;
    final private static int MASK = 123459876;

    // Required constructors
    public SimpleUniformDeviate()
    {
        // Nothing to do
    }

    public SimpleUniformDeviate(int seed)
    {
        super(seed);
    }
```

```
    // Implementation of abstract method
    public int nextValue()
    {
        m_nSeed ^= MASK; // Prevent zero seed

        // Use Schrage's method of multiplying
        int k = m_nSeed / IQ;
        m_nSeed = IA * (m_nSeed - k * IQ) - IR * k;

        if (m_nSeed < 0)
            m_nSeed += IM;

        return m_nSeed;
    }
}
```

In *SimpleUniformDeviate*, I've defined a set of constants used in the algorithm. *IA* and *IM* correspond to the factors in the formula; the *IR* and *IQ* values allow multiplication of 32-bit *int* values within 32 bits, thus avoiding the need to use long values to prevent overflow. Two constructors simply call the constructors for *UniformDeviate*. The implementation of *nextValue* uses the Park and Miller algorithm to update the seed, which is returned. I use L. Schrage's technique for multiplying integer values without overflow.

THE *BetterUniformDeviate* CLASS

Although the Park and Miller algorithm is an excellent tool, it also has limitations. Subsequent numbers will differ by only a factor of 16,807, the value of *IA*. So a very small seed will tend to stay that way, making it unlikely, for example, that 1 will be followed by 2,000,000,000. Mathematicians can also point out other weaknesses in *SimpleUniformDeviate*; although those differences might seem insignificant, they can cause difficulties in processes that expect millions of evenly distributed numbers.

The authors of the excellent volume *Numerical Recipes in C* suggest solutions to these problems that add some new features to the Park and Miller algorithm. They use an array of generated values, shuffling them around, effectively keeping a set of seeds rather than just one. The shuffling adds overhead that might not be necessary for some purposes, so I've implemented this "better" uniform deviate generator as another class, *BetterUniformDeviate*.

```
// Assign to package
package coyote.math;

// Class BetterUniformDeviate
final public class BetterUniformDeviate
    extends UniformDeviate
{
    // Constants used in algorithm
    final private static int IA   = 16807;
```

(continued)

```
final private static int IM   = 2147483647;
final private static int IQ   = 127773;
final private static int IR   = 2836;
final private static int NTAB = 32;
final private static int NDIV = (1+(IM-1)/NTAB);

// Variables
private int m_nY = 0;
private int m_nV[] = new int[NTAB];

// Method to implement table initialization
private void initTable()
{
    int j, k;

    // Prevent 0 seed
    if (-m_nSeed < 1)
        m_nSeed = 1;
    else
        m_nSeed *= -1;

    // Load the shuffle table
    for (j = NTAB + 7; j >= 0; j--)
    {
        k = m_nSeed / IQ;
        m_nSeed = IA * (m_nSeed - k * IQ) - IR * k;

        if (m_nSeed < 0)
            m_nSeed += IM;

        if (j < NTAB)
            m_nV[j] = m_nSeed;
    }

    m_nY = m_nV[0];
}

// Required constructors
public BetterUniformDeviate()
{
    initTable();
}

public BetterUniformDeviate(int seed)
{
    super(seed);
    initTable();
}
```

```
// Implementation of abstract method
public int nextValue()
{
    int j, k;

    k = m_nSeed / IQ;
    m_nSeed = IA * (m_nSeed - k * IQ) - IR * k;

    if (m_nSeed < 0)
        m_nSeed += IM;

    j = m_nY / NDIV;
    m_nY = m_nV[j];
    m_nV[j] = m_nSeed;

    return m_nSeed;
    }
}
```

BetterUniformDeviate has some similarities to *SimpleUniformDeviate*. Two additional constants, *NTAB* and *NDIV*, define size and elements in the shuffle table. The constructors call the private *initTable* function to load the shuffle table with an initial set of values. The *nextValue* method then initializes the table, performs the Park and Miller algorithm, and finally swaps the result of that calculation into an element of the shuffle table, returning the old table value as the new seed.

Now I've created a small hierarchy of classes. The *UniformDeviate* class implements the *NumericConstants* interface in order to access predefined constants. Then I derive two classes from *UniformDeviate* to implement a pair of algorithms for generating random numbers. *UniformDeviate* provides a set of common utility functions inherited by its subclasses. In a program, I can use polymorphism.

```
boolean simpleAlgor = true;

// User input might change simpleAlgor to false

UniformDeviate uniDev;

if (simpleAlgor)
    uniDev = new SimpleUniformDeviate();
else
    uniDev = new BetterUniformDeviate();

int n = uniDev.nextValue();
```

Java will "know" the actual type of the *uniDev* object and will call the appropriate implementation of *nextValue* automatically. Based on selections made by the user, my program can select the type of pseudorandom number generator to be used at run time.

New Classes for *java.lang*

In addition to allowing inner and local classes, version 1.1 of the Java specification makes a number of minor changes in the language. New *Short* and *Byte* classes in the *java.lang* package provide services similar to those found in the other type-wrapping classes such as *Integer* and *Float*. In light of these additions, the *Number* class gains two new methods, *byteValue* and *shortValue*.

Java now also specifies a *Void* class, for the sake of completeness. You cannot instantiate a *Void* object.

Some Object-Oriented Philosophy

Now that we've discussed the ways in which Java handles classes, it's time to consider the kinds of classes you want in your programs. Object-oriented programming shouldn't be a haphazard process; you need to do some thinking about what your applets and applications will do before you begin designing their components.

If you're developing a simple Java program, you probably won't be very concerned with program design. The basic applet is a single class, derived from *Applet*; no class hierarchy is involved. But when you intend to use Java for a large-scale project, it is essential that you do some up-front design. Experience has taught me that object-oriented programs require more planning than other types of computer programs. You need a clear understanding of the fundamental organization and requirements of a software project before you can begin to design an object-oriented program in Java. You won't be able to properly define classes and their relationships unless you thoroughly understand the application *before* you begin programming. An unplanned object-oriented program quickly becomes a swamp of illogical classes tangled with thickets of poorly designed class hierarchies. If you've done a thorough initial analysis, the necessary class structure should become obvious. Some of the things you need to know are what kinds of data the applet will process, what those processes are, and how the elements of data in your program are interrelated.

The approach you use to build a class hierarchy depends on your program design. Begin by determining the nature of the data structures used in the project. Find the similarities and differences between the data structures, and group similarities together to form the building blocks of base classes. Begin working with the actual data at first, and then begin studying the related operations. Instead of building a function flowchart, design a class hierarchy chart that shows the various data types and their relationships to each other. Similar data structures are virtually guaranteed to have similar processing requirements; recognizing those requirements will help you design classes effectively. In later chapters, I show some of the techniques I use to design class hierarchies.

The champions of object-oriented programming make some pretty big promises. They tell us that Java programs will be easier to build because existing components can be linked together quickly and easily, and that the use of objects will make debugging easier because problems can be isolated within encapsulated data types. Future changes, they promise, can be implemented merely by deriving new program components from the existing ones.

That's the theory, anyway. As I've worked with object-oriented programming languages such as Java, I've come to realize that the additional benefits of object-oriented programming require more design and planning on the part of the software developer. It takes time to analyze an application, identify its components, develop the relationships between those components, and create the network of classes. Many programmers "hack" programs together, for whatever reason. To effectively build a complex application in Java, however, a programmer needs a clear idea of the data types needed, how they will be used, and their relationships.

Onward

For programmers steeped in C++, Java code may appear very familiar. But don't fall into the trap of thinking that Java *is* C++. The two languages differ in many ways. In the next chapter, I look at the ways in which these two languages differ in features and syntax; you'll also see an example that converts a C++ class to Java.

 Java Is Not C++

This chapter provides a quick look at some of the more significant ways in which Java differs from C++, a language that many of you are probably familiar with. Java may look like C++, but it isn't C++. In trying to maintain backward compatibility with C, C++ inherited many non-object-oriented features that are now considered archaic, perhaps even clunky. And C++ has a long history; it evolved through several versions at AT&T Labs before being run through the international standardization process. Along the way, C++ became something of a "kitchen-sink" language, a language that tries to meet everyone's needs without concern for how all of its features fit together.

What's Different?

If you're a C++ programmer, you'll find that Java lacks the following features that you may have become accustomed to:

- Pointers and pointer arithmetic
- Method references and pointers
- Method prototypes (These are not needed by Java.)
- Operator overloading
- Multiple inheritance
- Templates
- The *virtual* keyword (This is implied in Java.)
- Default arguments
- Enumerated types
- Friend functions
- Unsigned types
- A preprocessor
- The *long double* type
- Explicitly inline methods (Java automatically inlines some methods.)
- The *goto* statement

It may seem that Java is missing a lot of features, but Java really doesn't suffer, because its design offers alternatives to or removes the need for many of those C++ features. I already covered some of the differences, such as the approach to references, in Chapter 2. Now, here are some Java features that you won't find in C++:

- ◆ Cross-platform portability
- ◆ Automatic garbage collection
- ◆ Static initializers
- ◆ Guaranteed type ranges
- ◆ A true *boolean* type
- ◆ The *byte* type
- ◆ Methods that can return arrays
- ◆ Object-oriented arrays
- ◆ Built-in Internet capability
- ◆ Standardized exceptions
- ◆ Universal tools for creating graphic interfaces

I find Java's syntax cleaner than that of C++; many features of C++ simply aren't needed in Java programs, which can infer or bypass many of C++'s more obscure syntactic features. The only two features of C++ that I really miss are default arguments (which allow you to use less code for similar methods) and operator overloading. You'll see how I handle those omissions later in this chapter.

Program Structure

In most programming languages, including C++, source code is compiled into a set of object modules, which are then linked to form the final piece of software. The code is compiled directly into the machine code for the hardware platform, and it won't run in another environment. An executable program compiled on a PC wouldn't run on a Macintosh unless it were recompiled, for example.

One of Java's goals was to allow its programs to be portable across existing and future platforms. To accomplish that goal, the designers of Java defined an abstract computer known as the *Java virtual machine* (JVM). When you compile a *.java* source file, the result is a *.class* file containing object code for the JVM. When it begins execution, the Java virtual machine loads the *.class* files associated with the applet or application being executed; linking occurs at run time. Some JVMs, including the one that comes with Microsoft Internet Explorer, employ a technique known as *Just-in-Time (JIT)* compiling. The JIT compiler converts the virtual machine code to native code for the PC that's running the Java program, thus making applets run far more quickly. And the JIT compilation is very speedy since it only has to translate from JVM code to native code, whereas a normal compiler must start from uncompiled source code.

C++ and Java Object Models

When it comes to turning source files into executable code, Microsoft Visual C++ and Microsoft Visual J++ differ in many ways.

◆ When you compile a C++ program, you're producing a file that contains machine code specific to a target hardware platform. Java produces "bytecode" output from your *.java* files; bytecode is a platform-independent machine language.

◆ Whereas a C++ program is executed directly by a computer's central processing unit, a Java program must be interpreted through the virtual machine. The virtual machine is similar, in this respect, to the p-code interpreter used to execute Microsoft Visual Basic programs.

◆ The C++ compiler produces a single object (*.obj*) file for each source (*.cpp*) file compiled; J++ will produce a separate bytecode (*.class*) file for the main class and each inner class in the source file.

◆ A final application in C++ is made up of several object files that are linked together. A Java applet or application consists of a set of *.class* files that reference each other and that are loaded as required by the virtual machine.

◆ You can create a native-code executable program from Java *.class* files by using the jexegen utility provided by Microsoft with the Java SDK. (jexegen is a free product separate from the Visual J++ compiler and is included on the CD-ROM accompanying this book.) The jexegen program is not a compiler; it binds relevant parts of the Java virtual machine to linked class files, creating a standalone program.

◆ A C++ application is linked to a library of standard functions and precompiled classes, which are either stored in a dynamic-link library or bound to the final executable during linking. In Java, the standard library consists of standard *.class* files (which are loaded at run time like any other *.class* files) and the built-in features of the Java virtual machine.

Types

Java types are either *reference types* or *primitive types*. The primitive types are the integers, characters, and floating-point numbers from which you build reference types. A reference type is simply a class; you create all reference objects with the *new* operator, and the objects are always accessed via references. The primitive types, such as *long* and *double*, act just like their C++ counterparts.

PRIMITIVE TYPES

Java does not support a *long double* type or any *unsigned* types. C++ types have suggested sizes and ranges, but the actual implementation of any type is left up to the compiler vendor. Thus, on some machines, an *int* might contain 16 bits, while on another platform *int*s may be 32 bits long. This is one of the most annoying attributes of C and C++, especially when you're trying to develop a portable application. You never know quite what your data types are going to look like, and many "portable" programs include long lists of conditional type definitions predicated on some macro that identifies the target system.

Java solves this problem by explicitly defining the bit length and range of its primitive numeric types, as shown in Table 3-1. Every Java virtual machine uses the bit sizes and ranges in this table.

TABLE 3-1
Numeric Type Sizes and Ranges

Group	Type	Bits	Minimum Value	Maximum Value
Integer	byte	8	−128	127
	short	16	−32,768	32,767
	int	32	−2,147,483,648	2,147,483,647
	long	64	−9,223,372,036,854,775,808	9,223,372,036,854,775,807
	char	16	0	65,535
Floating	float	32	$\approx\pm1.40130 \times 10^{-38}$	$\approx\pm3.40282 \times 10^{38}$
	double	64	$\approx\pm2.22507 \times 10^{-308}$	$\approx\pm1.79769 \times 10^{308}$

The *byte* type is new; it replaces the C++ *char* type often used for small integers. Java's *char* type is 16 bits long, twice the size of its C++ counterpart; it has been expanded to handle the Unicode character set, a 65,535-character superset of the old 7-bit ASCII character set. The first 127 characters in Unicode are the old ASCII characters, retained for compatibility with existing programs. But the larger Unicode character set allows for the inclusion of non-Latin alphabets, standard mathematical characters, and other symbols that just won't fit into the 256 slots available with the 8-bit *char* type. And since Java intrinsically supports Unicode, programmers no longer have to figure out how to mix the large character set with older ASCII-based code—a requirement of many Windows-based programs.

One of the great advantages of Java's Unicode support is that it allows you to create identifiers with characters other than numbers and the letters *A* through *Z*. You can use *any* Unicode character in an identifier, with the exception of the space and reserved Java symbols such as parentheses and numeric operators. So your programs can have identifiers such as *København*, *Cæsar*, or *Bòrd* ("table" in Scots Gaelic).

Java defines a *boolean* type, similar to the *bool* type provided in standard C++. But Java's *boolean* type isn't a numeric value; you can't equate it to 0 (for false) and nonzero (for true) as you can with C and C++ logical values. A *boolean* type can have only one of two values, *true* or *false*, which are reserved words in Java. If you are accustomed to using numeric values in your C++ logical statements, you'll have to change your coding style for Java. For example, the following is a legal construct in C.

```
int flag = 1;

if (flag)
{
    // Do something
}
```

Java will reject such code, complaining that *flag* isn't a logical value. For Java programs, you'll need to change the code.

```
int flag = 1;

if (flag != 0)
{
    // Do something
}
```

When cutting and pasting code from C++ to Java, you'll want to check any conditional statements inside *if*, *while*, and especially *for* loops for this situation.

Arrays

An array in C++ is essentially a linear block of memory that contains a series of elements. Unless you check indexes yourself, C++ will not object if you index outside the bounds of an array. And most old-time C programmers pride themselves on their knowledge of how to use pointers to provide high-performance access to array elements. But C++ arrays fall short when you want to return an array from a method: You can't do so unless you use a pointer.

All that changes in Java, in which an array is actually a kind of object. A Java method can return an array because it will be returning only a reference and not the array data itself. All arrays in Java are dynamically created via the *new* operator and automatically act as if they inherit the methods defined by the *Object* class; arrays also implement the *Cloneable* interface. Every array knows how many components it has, and Java will throw an exception if you address a component beyond an array's bounds. As in C++ arrays, the first component in a Java array is the 0th component; you cannot use negative array indexes. And you don't really need to worry about how Java organizes the elements of an array because you can reference those components only through indexes.

Java also allows a slightly different syntax for array declaration.

```
int Array [];  // C++-style declaration
int [] Array;  // Java-style declaration
```

You do not specify the number of components when you declare a Java array; the empty brackets merely specify that the object is an array. The number of bracket pairs defines the level of nesting; Java, like C++, allows the use of arrays of arrays to simulate some of the functionality of multidimensional matrices.

```
int []      Array1;  // An array of ints
int [][]    Array2;  // An array of arrays of ints
int [][][]  Array3;  // An array of arrays of arrays of ints
int []      a1, a2;  // Two arrays of ints
```

The statements above don't create arrays or allocate any memory; they just create references to arrays. As you would for any object, you call *new* to generate the components of an array.

```
int []      Array1 = new int[10];
int [][]    Array2 = new int[5][5];
int [][][]  Array3 = new int[7][3][12];
```

An array initializer both creates an array and fills its components with specified values.

```
float [] Array1 = { 1, 2, 3, 4, 5 }; // Array1 references a
                                     // five-element array
```

An array is just like any other object when it comes to memory management; the Java virtual machine will free the space used by any array that can no longer be reached through any reference.

To find the number of components in an array, use the *length* field (treated as public and final) that is part of all Java arrays.

```
void zeroOut(int [] array)
{
    for (int i = 0; i < array.length; ++i)
        array[i] = 0;
}
```

Every array also has a *clone* method that makes the copying of arrays quite simple.

```
int [] prime = { 0, 1, 2, 3, 5, 7, 11 };
int [] prime2 = (int [])prime.clone();
```

Casting *clone* to an integer array is required because *clone* is actually a polymorphic method (inherited implicitly from *Cloneable*) that the array overrides; the result of *clone* is a reference to *Object*.

Strings and Characters

In Java, an array of *char*s is not a *String* object, and neither a *String* object nor a *char* array has a null (0) character terminator—or any other terminating character, for that matter. This is quite different from the way things are in C++. So what, exactly, is *String* in Java? It's a class, like almost everything else in Java. If you're familiar with the C++ *string* class or the library of string methods in the C header file *string.h*, you'll have little trouble understanding the *String* class just by looking at its class definition.

```
public final class String extends Object
{
    // Constructors
    public String();
    public String(byte  ascii [], int  hibyte);
    public String(byte  ascii [], int  hibyte,
                    int  offset, int  count);
    public String(char  value []);
    public String(char  value [], int  offset,
                    int  count);
    public String(String  value);
    public String(StringBuffer  buffer);

    // Methods
    public char charAt(int  index);
    public int compareTo(String  anotherString);
    public String concat(String  str);
    public static String copyValueOf(char  data []);
    public static String copyValueOf(char  data [],
                                    int  offset, int count);
    public boolean endsWith(String  suffix);
    public boolean equals(Object  anObject);
    public boolean equalsIgnoreCase(String  anotherString);
    public void getBytes(int srcBegin, int srcEnd,
                    byte dst[], int dstBegin);
    public void getChars(int srcBegin, int srcEnd,
                    char dst[], int dstBegin);
    public int hashCode();
    public int indexOf(int  ch);
    public int indexOf(int  ch, int  fromIndex);
    public int indexOf(String  str);
    public int indexOf(String  str, int  fromIndex);
    public String intern();
    public int lastIndexOf(int  ch);
    public int lastIndexOf(int  ch, int  fromIndex);
    public int lastIndexOf(String  str);
    public int lastIndexOf(String  str, int  fromIndex);
```

```
public int length();
public boolean regionMatches(boolean ignoreCase,
                             int toffset,
                             String other, int ooffset,
                             int len);
public boolean regionMatches(int  toffset,
                             String  other,
                             int  ooffset, int  len);
public String replace(char  oldChar, char  newChar);
public boolean startsWith(String  prefix);
public boolean startsWith(String  prefix, int toffset);
public String substring(int  beginIndex);
public String substring(int  beginIndex, int endIndex);
public char[] toCharArray();
public String toLowerCase();
public String toString();
public String toUpperCase();
public String trim();
public static String valueOf(boolean  b);
public static String valueOf(char  c);
public static String valueOf(char  data []);
public static String valueOf(char  data [], int  offset,
                             int  count);
public static String valueOf(double  d);
public static String valueOf(float  f);
public static String valueOf(int  i);
public static String valueOf(long  l);
public static String valueOf(Object  obj);
}
```

All text literals in a program are *String* objects; as such, they are constants that cannot be changed. And you can't use the *String* class as a superclass because it is defined as final. So what good is the *String* class? Plenty! The class defines a set of methods that essentially replace all of C's library methods.

You construct *String* objects from a series of values, using the + concatenation operator.

```
int age = 35;
String name = "John Doe";

String s1 = name + " is " + age + " years old";
```

The statement above generates the string "John Doe is 35 years old" from its components. The Java compiler knows how to convert each member of the concatenation list into a *String* object, using the *toString* method each data type implicitly inherits from the *Object* class.

Since *String* objects are constants, Java uses another class when implementing the + operator: *StringBuffer*. That class uses the following methods to define a mutable string of characters.

```
public class StringBuffer extends Object
{
    // Constructors
    public StringBuffer();
    public StringBuffer(int  length);
    public StringBuffer(String  str);

    // Methods
    public StringBuffer append(boolean  b);
    public StringBuffer append(char  c);
    public StringBuffer append(char  str []);
    public StringBuffer append(char  str [], int  offset,
                                int  len);
    public StringBuffer append(double  d);
    public StringBuffer append(float  f);
    public StringBuffer append(int  i);
    public StringBuffer append(long  l);
    public StringBuffer append(Object  obj);
    public StringBuffer append(String  str);
    public int capacity();
    public char charAt(int index);
    public void ensureCapacity(int  minimumCapacity);
    public void getChars(int  srcBegin, int  srcEnd,
                          char  dst [], int  dstBegin);
    public StringBuffer insert(int  offset, boolean  b);
    public StringBuffer insert(int  offset, char  c);
    public StringBuffer insert(int  offset, char  str []);
    public StringBuffer insert(int  offset, double  d);
    public StringBuffer insert(int  offset, float  f);
    public StringBuffer insert(int  offset, int  i);
    public StringBuffer insert(int  offset, long  l);
    public StringBuffer insert(int  offset, Object  obj);
    public StringBuffer insert(int  offset, String  str);
    public int length();
    public StringBuffer reverse();
    public void setCharAt(int  index, char  ch);
    public void setLength(int  newLength);
    public String toString();
}
```

Behind the scenes, Java compiles the string concatenation shown earlier into the following sequence.

```
StringBuffer temp = new StringBuffer(name);
temp.append(" is ");
temp.append(age);
temp.append(" years old");

String s1 = temp.toString();
```

The concatenation operator is simply a notation convenience, making the actual programs look nicer.

Your own classes can define methods to return *String* objects, as I did in this method I created to display *Polynomial* objects.

```
// Display polynomial as string
String stringPoly(Polynomial p)
{
    StringBuffer s = new StringBuffer("[");

    for (int i = p.getDegree() - 1; i >= 0; --i)
        s.append(p.getCoeff(i) + " ");

    s.append("]");

    return s.toString();
}
```

A *StringBuffer* object is limited in capability when compared to a *String* object; essentially, a *StringBuffer* object is meant to have new items appended to or inserted into its text. You can convert a *StringBuffer* object to a *String* object at any time via the *toString* method.

Converting a C++ Program to Java

If you look at the typical applets that are currently circulating on the Internet, you'll find that they're usually small and that few use Java's object-oriented facilities. Until recently, Java programmers thought small, producing mostly interesting graphical applets or coming up with ways to make imagemaps work better. But I think people are selling Java short, failing to see its potential as a mainstream application development tool. So I'm going to show you how I've converted one part of my class library from C++ to Java to demonstrate how well Java works for larger applications.

Changing a piece of code from C++ to Java isn't a task to be taken lightly. After almost a decade of writing C++ programs, I found that many of my assumptions about how Java works were just flat-out *wrong*. I'm going to lead you through the conversion of a C++ class into Java, showing you some of the tricks and traps that I encountered. I'll explain the application and show you the C++ implementation before going on to describe the issues involved in converting the code to Java.

Fractions

Java intrinsically supports integer (whole) and floating-point (decimal fraction) numbers. One type of value is noticeably absent: the true fraction, known formally as a *rational number*. If we have floating-point numbers, why do we need true fractions? For the most part, the *float* and *double* types are more than adequate for most computational tasks. But in some cases, a true fractional representation can be invaluable. For example, the fraction 1/3 cannot be represented accurately by a floating-point number since it is an infinite sequence beginning with 0.3333333.... And many calculations, such as those involving the English measurement system, use fractions.

When we were kids, many of us hated learning about fractions in school because working with them seemed arcane. Try adding 7/33 and 1/3; it takes a few moments to remember how to create a common denominator before adding the numerators and reducing the resulting fraction. Some calculators, including mine, can handle fraction math—and if a calculator can do it, so can a Java program.

The C++ *Fraction* Class

I wrote a basic *Fraction* class in C++ several years ago, and I'll use it as the basis for creating an equivalent Java class. *Fraction* is a C++ class template that instantiates a type-specific class based on a parameter. The template definition follows.

```
#include "stdlib.h"
#include "math.h"
#include "iostream.h"

namespace Coyote {

template
    <
    class T
    >
    class Fraction
        {
        public:
            // Constructors
            Fraction();
            Fraction(const Fraction<T> & r);
            Fraction(T num, T den = 1);

            // Assignment operator
            Fraction<T> & operator =
                (const Fraction<T> & r);

            // Conversion operators
            operator float() const;
            operator double() const;

            // Assignment of numerator and denominator
            Fraction<T> & assign(T num, T den = 1);

            // Negate
            Fraction<T> operator - () const;

            // Basic four operators
            friend Fraction<T> operator +
                (
                const Fraction<T> & r1,
                const Fraction<T> & r2
                );
```

```
        friend Fraction<T> operator -
            (
            const Fraction<T> & r1,
            const Fraction<T> & r2
            );

        friend Fraction<T> operator *
            (
            const Fraction<T> & r1,
            const Fraction<T> & r2
            );

        friend Fraction<T> operator /
            (
            const Fraction<T> & r1,
            const Fraction<T> & r2
            );

        // Shorthand operators
        Fraction<T> operator += (const Fraction<T> & r);
        Fraction<T> operator -= (const Fraction<T> & r);
        Fraction<T> operator *= (const Fraction<T> & r);
        Fraction<T> operator /= (const Fraction<T> & r);

        // Interrogation functions
        T getNumer() const;
        T getDenom() const;

    // Stream input/output
    friend istream & operator >>
        (
        istream & strm,
        Fraction<T> & r
        );

    friend ostream & operator <<
        (
        ostream & strm,
        const Fraction<T> & r
        );

    // Interrogators
    float asFloat();
    double asDouble();

protected:
    T Numer;
    T Denom;
```

(continued)

```
    private:
        // Reduce fraction and adjust sign
        void reduce();

        // Greatest common divisor
        static T gcd(T x, T y);

        // Least common multiple
        static T lcm(T x, T y);
    };

typedef Rational<long>  LongRational;
typedef Rational<short> ShortRational;
template
    <
    class T
    >
    inline Rational<T>::Rational()
        {
        Numer = 0;
        Denom = 0;
        }

template
    <
    class T
    >
    inline Rational<T>::Rational
        (
        const Rational<T> & r
        )
        {
        Numer = r.Numer;
        Denom = r.Denom;
        }

template
    <
    class T
    >
    inline Rational<T> & Rational<T>::operator =
        (const Rational<T> & r)
        {
        Numer = r.Numer;
        Denom = r.Denom;
        return *this;
        }
```

```
template
    <
    class T
    >
    inline Rational<T> Rational<T>::operator - () const
        {
        Rational<T> result = *this;
        result.Numer = -result.Numer;
        return result;
        }

template
    <
    class T
    >
    Rational<T>::Rational(T num, T den)
        {
        if (den == 0)
            num = 0;

        Numer = num;
        Denom = den;

        Reduce();
        }

template
    <
    class T
    >
    Rational<T> & Rational<T>::operator ()
        (
        T num,
        T den
        )
        {
        if (den == 0)
            num = 0;

        Numer = num;
        Denom = den;

        Reduce();

        return *this;
        }
```

(continued)

```
template
    <
    class T
    >
    Rational<T> operator + (const Rational<T> & r1,
                            const Rational<T> & r2)
        {
        Rational<T> result;

        result.Denom =
            Rational<T>::LCM(r1.Denom,r2.Denom);

        result.Numer =
            r1.Numer * (result.Denom / r1.Denom)
          + r2.Numer * (result.Denom / r2.Denom);

        result.Reduce();
        return result;
        }

template
    <
    class T
    >
    Rational<T> operator - (const Rational<T> & r1,
                            const Rational<T> & r2)
        {
        Rational<T> result;

        result.Denom =
            Rational<T>::LCM(r1.Denom,r2.Denom);

        result.Numer =
            r1.Numer * (result.Denom / r1.Denom)
          - r2.Numer * (result.Denom / r2.Denom);

        result.Reduce();
        return result;
        }

template
    <
    class T
    >
    Rational<T> operator * (const Rational<T> & r1,
                            const Rational<T> & r2)
        {
        Rational<T> result;
        result.Numer = r1.Numer * r2.Numer;
        result.Denom = r1.Denom * r2.Denom;
```

```
        result.Reduce();
        return result;
        }

template
    <
    class T
    >
    Rational<T> operator / (const Rational<T> & r1,
                            const Rational<T> & r2)

        {
        Rational<T> result;
        result.Numer = r1.Numer * r2.Denom;
        result.Denom = r1.Denom * r2.Numer;
        result.Reduce();
        return result;
        }

template
    <
    class T
    >
    Rational<T> Rational<T>::operator +=
        (const Rational<T> & r)
        {
        *this = *this + r;
        return *this;
        }

template
    <
    class T
    >
    Rational<T> Rational<T>::operator -=
        (const Rational<T> & r)
        {
        *this = *this - r;
        return *this;
        }

template
    <
    class T
    >
    Rational<T> Rational<T>::operator *=
        (const Rational<T> & r)
        {
        *this = *this * r;
        return *this;
        }
```

(continued)

```
template
    <
    class T
    >
    Rational<T> Rational<T>::operator /=
        (const Rational<T> & r)
        {
        *this = *this / r;
        return *this;
        }
template
    <
    class T
    >
    Rational<T>::operator float() const
        {
        float result;

        if (Denom == 0)
            {
            if (Numer == 0)
                result = 0.0F;
            else
                result = (float)HUGE_VAL;
            }
        else
            result = (float)Numer /
                     (float)Denom;

        return result;
        }

template
    <
    class T
    >
    Rational<T>::operator double() const
        {
        double result;

        if (Denom == 0)
            {
            if (Numer == 0)
                result = 0.0;
            else
                result = HUGE_VAL;
            }
        else
            result = (double)Numer /
                     (double)Denom;
```

```
        return result;
        }

template
    <
    class T
    >
    istream & operator >> (istream & strm,
                            Rational<T> & r)

        {
        T n, d;
        char c;

        strm >> n >> c;

        if (c == '/')
            strm >> d;
        else
            {
            strm.putback(c);
            d = 1;
            }

        r = Rational(n,d);

        return strm;
        }

template
    <
    class T
    >
    ostream & operator << (ostream & strm,
                            const Rational<T> & r)
        {
        strm << r.Numer << "/" << r.Denom;
        return strm;
        }

template
    <
    class T
    >
    inline T Rational<T>::GetNum() const
        {
        return Numer;
        }
```

(continued)

```
template
    <
    class T
    >
    inline T Rational<T>::GetDen() const
        {
        return Denom;
        }

template
    <
    class T
    >
    void Rational<T>::Reduce()
        {
        // check for zero numerator
        if (Numer == 0)
            {
            Denom = 0;
            return;
            }
        else
            if (Denom == 0)
                {
                Numer = 0;
                return;
                }

        if ((Numer > 0) && (Denom < 0))
            {
            Numer = -Numer;
            Denom = -Denom;
            }
        else
            {
            if ((Numer < 0) && (Denom < 0))
                {
                Numer =  Numer;
                Denom = -Denom;
                }
            }

        T div = GCD(Numer,Denom);

        Numer /= div;
        Denom /= div;
        }
```

```
template
    <
    class T
    >
    T Rational<T>::LCM(T x, T y)

        {
        x = labs(x);
        y = labs(y);

        if (x == y)
            return x;
        else
            {
            if (x < y)
                return (y / GCD(x, y)) * x;
            else
                return (x / GCD(y, x)) * y;
            }
        }

template
    <
    class T
    >
    T Rational<T>::GCD(T x, T y)
        {
        x = labs(x);
        y = labs(y);

        T temp;

        while (y != 0)
            {
            temp = x % y;
            x = y;
            y = temp;
            }

        return x;
        }

} // end namespace Coyote
```

The Java *Fraction* Class

I obviously can't just copy the C++ code into a *.java* file and expect it to compile and run! To begin with, the C++ *Fraction* class is a template, and Java doesn't support templates. I considered basing my Java class on the standard *Integer* class, but I need to perform calculations with the numerator and the denominator, and *Integer* doesn't support mathematical operations. So I settled on using the Java *long* type, a 64-bit signed integer type.

Of course, Java doesn't use include files (it doesn't even have a preprocessor), so I could eliminate those lines. Because my C++ class was part of the namespace *Coyote*, I defined the Java class as a member of the package *coyote.math*. Here is the first part of my Java class.

```java
package coyote.math;

//
//
// Fraction
//
//
public class Fraction
{
    //-----------------------
    // Fields
    //-----------------------
    protected long m_nNumer;
    protected long m_nDenom;

    //-----------------------
    // Methods
    //-----------------------

    // Reduce
    protected void reduce()
    {
        // Handle 0 in numerator or denominator
        if (m_nNumer == 0L)
        {
            m_nDenom = 0L;
            return;
        }
        else
        {
            if (m_nDenom == 0L)
            {
                m_nNumer = 0L;
                return;
            }
        }
```

```
        // Adjust signs
        if (m_nDenom < 0L)
        {
            m_nNumer = -m_nNumer;
            m_nDenom = -m_nDenom;
        }
        // Reduce by gcd
        long div = gcd(m_nNumer, m_nDenom);

        m_nNumer /= div;
        m_nDenom /= div;
    }

    // Greatest common divisor
    public static long gcd(long x, long y)
    {
        x = Math.abs(x);
        y = Math.abs(y);

        long temp;

        while (y != 0L)
        {
            temp = x % y;
            x = y;
            y = temp;
        }

        return x;
    }

    // Least common multiple
    public static long lcm(long x, long y)
    {
        x = Math.abs(x);
        y = Math.abs(y);

        if (x == y)
            return x;
        else
        {
            if (x < y)
                return (y / gcd(x, y)) * x;
            else
                return (x / gcd(y, x)) * y;
        }
    }
```

⋮

The *reduce* method uses the *gcd* (greatest common divisor) static method to perform reduction on a *Fraction* object. The *Fraction* class also provides an *lcm* (least common multiple) static method. I could have defined *gcd* and *lcm* as private members, but then they wouldn't have been available for the calculation of a common multiple or denominator outside the scope of *Fraction*. Several of the Java API classes follow this pattern, exporting useful utility functions as static methods for general use.

Because Java lacks default arguments, I needed to add an extra constructor and assignment operator to handle the case in which I assign just a numerator to a *Fraction* object.

⋮

```java
// Default constructor
public Fraction()
{
    m_nNumer = 0L;
    m_nDenom = 0L;
}

// Copy constructor
public Fraction(Fraction f)
{
    m_nNumer = f.m_nNumer;
    m_nDenom = f.m_nDenom;

    reduce();
}

// Other constructors
public Fraction(long n, long d)
{
    m_nNumer = n;
    m_nDenom = d;

    reduce();
}

public Fraction(long n)
{
    m_nNumer = n;
    m_nDenom = 1L;
}

// Assignment
public void assign(long n, long d)
{
    m_nNumer = n;
    m_nDenom = d;

    reduce();
}
```

```
    public void assign(long n)
    {
        m_nNumer = n;
        m_nDenom = 1L;
    }
```
⋮

I couldn't keep the operator methods from C++, much as I wanted to. Java does not support the definition of operator methods, which is too bad because operator methods improve the readability of programs by making formulas look "normal." But since I didn't have operator methods available, I defined named methods for the basic mathematical operations.

⋮

```
    // Negate
    public Fraction negate()
    {
        return new Fraction(-m_nNumer, m_nDenom);
    }

    // Add
    public Fraction add(Fraction f)
    {
        Fraction result = new Fraction();

        result.m_nDenom = lcm(m_nDenom, f.m_nDenom);

        result.m_nNumer =
                m_nNumer * (result.m_nDenom /   m_nDenom)
                + f.m_nNumer * (result.m_nDenom / f.m_nDenom);

        result.reduce();
        return result;
    }

    // Subtract
    public Fraction sub(Fraction f)
    {
        Fraction result = new Fraction();

        result.m_nDenom = lcm(m_nDenom, f.m_nDenom);

        result.m_nNumer =
                m_nNumer * (result.m_nDenom /   m_nDenom)
                - f.m_nNumer * (result.m_nDenom / f.m_nDenom);

        result.reduce();
        return result;
    }
```

(continued)

```
// Multiply
public Fraction mul(Fraction f)
{
    Fraction result =
        new Fraction(m_nNumer * f.m_nNumer,
                     m_nDenom * f.m_nDenom);
    result.reduce();
    return result;
}

// Divide
public Fraction div(Fraction f)
{
    Fraction result =
        new Fraction(m_nNumer * f.m_nDenom,
                     m_nDenom * f.m_nNumer);
    result.reduce();
    return result;
}
```
⋮

The interrogation and conversion methods work much the same in Java as they did in C++. But I couldn't translate the C++ stream operators << and >> into Java, so I replaced them with an overload of the *asString* method that *Fraction* automatically inherits from *Object*.

NOTE

All Java classes are subclasses of *Object*; if you do not include an *extends* clause in your class definition, Java will automatically assume *extends Object*.

The following code is for the interrogation and conversion methods.

⋮
```
// Get as a float
public float asFloat()
{
    return (float)m_nNumer / (float)m_nDenom;
}

// Get as a double
public double asDouble()
{
    return (double)m_nNumer / (double)m_nDenom;
}

// Get as a string
public String asString()
{
    return m_nNumer + "/" + m_nDenom;
}
```

```
    // Interrogate
    public long getNumer()
    {
        return m_nNumer;
    }

    public long getDenom()
    {
        return m_nDenom;
    }
}   // End class Fraction
```

Here's an example of a method that uses the *Fraction* class; it's part of the *RationalTest* applet, which you can find in the \ActiveVJ\Chap03 directory. Remember, if you intend to include the *Fraction* class in your application, you'll need to add an *import coyote.math.** declaration at the beginning of your *.java* source file.

```
public void paint(Graphics g)
{
    Fraction r1 = new Fraction(1L, 2L);
    Fraction r2 = new Fraction();
    Fraction r3;

    r2.assign(21, 31);

    r3 = r1.add(r2);
    g.drawString(r1.asString() + " + " +
                r2.asString() + " = " +
                r3.asString(),
                10, 20);

    r3 = r1.sub(r2);
    g.drawString(r1.asString() + " - " +
                r2.asString() + " = " +
                r3.asString(),
                10, 40);

    r3 = r1.mul(r2);
    g.drawString(r1.asString() + " * " +
                r2.asString() + " = " +
                r3.asString(),
                10, 60);

    r3 = r1.div(r2);
    g.drawString(r1.asString() + " / " +
                r2.asString() + " = " +
                r3.asString(),
                10, 80);

    r1.assign(7, 12);
    r2.assign(6, 7);
```

(continued)

```
        r3 = r1.add(r2);
        g.drawString(r1.asString() + " + " +
                r2.asString() + " = " +
                r3.asString(),
                10, 100);

        r3 = r1.sub(r2);
        g.drawString(r1.asString() + " - " +
                r2.asString() + " = " +
                r3.asString(),
                10, 120);

        r3 = r1.mul(r2);
        g.drawString(r1.asString() + " * " +
                r2.asString() + " = " +
                r3.asString(),
                10, 140);

        r3 = r1.div(r2);
        g.drawString(r1.asString() + " / " +
                r2.asString() + " = " +
                r3.asString(),
                10, 160);

        g.drawString("as double = " + r3.asDouble(),
                10, 180);
        g.drawString("as float  = " + r3.asFloat(),
                10, 200);
    }
```

Translating code from C++ to Java requires you to change the way you think about some things, but it isn't an onerous task. In general, you'll find that your C++ template classes can be defined either as class hierarchies in terms of Java's *Object* class or as type-specific classes. And although default arguments and operator methods are convenient, you can write code without them.

Onward

Next I put the ideas from Chapters 1 through 3 into action by developing a complete object-oriented Java application. In the next chapter, I discuss the design process and use classes, interfaces, polymorphism, and other techniques to show how Java can be used to create a flexible set of software components.

4 Java at Work

n this chapter, I put the concepts from Chapters 1 through 3 to work by using Microsoft Visual J++ to develop an object-oriented application in Java. The typical one-class applet doesn't need to be very object-oriented; to really see what Java can do, you need to consider a fairly complex application that involves several classes and interfaces. In the example in this chapter, I develop such an application to solve a specific complicated problem. In the course of this program's development, I also construct a generic class package that can be used to solve many different types of problems.

The Problem

Computers are deterministic devices; most algorithms, by their very nature, proceed by executing a predefined sequence of operations. But sometimes a problem can't easily be solved by a deterministic algorithm; its solution set may be too large, or you may have no clue as to what the best solution is. Network optimization, large database searches, and optimal path determination often involve solution sets that cannot be examined practically by deterministic algorithms.

Here's an example of this sort of problem. Let's say that I've been given a Java class named *BlackBox*. I don't know where the source code is; all I have is the *BlackBox.class* file and the following definition of the public interface.

```
public final class BlackBox
{
    public static int test(int n);
}
```

Without the source code, it's difficult to know what is going on inside *BlackBox.test*; I can only feed it values and examine the associated output. Although no one knows what is going on inside the box, I have been given some information about the *test* method: Its output is a value from 0 through 32. Only one (unknown) input value generates the output value 32; all other values produce some number less than that. There does not appear to be an obvious mathematical correspondence between input values and their output values.

My task is to find the input value that produces the output value 32—in other words, to maximize the output of the black box. The brute force approach would be to test *BlackBox* with all 4,294,967,296 possible *int* values. The problem with such an approach isn't that it won't find the answer; assuming that the above facts are correct, one of the input values *will* generate the answer 32. Where brute force falls on its face is in the length of time it might take to find the answer. The loop might find the answer after a few loops, but it might take *billions* of loops.

The Tool: A Genetic Algorithm

A more effective approach would be to use a *genetic algorithm*. In its most basic sense, a genetic algorithm (GA) creates a set of solutions, tests them against a given problem, and then "breeds" a new set of solutions based on some measure of success. This is how natural evolution takes place; think of a biological species as life's solution to the problem of exploiting a niche. When you use a genetic algorithm, you "evolve" a solution to some specific problem, such as finding an optimal path, by emulating nature. Fortunately, the software universe is far less complex than the biological world, and no piece of software can—or needs to—incorporate all of life's techniques. Whereas living things need to develop flexible roles to survive in variable environments, computer algorithms often only need to find a specific answer to a fixed question.

Computer scientists still debate the precise definition of the genetic algorithm. In the broadest sense, a GA creates a set of solutions that reproduce based on their fitness in a given environment. The process follows this pattern:

1. **Initialization**   Create a starting population of random solutions. These are called *chromosomes*.

2. **Fitness testing**   Assign to each chromosome in the population a fitness value based on how it performs in response to the problem.

3. **Reproduction**   Chromosomes with higher fitness values are more likely to parent the optimal solution during reproduction. Use a *roulette wheel* to select parents; combine parts of the parents through *reproduction* to produce a new child. Make random changes in the child through *mutation* before it is assigned to the new problem. Select different reproduction and mutation operators using a roulette wheel.

4. **Creation of the next generation**   If the optimal solution has been found, the process is finished. Otherwise, replace the old set of chromosomes with the newly generated children. A *generation* is complete, and the process iterates to step 2.

That sequence implements, in a very simplistic way, the concept of survival of the fittest. The reproductive success of a solution is proportional to the fitness value assigned to it during evaluation. Of course, in this stochastic process, the least fit solution always has a small chance at reproduction, whereas the most fit solution may not reproduce at all. The outcome of a genetic algorithm is based on probability, just as biological success is grounded in chance. By "homing in on" a solution through fitness selection, a GA can dramatically reduce the size of the solution set.

Preliminary Design

Although this example presents a specific problem to be solved, namely the optimization of the output of *BlackBox.test*, I've also defined a more general goal: the creation of a set of extensible, polymorphic classes that allow the easy implementation of any genetic algorithm. Figure 4-1 on the following page shows the hierarchy of the class package I developed, *coyote.genetic*, using the same notation the Java documents use to describe the Java API packages.

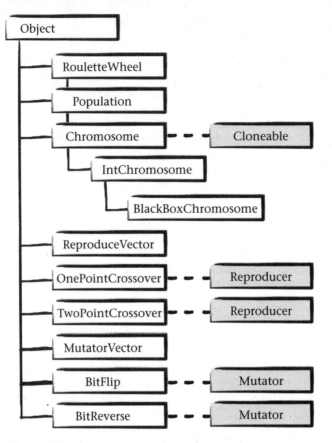

Figure 4-1. *The* coyote.genetic *package.*

The rectangles represent classes, with solid lines showing their ancestry. Thus, the *BlackBoxChromosome* class is a subclass of *IntChromosome*, which is a subclass of *Chromosome*, which in turn is derived from *Object*. The shaded rectangles represent interfaces implemented by various classes, as indicated by the dashed lines. For example, *BitFlip* is a subclass of *Object* that implements the *Mutator* interface.

Why did I design my hierarchy this way? In many cases, the design of a package is a matter of personal preference and philosophy—and, as with all philosophy, there often isn't a "right" or "wrong" way of doing things. The best way to start your design is usually to write down what your application does. A simple text description, perhaps a numbered list, is adequate for the task. Then examine your description for key components and processes.

For my genetic algorithm system, I began by examining the four-step process outlined above. I looked for nouns and verbs: *population, chromosome, reproduce,* and so on. A noun almost always becomes a class. A verb becomes a class if it acts on several types of nouns; it becomes a method if it seems tied directly to a class. For example, the process of *using the roulette wheel* is a class because it applies to selecting parent chromosomes and to choosing reproduction and mutation operators. But the concept of *creating a generation* affects only a population, so I defined it as a method for the population class. Because there is a set of choices for reproduction and mutation operators, I created abstract superclasses for both operations.

The outline of my program told me that "fitness" is a property of all chromosomes, which indicated that I should once more use a superclass to encapsulate a common feature of several types. Having created my basic class hierarchy, I now understand what my approach should be during development.

The Solution

A genetic algorithm is just the ticket for solving problems such as the one posed by *BlackBox*. The solutions—known as *chromosomes* in GA terminology—will be *int* values, and their fitness will be determined by testing them with the *BlackBox.test* method. Think of these *int*s as the binary equivalents of DNA-based chromosomes. The genetic algorithm will need to define a set of *int*s—the population—from which the more successful *int*s will be selected to create a new set of solutions. It will need to include operations that will combine parent chromosomes and mutate their children. And I want to make all of this object-oriented and polymorphic so that my genetic algorithm system can be used to solve the widest possible set of problems.

Chromosomes

I've already identified two generic concepts: populations and chromosomes. The population concept applies to all chromosomes, regardless of type. With that in mind, I defined an abstract *Chromosome* class that encapsulates the common elements of all chromosome types: a fitness value and an abstract method that evaluates the chromosome.

```
package coyote.genetic;

import coyote.math.*;

//
//
// Chromosome
//
//
public abstract class Chromosome implements Cloneable
{

    //----------------------
    // Fields
    //----------------------

    // Fitness value
    protected float m_fitness;

    // Predefined exception objects
    static private final RuntimeException m_err1 =
        new RuntimeException
                ("Chromosome: incompatible types");
```

(continued)

```
//----------------------
// Methods
//----------------------

// Constructor
public Chromosome()
{
    m_fitness = 0.0F;
}

// Copy constructor
public Chromosome(Chromosome c)
{
    m_fitness = c.m_fitness;
}

// Interrogator
public float getFitness()
{
    return m_fitness;
}


// Verify compatible chromosomes
protected void verify(Chromosome c)
{
    if (this.getClass() !/ c.getClass())
        throw m_err1;
}

// Compute fitness
abstract public float testFitness();


// Return a clone of this object
public Object clone()
    throws CloneNotSupportedException
{
    return super.clone();
}


}
```

The *Chromosome* class states that a common attribute of all subclasses is a *float* value representing the fitness of a specific chromosome. A subclass designed to solve a specific task will implement the *testFitness* method according to its needs, returning and storing the fitness value. Because many problems involve the search for solutions that can be mapped onto a 32-bit *int* chromosome, I created *IntChromosome* as a subclass of *Chromosome*.

```java
package coyote.genetic;

import coyote.math.*;

//
//
// IntChromosome
//
//
public abstract class IntChromosome extends Chromosome
{

    //-----------------------
    // Fields
    //-----------------------

    // Genes for this chromosome
    protected int m_genes;

    //-----------------------
    // Methods
    //-----------------------

    // Constructor
    public IntChromosome()
    {
        super();
        m_genes = GARand.rand.nextValue();
    }

    // Copy constructor
    public IntChromosome(IntChromosome ic)
    {
        super(ic);
        m_genes = ic.m_genes;
    }

    // Get genes
    public int getGenes()
    {
        return m_genes;
    }

    // Set genes
    public int setGenes(int g)
    {
        int x = m_genes;
        m_genes = g;
        return x;
    }
```

(continued)

```
                    // Display as string
                    public String toString()
                    {
                        return "gene: " +
                                Integer.toHexString(m_genes) +
                                ", fit = " +
                                m_fitness;
                    }

                }
```

IntChromosome is still an abstract class that implements a generic chromosome that is a 32-bit *int* value; the actual implementation of *testFitness* is application-specific. You can think of *IntChromosome* as a refinement of *Chromosome*, defining a more specific variant of its parent. Now, from *IntChromosome*, I can create a class whose particular task is to optimize the output of *BlackBox.test*.

```
package coyote.genetic;

import coyote.math.*;

//
//
// BlackBoxChromosome
//
//
public final class BlackBoxChromosome
    extends IntChromosome
{

    //-----------------------
    // Methods
    //-----------------------

    // Constructor
    public BlackBoxChromosome()
    {
        super();
    }

    // Copy constructor
    public BlackBoxChromosome(BlackBoxChromosome bbc)
    {
        super(bbc);
    }

    // Test fitness
    public float testFitness()
    {
        m_fitness = BlackBox.test(m_genes);

        return m_fitness;
    }
```

```
    // Clone
    public Object clone()
    {
        return new BlackBoxChromosome(this);
    }
}
```

Chromosome implements the Java API's *Cloneable* interface; complete subclasses such as *BlackBoxChromosome* should implement the *clone* method to duplicate themselves.

As far as the *Population* class (described later) is concerned, the actual data that defines a chromosome is unimportant; the population needs to know only how fit the chromosome is. The *Population* class simply uses *Chromosome* objects through a polymorphic interface. But before I implement the *Population* class, a few more pieces are required.

Roulette Wheels

A simulated roulette wheel is an excellent tool for selecting parents based on their fitness. You've probably seen a standard gambler's roulette wheel—a spinning circle divided into 37 or 38 equal-size, pie-shaped sections. The croupier sets the wheel spinning and at the same time throws a marble into the bowl in the direction opposite to that in which the wheel is moving; the marble goes round and round, bounces about, and finally comes to rest in one of the numbered sections.

In a genetic algorithm, chromosomes from the parent generation are placed around the wheel. Chromosomes occupy more or fewer slots depending on their relative fitness; each equal-size slot on the wheel represents a fitness point. The total number of slots on the wheel is equal to the total number of fitness points of the population. The chromosomes with the largest fitness values tend to be the most likely resting places for the marble since they occupy more slots. Essentially, the simulated roulette wheel generates a random number that is some fraction of the total fitness of the parent population; then, starting from an arbitrary fixed point, it counts around the wheel until it finds the selected fitness point slot. The chromosome that occupies that slot is then selected for reproduction.

Let's look at a small example with a population of five. Table 4-1 shows this population and its corresponding fitness values. The total fitness of this population is 60. Figure 4-2 on the following page shows how these chromosomes would be distributed around the roulette wheel.

TABLE 4-1
A Hypothetical Population and Its Fitness Values

Chromosome	Fitness Value
10110110	20
10000000	5
11101110	15
10010011	8
10100010	12

Fitness points

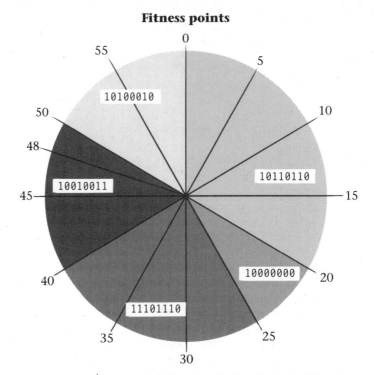

Figure 4-2. *An example roulette wheel showing the distribution of five chromosomes.*

Chromosome 10110110 occupies slots 1 through 20 and has a 34 percent chance of being selected as a parent, whereas 10000000 occupies only five slots (21 through 25) and has only an 8 percent chance of generating a new chromosome. Each chromosome in a new generation will be parented by chromosomes selected from the old generation. The selection of five pairs of parents requires the algorithm to generate ten random numbers in the range 1 through 60. For example, if the algorithm generates the values 44 and 31, the chromosomes selected are 10010011 (which occupies slots 40 through 48) and 11101110 (which occupies slots 25 through 40). The complete selection results are shown in Table 4-2.

TABLE 4-2
Roulette Wheel Selection of Parent Chromosomes

Random Numbers	Father Chromosome	Mother Chromosome
44, 31	10010011	11101110
5, 32	10110110	11101110
49, 3	10100010	10110110
18, 27	10110110	11101110
22, 54	10000000	10100010

The chromosomes with the highest fitness values, 10110110 and 11101110, each parent three members of the new population; even the chromosomes with the lowest fitness values will be parents once.

I implemented the *RouletteWheel* class using the following code.

```
package coyote.genetic;

import java.util.*;
import coyote.math.*;

//
//
// RouletteWheel
//
//
public final class RouletteWheel
{

    //-----------------------
    // Fields
    //-----------------------

    // Table of weights
    private FloatVector m_weights;

    // Total "weight" of all indexes
    private float m_totalWt;

    // Predefine exceptions
    static private final IllegalArgumentException m_err1 =
        new IllegalArgumentException
            ("RouletteWheel: negative weight");

    static private final IllegalArgumentException m_err2 =
        new IllegalArgumentException
            ("RouletteWheel: nonpositive total weight");

    //-----------------------
    // Methods
    //-----------------------

    // Constructors
    public RouletteWheel()
    {
        m_weights = new FloatVector();
    }

    public RouletteWheel(float [] wtList)
    {
        m_weights = new FloatVector();
```

(continued)

```
        for (int i = 0; i < wtList.length; ++i)
            addWeight(wtList[i]);
    }

    // Copy constructor
    public RouletteWheel(RouletteWheel rw)
    {
        m_weights = new FloatVector(rw.m_weights);
        m_totalWt = rw.m_totalWt;
    }

    // Interrogation methods
    public float getWeight(int n)
    {
        return m_weights.floatAt(n);
    }

    public float getTotalWeight()
    {
        return m_totalWt;
    }

    public FloatVector getWeightTable()
    {
        return m_weights;
    }

    // Change a specific weight
    public float setWeight(int n, float w)
    {
        if (w < 0.0F)
            throw m_err1;

        float result = m_weights.floatAt(n);

        m_weights.setFloatAt(n, w);

        m_totalWt -= result + w;

        if (m_totalWt <= 0.0F)
            throw m_err2;

        return result;
    }

    // Add a new weight to the table
    public void addWeight(float w)
    {
```

```
        if (w <= 0.0F)
            throw m_err1;

        m_weights.addFloat(w);
        m_totalWt += w;
    }

    // Get a randomly selected index
    public int getIndex()
    {
        if (m_totalWt <= 0.0F)
            throw m_err2;

        float s = GARand.rand.nextFloat() * m_totalWt;

        int i = 0;

        while (true)
        {
            if (i >= m_weights.size())
                break;

            s -= m_weights.floatAt(i);

            if (s < 0.0)
                break;

            ++i;
        }

        return i;
    }

}
```

Now that I have a tool for selecting parent chromosomes, I need to consider how reproduction occurs.

Reproduction

Reproduction creates a new chromosome from two parents. The most common technique for this is known as *crossover,* and it comes in two flavors. In *one-point crossover,* the program combines a pair of parents by randomly selecting a point at which pieces of the parents' bit strings are swapped. Table 4-3 shows four examples of one-point crossover, using the chromosomes from Table 4-1. The vertical bar in the child chromosome indicates the point of crossover.

TABLE 4-3
Examples of One-Point Crossover

Father Chromosome	Mother Chromosome	Crossover Point	Child Chromosome
10010011	10110110	3	100|10110
10000000	10110110	6	100000|10
10110110	11101110	2	10|101110
10110110	11101110	5	10110|110

Another technique is *two-point crossover,* which swaps the middle of one parent with the middle of another, using two randomly selected bit positions to indicate the beginning and end of the swap section. Table 4-4 shows how two-point crossover works.

TABLE 4-4
Examples of Two-Point Crossover

Father Chromosome	Mother Chromosome	Crossover Point 1	Crossover Point 2	Child Chromosome
10010011	**10110110**	3	6	100|**1011**|1
10000000	**10110110**	0	4	**10110**|000
10110110	**11101110**	2	3	10|**10**|0110

Crossover allows the mixing of attributes from different chromosomes. Some experts define genetic algorithms as only those processes that include some form of crossover. Although such a dogmatic viewpoint is arguable, my research shows that crossover does enhance the performance of genetic algorithms.

Schemata

In association with crossover, there is also the theory of *schemata,* which are sets of bits that provide building blocks or components for high-fitness chromosomes. John Holland, inventor of the genetic algorithm at the University of Michigan, determined that crossover mixes schemata from the chromosomes with the highest fitness values, thus increasing the frequency of valuable schemata within a population.

Different types of chromosomes will require different algorithms and techniques for reproduction. Chromosome reproduction is an example of a common process that has several possible implementations—a clear indication that I need to design with polymorphic types in mind. I defined a simple interface, *Reproducer,* to declare the abstract function *reproduce* common to all reproduction operators.

```
package coyote.genetic;

//
//
// Reproducer
//
//
public interface Reproducer
{

    //-----------------------
    // Methods
    //-----------------------

    Chromosome reproduce(Chromosome father,
                          Chromosome mother);
        throws CloneNotSupportedException;
}
```

Remember, all interface methods are *abstract*, which means that they are polymorphic. I can now define any number of reproduction operators, all of them implementing *Reproducer* so they can be treated in a polymorphic fashion. Such is the essence of object-oriented programming, in which you define common concepts that can be used through interfaces and other abstract definitions. The *OnePointCrossover* class implements the *Reproducer* interface for *IntChromosomes*, checking its polymorphic arguments to ensure that it is operating on the appropriate type of chromosome.

```
package coyote.genetic;

//
//
// OnePointCrossover
//
//
public class OnePointCrossover implements Reproducer
{

    //-----------------------
    // Fields
    //-----------------------

    private static RuntimeException m_err1 =
        new RuntimeException
            ("OnePointCrossover: incompatible chromosomes");

    //-----------------------
    // Methods
    //-----------------------

    public Chromosome reproduce(Chromosome father,
                                 Chromosome mother)
```

(continued)

```
                        throws CloneNotSupportedException

        {
            if ((father instanceof IntChromosome)
            &&  (mother instanceof IntChromosome))
            {
                IntChromosome child =
                    (IntChromosome)father.clone();

                int fg = ((IntChromosome)father).getGenes();
                int mg = ((IntChromosome)mother).getGenes();

                int mask =
                    0xFFFFFFFF << GARand.rand.nextValue(0, 32);

                child.setGenes((fg & mask) | (mg & (~mask)));

                return child;
            }
            else
                throw m_err1;
        }


    }
```

The *TwoPointCrossover* class also implements *Reproducer*.

```
    package coyote.genetic;

    //
    //
    // TwoPointCrossover
    //
    //
    public class TwoPointCrossover implements Reproducer
    {

        //-----------------------
        // Fields
        //-----------------------

        private static RuntimeException m_err1 =
            new RuntimeException
                ("TwoPointCrossover: incompatible chromosomes");

        //-----------------------
        // Methods
        //-----------------------

        public Chromosome reproduce(Chromosome father,
                                    Chromosome mother)
            throws CloneNotSupportedException
```

```
{
    if ((father instanceof IntChromosome)
    && (mother instanceof IntChromosome))
    {
        IntChromosome child =
            (IntChromosome)father.clone();

        int fg = ((IntChromosome)father).getGenes();
        int mg = ((IntChromosome)mother).getGenes();

        int p1 = GARand.rand.nextValue(0, 32);
        int p2 = 0;

        do
        {
            p2 = GARand.rand.nextValue(0, 32);
        }
        while (p2 == p1);

        // Swap if needed
        if (p2 > p1)
        {
            int temp = p1;
            p1 = p2;
            p2 = temp;
        }

        int mask = (0xFFFFFFFF << p1) |
                   (0xFFFFFFFF >>> (31 - p2));

        child.setGenes((fg & mask) | (mg & (~mask)));

        return child;
    }
    else
        throw m_err1;
}


}
```

NOTE

You might have noticed my use of the >>> unsigned shift operator (which does not exist in C++) in *TwoPointCrossover.reproduce*. In my initial implementation, I used only the >> operator, which does a *signed* right shift, filling the left bits of the result with 1s! I wanted Java to fill the shifted value with 0 bits on the left, so I needed to use the >>> operator.

Genetic algorithms can employ more than one form of reproduction, and I wanted a flexible system that allowed me to use any number of reproduction operators, each "weighted" to influence the chance of its being selected. The efficacy of a given reproductive operator often depends on the nature of the problem being solved; for example, you might want one-point crossover to happen twice as often as two-point crossover. Knowing how to set the ratios between various operators is largely a matter of experience; in general, two-point crossover works best when you are solving problems with short schemata, whereas one-point crossover is most efficacious when you are working with larger schemata (which would be broken up with two-point crossover). The *ReproducerVector* class is a wrapper around the standard API *Vector* class; it uses a *RouletteWheel* object to randomly select a reproduction operator from a dynamic list.

```java
package coyote.genetic;

import java.util.*;

//
//
// ReproducerVector
//
//
public class ReproducerVector
{

    //-----------------------
    // Fields
    //-----------------------

    // List of Reproducer objects
    protected Vector m_reproducers;

    // Roulette wheel for choosing reproducers
    protected RouletteWheel m_chooser;

    // Exceptions
    private RuntimeException m_err1 =
        new RuntimeException
            ("ReproducerVector: empty vector");

    //-----------------------
    // Methods
    //-----------------------

    // Constructor
    public ReproducerVector()
    {
        m_reproducers = new Vector();
        m_chooser     = new RouletteWheel();
    }
```

```
    // Install a new reproducer
    public void addReproducer(Reproducer m, float w)
    {
        m_reproducers.addElement(m);
        m_chooser.addWeight(w);
    }

    // Select a reproducer by roulette wheel
    public Reproducer select()
    {
        if (m_reproducers.size() == 0)
            throw m_err1;

        return (Reproducer)
            m_reproducers.elementAt(m_chooser.getIndex());
    }

}
```

One last point: both crossover classes (and other components in the *coyote.genetic* package) use a common random number generator, which I've defined in the all-static, all-public *GARand* class.

```
package coyote.genetic;

import coyote.math.*;

//
//
// GARand
//
//
public class GARand
{

    // "Random number" generator
    public static BetterUniformDeviate rand;

    static
    {
        rand = new BetterUniformDeviate();
    }

}
```

The single *BetterUniformDeviate* object in *GARand* encapsulates a common tool used by several *coyote.genetic* classes.

Mutation

The final step in reproduction is mutation, which involves the random change of one or more bits in each chromosome of the new population. The primary purpose of mutation is to increase variation in a population; mutation is most important in populations in which the initial solution set is a small subset of all possible solutions. It is possible, for example, for every instance of an essential bit to be 0 in the initial population. In such a case, crossover could never set that bit to 1; mutation, however, *could* set that bit.

As with reproduction, I created a superinterface—*Mutator*—to provide the method that must be defined by every mutation operator.

```
package coyote.genetic;

//
//
// Mutator
//
//
public interface Mutator
{

    //------------------------
    // Methods
    //------------------------

    Chromosome mutate(Chromosome c)
        throws CloneNotSupportedException;
}
```

Programmers use various techniques to mutate chromosomes. A common system sets a probability that any given bit will be changed; a test is performed for each bit to see whether its value should be changed. Such a system requires the generation of many random numbers, which degrades program performance. For example, a population of 50 *int* chromosomes would use 1600 random values in doing mutation on a bit-by-bit basis!

For my application, I defined two forms of mutation. The *BitFlip* mutator selects a bit that will have its value "flipped," or complemented.

```
package coyote.genetic;

//
//
// BitFlip
//
//
public class BitFlip implements Mutator
{

    //------------------------
    // Fields
    //------------------------

    private static RuntimeException m_err1 =
        new RuntimeException
            ("BitFlip: incompatible chromosomes");
```

```
//----------------------
// Methods
//----------------------

public BitFlip()
{
    super();
}

public Chromosome mutate(Chromosome c)
    throws CloneNotSupportedException
{
    if (c instanceof IntChromosome)
    {
        IntChromosome x = (IntChromosome)c.clone();

        int g    = x.getGenes();
        int mask = 1 << GARand.rand.nextValue(0, 32);

        if ((g & mask) != 0)
            g &= ~mask;
        else
            g |= mask;

        x.setGenes(g);

        return x;
    }
    else
        throw m_err1;
}

}
```

A second type of mutation reverses the order of the bits in an *IntChromosome* object. This corresponds to a natural process that inverts genes within a DNA chromosome. The following defines the *BitReverse* class.

```
package coyote.genetic;

//
//
// BitReverse
//
//
public class BitReverse implements Mutator
{

    //----------------------
    // Fields
    //----------------------
```

(continued)

```
private static RuntimeException m_err1 =
    new RuntimeException
        ("BitReverse: incompatible chromosome");


//------------------------
// Methods
//------------------------

public BitReverse()
{
    super();
}

public Chromosome mutate(Chromosome c)
    throws CloneNotSupportedException
{
    if (c instanceof IntChromosome)
    {
        IntChromosome x = (IntChromosome)c.clone();

        int g1 = x.getGenes();
        int g2 = 0;

        int m1 = 0x00000001;
        int m2 = 0x80000000;

        for (int i = 0; i < 32; ++i)
        {
            if ((g1 & m1) != 0)
                g2 |= m2;

            m1 <<= 1;
            m2 >>>= 1;
        }

        x.setGenes(g2);

        return x;
    }
    else
        throw m_err1;
}

}
```

As with reproduction operators, I wanted to define a list of mutators for a given population so that I could give a weight to each mutator to control its relative prevalence. The *MutatorVector* class, shown here, is similar in scope and design to the *ReproducerVector* class described above.

```
package coyote.genetic;

import java.util.*;
```

```
//
//
// MutatorVector
//
//
public class MutatorVector
{

    //-----:-----------------
    // Fields
    //-----------------------

    // List of mutator objects
    protected Vector m_mutators;

    // Roulette wheel for choosing mutators
    protected RouletteWheel m_chooser;

    // Exceptions
    private RuntimeException m_err1 =
        new RuntimeException("MutatorVector: empty vector");


    //-----------------------
    // Methods
    //-----------------------

    // Constructor
    public MutatorVector()
    {
        m_mutators = new Vector();
        m_chooser  = new RouletteWheel();
    }

    // Install a new mutator
    public void addMutator(Mutator m, float w)
    {
        m_mutators.addElement(m);
        m_chooser.addWeight(w);
    }

    // Select a mutator by roulette wheel
    public Mutator select()
    {
        if (m_mutators.size() == 0)
            throw m_err1;

        return (Mutator)
            m_mutators.elementAt(m_chooser.getIndex());
    }
}
```

Now that I have all my tools in place, I need to define a population and the process that performs the genetic optimization of *BlackBox.test*.

Populations

Tying all of these concepts together is the *Population* class, which deals with a generic array of *Chromosome* objects. When you construct a *Population* object, you provide it with an array of chromosomes, vectors of mutator and reproduction operators, and a probability that mutation will occur. To execute a cycle of fitness testing, reproduction, and mutation, call the *nextGeneration* method. Here is the *Population* class definition.

```
package coyote.genetic;

import coyote.math.*;

//
//
// Population
//
//
public class Population
{

    //-----------------------
    // Fields
    //-----------------------

    // Vector of chromosomes
    protected Chromosome [] m_pop;

    protected float m_fBestFit = 0.0F;

    // Vectors of operators
    private MutatorVector    m_mutators;
    private ReproducerVector m_reproducers;

    // Probabilities
    private float m_fMuteRate;

    //-----------------------
    // Methods
    //-----------------------

    // Constructor
    public Population(   Chromosome [] cv,
                          MutatorVector mv,
                        ReproducerVector rv,
                                float muteRate)
    {
        m_pop         = cv;
        m_mutators    = mv;
        m_reproducers = rv;

        m_fMuteRate = muteRate;
    }
```

```java
// Copy constructor
public Population(Population p)
{
    m_pop        = p.m_pop;
    m_mutators   = p.m_mutators;
    m_reproducers = p.m_reproducers;
    m_fMuteRate  = p.m_fMuteRate;
}


// Interrogator
public float getBestFit()
{
    return m_fBestFit;
}


// Compute next generation
public String nextGeneration()
    throws CloneNotSupportedException
{
    int i;
    int best_i = 0;
    float best_f = Float.MIN_VALUE;
    float f;

    // Create a roulette wheel for this population
    RouletteWheel rw = new RouletteWheel();

    // Test fitness for each chromosome
    for (i = 0; i < m_pop.length; ++i)
    {
        // Compute new fitness
        f = m_pop[i].testFitness();

        // Add fitness to roulette wheel
        rw.addWeight(f);

        // Is this the best so far?
        if (f > best_f)
        {
            best_f = f;
            best_i = i;
        }
    }

    m_fBestFit = best_f;

    // Create string from best chromosome
    String result = m_pop[best_i].toString();
```

(continued)

```
// Create new population
Chromosome [] new_pop =
    new Chromosome [m_pop.length];

// Copy best into new population
new_pop[0] = m_pop[best_i];

// Fill remainder of new population
// by reproduction and mutation
Chromosome c;

for (i = 1; i < m_pop.length; ++i)
{
    // Reproduction
    c = m_reproducers.select().reproduce
            (m_pop[rw.getIndex()],
             m_pop[rw.getIndex()]);

    // Mutation
    if (GARand.rand.nextFloat() < m_fMuteRate)
        c = m_mutators.select().mutate(c);

    // Store new chromosome
    new_pop[i] = c;
}

m_pop = new_pop;

// Return string
return result;
    }
}
```

Population.nextGeneration keeps the best chromosome from the parent generation in the new population. This is called *elitist selection*, which always copies the most fit chromosome into the next generation, guaranteeing that the current best solution to a problem survives, and ensuring that populations never lose ground on fitness.

Population's *nextGeneration* method processes one cycle: fitness testing and reproduction. The *String* object returned by *nextGeneration* contains the hexadecimal representation and fitness value of the best chromosome from the parent generation. *Population* is a generic process because it is written in terms of polymorphic superclasses.

The GATest Application

Now that the *coyote.genetic* package is in place, it's a simple matter to implement a Java application that will find the solution to the *BlackBox* problem. I created GATest to achieve this purpose, but GATest can also be used in a more general manner to explore the effects of different forms of mutation and reproduction on a genetic algorithm. The applet allows the user to input a population size, the number of generations to run, and the relative chances of different reproducers and mutators.

GATest

```
import java.applet.*;
import java.awt.*;
import coyote.genetic.*;
import coyote.math.*;
import GATestFrame;

public class GATest extends Applet
{

    //----------------------
    // Fields
    //----------------------

    // Visual components
    Button    ctlGo;
    TextField ctlMute;
    TextField ctlPop;
    TextField ctlGen;
    TextField ctlBit;
    TextField ctlCros;
    List      ctlList;

    Label     lblMute;
    Label     lblPop;
    Label     lblGen;
    Label     lblBit;
    Label     lblCros;
    Label     lblMsg;


    //----------------------
    // Methods
    //----------------------

    public GATest()
    {
    }
```

(continued)

```
public String getAppletInfo()
{
    return "Name: GATest\r\n" +
           "Author: Scott Robert Ladd\r\n" +
           "Created with Microsoft Visual J++ " +
           "Version 1.1";
}

public static void main(String args[])
{
    // Create window to contain applet GATest
    GATestFrame frame = new GATestFrame("GATest");

    // Show frame
    frame.show();
    frame.hide();
    frame.resize(frame.insets().left +
                 frame.insets().right  + 400,
                 frame.insets().top +
                 frame.insets().bottom + 250);

    // Start the applet within the frame window
    GATest applet_GATest = new GATest();

    frame.add("Center", applet_GATest);
    applet_GATest.init();
    applet_GATest.start();
    frame.show();
}

public void init()
{
    // Resize display
    setLayout(null);
    resize(400, 250);

    // Create controls
    ctlGo   = new Button("Go");
    add(ctlGo);
    ctlGo.reshape(220, 10, 60, 23);

    ctlPop  = new TextField("200");
    add(ctlPop);
    ctlPop.reshape(220, 40, 40, 23);

    lblPop = new Label("Population");
    add(lblPop);
    lblPop.reshape(265, 40, 100, 23);
```

```
        ctlGen  = new TextField("100");
        add(ctlGen);
        ctlGen.reshape(220, 70, 40, 23);

        lblGen = new Label("Generations");
        add(lblGen);
        lblGen.reshape(265, 70, 100, 23);

        ctlMute = new TextField("2.5");
        add(ctlMute);
        ctlMute.reshape(220, 100, 40, 23);

        lblMute = new Label("% Mutation");
        add(lblMute);
        lblMute.reshape(265, 100, 100, 23);

        ctlBit = new TextField("2");
        add(ctlBit);
        ctlBit.reshape(220, 130, 40, 23);

        lblBit = new Label(": 1 Flip/Rev Ratio");
        add(lblBit);
        lblBit.reshape(265, 130, 100, 23);

        ctlCros = new TextField("1");
        add(ctlCros);
        ctlCros.reshape(220, 160, 40, 23);

        lblCros = new Label(": 1 1X/2X Ratio");
        add(lblCros);
        lblCros.reshape(265, 160, 100, 23);

        ctlList = new List();
        add(ctlList);
        ctlList.reshape(10, 10, 200, 200);

        lblMsg = new Label("Genetic Algorithm Example");
        add(lblMsg);
        lblMsg.reshape(10, 225, 300, 23);

    }

public void destroy()
{
    // Nothing to do
}
```

(continued)

```
public void paint(Graphics g)
{
    // Nothing to do
}

public void start()
{
    // Nothing to do
}

public void stop()
{
    // Nothing to do
}

public boolean action(Event event, Object obj)
{
    if (event.target == ctlGo)
    {
        try
        {
        lblMsg.setText("Initializing...");

        // Get parameters
        int pop =
            Integer.parseInt(ctlPop.getText());

        if (pop < 2)
        {
            lblMsg.setText
                ("Population must be >= 2!");
            return true;
        }

        int gen =
            Integer.parseInt(ctlGen.getText());

        if (gen < 2)
        {
            lblMsg.setText("Generations must be >= 2!");
            return true;
        }

        float mut =
            Float.valueOf(ctlMute.getText()).floatValue();
        mut /= 100.0F;

        if ((mut < 0.0F) || (mut > 1.0F))
        {
```

```
        lblMsg.setText
            ("% Mutation must be > 0 and < 100!");
        return true;
    }

    float bRatio =
        Float.valueOf(ctlBit.getText()).floatValue();

    if (bRatio <= 0.0F)
    {
        lblMsg.setText("Flip/Rev ratio must be > 0!");
        return true;
    }

    bRatio = bRatio / (bRatio + 1.0F) * 100.0F;

    float xRatio =
        Float.valueOf(ctlCros.getText()).floatValue();

    if (xRatio <= 0.0F)
    {
        lblMsg.setText("1X/2X ratio must be > 0!");
        return true;
    }

    xRatio = xRatio / (xRatio + 1.0F) * 100.0F;

    // Disable Go control
    ctlGo.disable();
    ctlList.clear();

    // Construct vector of chromosomes
    Chromosome [] cv = new Chromosome [pop];

    for (int i = 0; i < pop; ++i)
        cv[i] = new BlackBoxChromosome();

    // Construct vector of mutators
    MutatorVector mv = new MutatorVector();
    mv.addMutator(new BitFlip(), bRatio);
    mv.addMutator(new BitReverse(), 100.0F - bRatio);

    // Construct vector of reproducers
    ReproducerVector rv = new ReproducerVector();
    rv.addReproducer(new OnePointCrossover(), xRatio);
    rv.addReproducer
        (new TwoPointCrossover(), 100.0F - xRatio);
```

(continued)

```
                // Construct population
                Population p = new Population(cv, mv, rv, mut);

                // Run generations
                int g;

                for (g = 1; g <= gen; ++g)
                {
                    lblMsg.setText("Generation: " + g);
                    ctlList.addItem((g < 10 ? "0" : "") + g +
                                    ": " + p.nextGeneration());

                    if (p.getBestFit() == 32)
                        break;
                }

                // Disable Go control
                ctlGo.enable();

                if (p.getBestFit() == 32)
                    lblMsg.setText
                        ("Found 32 in generation " + g + "!");
                else
                    lblMsg.setText("Failure! Oh, the shame...");

                return true;
            }
            catch (Exception x)
            {
                lblMsg.setText(x.toString());
                return true;
            }
        }

        return false;
    }

}
```

The meat of GATest is in the *action* method, in which a click of the Go button starts the genetic algorithm. The routine extracts and verifies data entered into the controls; it then allocates an array of *BlackBoxChromosome*s. After creating vectors of mutators and reproducers, *action* constructs a *Population* object. Then the main loop calls *p.nextGeneration* for a specified number of cycles, or until the best chromosome has the fitness value 32. For each generation, the program appends a new line to the list box, describing the best chromosome and its fitness value. The application displays its status (or an exception message) in a label at the bottom of its display. From Microsoft Internet Explorer, the GATest display looks something like the screen shown in Figure 4-3.

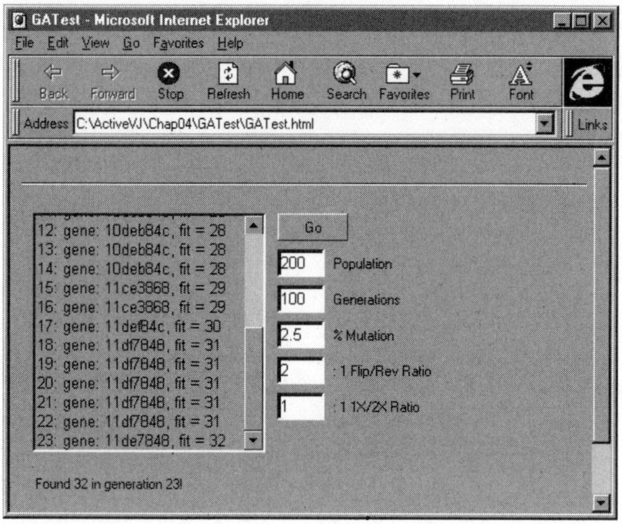

Figure 4-3. *The GATest applet in operation.*

How well do GATest and the *coyote.genetic* package work? With the program's default parameters, GATest will zero in on the correct value by the thirtieth generation, on average. In doing so, the genetic algorithm tests about 60,000 values (chromosomes) against *BlackBox.test*—a far cry from the billions of values that might need to be tried by a deterministic algorithm.

Here is the actual implementation of the *BlackBox* class.

```
package coyote.genetic;

//
//
// BlackBox
//
//
public final class BlackBox
{

    //-----------------------
    // Fields
    //-----------------------

    static int m_Secret = 299792456;

    //-----------------------
    // Methods
    //-----------------------

    public static int test(int n)
    {
        int fit  = 0;
        int mask = 1;
```

(continued)

```
        for (int i = 0; i < 32; ++i)
        {
            if ((n & mask) == (m_Secret & mask))
                ++fit;

            mask <<= 1;
        }

        return fit;
    }


}
```

The action that *BlackBox.test* performs is to compare an input value, bit by bit, with a hidden constant. The fitness value is a count of the matching bits. That's why only one *int* value returns the maximum fitness value, 32.

I've defined GATest with a *main* method that creates a frame for displaying the applet. This allows you to run the applet with a Java viewer—or you can use a tool such as Microsoft *jexegen* to turn GATest into a standalone Win32 application.

Rules of Thumb

You'll need to experiment with GAs for a while before they become somewhat intuitive. I certainly haven't covered the subject of genetic algorithms in much depth in this chapter because this book's focus is on Java programming. You'll find several references in the bibliography that will take you further. To end this discussion, I pass along some of the things I've learned from working with genetic algorithms, providing a few rules of thumb to help you effectively evolve solutions to problems.

♦ Chromosome evaluation and fitness calculation are the most time-consuming components of a genetic algorithm. If you optimize your fitness function, your genetic algorithm will run much more quickly.

♦ In a 4-bit chromosome, only 16 possibilities exist; crossover probably won't create any new chromosome variations in such an environment because all possibilities are probably represented, even in a small population. Mutation, in turn, has less effect on longer chromosomes; changing one bit in a 256-bit string has less influence than flipping a single bit in a 16-bit chromosome does.

♦ Too much mutation eliminates the value of selection by fitness. Simply put, a high mutation rate produces a stochastic population that never allows crossover to select important schemata because the schemata are too often altered by mutation.

♦ Too little mutation, on the other hand, limits diversity so much that the population never evolves at all.

- Small populations tend to become dominated by a single strategy and lack the robustness required to adapt. This is reflected in the old theory that no (biological) species can survive if its population count is below a certain minimum.

- A small population has another influence on genetic algorithms: it dilutes the influence of high fitness values on reproductive success. In a population of 10 chromosomes in which one has the fitness value 9 and the others have the fitness value 1, half of all parents will probably be selected from the 9 relatively unfit chromosomes, even though the best chromosome is 9 times more fit.

- For more complicated and difficult problems (such as a very small peak in a very large search space), use a large population. Large populations process more slowly than smaller ones, but they also cover more ground and have more schemata to exchange.

- Always use elitist selection. You're working with a computer, not nature, and you should not find it necessary to kill the best specimen by accident just because Mother Nature does.

- Long runs with large populations show more interesting behavior than do short runs with small populations.

- On the other hand, if your fitness landscape is very broad and flat, you'll find that large populations tend to drown out minor differences in fitness. This is where linear normalization becomes important. Linear normalization emphasizes the reproductive chances of the most fit chromosomes in a population. It accomplishes this by changing fitness values to reflect a weighted gradation of values.

- Populations of 100 or 200 individuals seem most useful, but I've gone as low as 50 and as high as 10,000 (and boy, was the latter run SLOW!)

Onward

Now it's time to move on to Part 2, in which I begin looking at Java in terms of its interaction with the elements of a web page. Java applications can communicate with ActiveX components, dynamic-link libraries, and Microsoft Visual Basic, Scripting Edition, building powerful compound documents from disparate components. Using Java in this way extends its power as an application development tool.

Part 2

Component-Oriented Java

Capital

Fluted Shaft

Base

5

Java
and ActiveX

A t first, web pages were unexciting displays of text, but they didn't stay that way for long. Developers soon began to add new features such as graphics, animation, and scripts to enliven their web pages and make them interactive. Java, the latest technology to add functionality to the Internet, enables web pages to interact with other software components.

Active Content

An HTML document that has multiple components that interact with one another is said to have *active content*. In a way, active content is an extension of object-oriented programming: the components communicate with one another by way of public interfaces. You can think of HTML as the binder that holds all these components together, making them aware of one another and passing information back and forth among them. Such interoperability requires the component interfaces to conform to a widely accepted standard. The Component Object Model (COM) is the standard that was developed for this purpose. COM is described in detail later in this chapter and even more thoroughly in Chapter 6, but first some background discussion is in order.

A Bit of History

A few years ago, Microsoft introduced Object Linking and Embedding, a component standard for the Windows operating system. Known by its initials, *OLE*, this technology provided two techniques—linking and embedding—that an application could use to work with another application's document:

- When an object—a spreadsheet or a graphic image, for instance—was **linked** to another application, the item would automatically be updated in the containing document when it was changed in the original application. Linked objects were very useful for complex documents that were developed with a variety of tools.

- Double-clicking on an object **embedded** in a container document would open another application within the container application that could be used to edit the object. The embedded application could use the container application's menus, client area, and so on, essentially taking over while the embedded object was being edited.

Later Microsoft extended the OLE definition to allow the creation of OLE controls. A control is a small, well-defined mini-application that performs a specific task; a developer could build an application by hooking together several OLE controls, even ones built in different languages. Again, this is a very object-oriented concept: the ability to define discrete parts of a program and then link them into complete applications. OLE controls, which can be built in Microsoft Visual Basic or C++ or licensed from an outside vendor, provide power and flexibility in program design. A developer can use a set of OLE controls to provide a consistent design—and share code—among applications.

Enter ActiveX

The World Wide Web was waiting for a distributed technology such as OLE. Web pages were already built from components such as graphic images and text blocks; the next step was to automate HTML documents by adding software components.

But OLE controls have one serious drawback: they tend to be large, at least for use on a network in which components must be transferred across phone or intranet lines. So Microsoft developed a refined version of the OLE control standard that allows developers to produce smaller components.

The result of that refinement is ActiveX technology, which facilitates the use of components in a network environment. Unlike OLE, ActiveX is optimized for the transfer of components; ActiveX allows you to download a control and its associated data asynchronously, and ActiveX controls have less overhead than their OLE counterparts, which results in smaller code modules. A web page can contain several embedded ActiveX controls, using Microsoft Visual Basic, Scripting Edition, or Java to communicate with them. Before I get into the programming details, let's look at how components communicate with one another.

Confusion About ActiveX and Java

Industry publications are often filled with erroneous comparisons of Microsoft's ActiveX technology and Java. Simply put, these two supposed competitors aren't the same thing: ActiveX is a binary standard for intercomponent communication; Java is a programming language. Microsoft has extended its virtual machine to support the easy use of ActiveX controls in Java applications and defines techniques for making Java components available through the COM mechanism.

Even the Java Beans specification (see Chapter 8) is not in conflict with ActiveX. If anything, Java Beans is a higher-level component definition that was designed for compatibility with several component standards, including ActiveX and OpenDoc. In essence, many pundits are looking for a conflict where there is none.

COM Basics

The standard that all interactive components conform to is called the Component Object Model, or COM. Objects use the COM standard to expose some of their features to other components and to access the exposed features of other components. I'll give you a brief introduction to COM here; Chapter 6 provides an indepth discussion.

INTERFACES

A COM component exposes sets of methods and fields through one or more interfaces. The term "expose" means to define an object field or method so that it is visible outside the component's definition. For example, the public methods and fields of a Java class define the interface that the class exposes for use by outside classes. But not all Java classes are COM objects; the operating system must be made aware of the interface and be told how to run the associated code. That is accomplished with an Object Description Language (ODL) file that describes the interfaces for COM objects. Each ODL description compiles into a type library (TLB) file containing information about the component's interfaces. When a new COM component is added to your system, an entry describing the methods and fields exposed by the new object type will be created in the system registry. Type libraries will be discussed a bit more in subsequent chapters.

All interfaces for COM objects are subclasses of *IUnknown*, which defines three universal interface methods: *QueryInterface*, *AddRef*, and *Release*. The first of these, *QueryInterface*, allows the user of an interface to use an interface-specific ID code to request a pointer to a different interface on that object. However, an object does not have to provide references to all of its interfaces through *QueryInterface*. For example, you might want to keep private an interface used only to debug code, or your company might want to limit access to a proprietary interface included in an otherwise public COM component.

The *AddRef* and *Release* methods together provide a rudimentary mechanism for garbage collection among COM components. However, the removal of unused components isn't automatic. COM was designed to produce small, fast components, so the elimination of unnecessary components was left as a manual process. Whenever you create an interface reference, you should call *AddRef* to increment a reference count for that interface. When an interface is no longer needed, make a call to *Release* to decrement the reference count. If the reference count for each of its interfaces is 0, the component knows that it is no longer being accessed and can remove itself from memory.

In some implementations, *AddRef* and *Release* manage a reference count for the entire object instead of each interface; a 0 reference count causes the removal of the object.

AGGREGATION

You can think of *aggregation* as the COM version of inheritance. Quite often, you'll have an existing COM object that you want to extend. Instead of changing the original component's source code, you can extend its functions by creating a new

Marshaling

When more than one process is active, a COM object can be in use in several execution threads at the same time. To avoid conflicts, COM implements *marshaling,* which is the packaging of parameters so that method calls can be invoked across thread boundaries with safety. This works in both standalone and distributed environments; in the latter case, the boundary is not between threads on the same machine, but between threads executing on separate but connected systems. COM also packages the return values for interthread components. Calls to COM will be like any other function calls.

For Java COM objects, marshaling is largely a hidden process managed by the operating system. Packaging goes on behind the scenes and ensures that communication across threads is reliable.

"wrapper" COM type. Again, this is very object-oriented; you can expand on existing code simply by knowing the base component beneath its COM definition. The original component can be written in any language—Visual Basic, C++, or whatever—and the extended COM type can also be constructed in any language. It's the ultimate in flexibility and code reuse!

Linking Active Content and Java

The COM standard might seem foreign to Java, but the two technologies are completely compatible. Java uses COM to communicate with and implement ActiveX controls.

Visual Basic, Scripting Edition, and Java Applets

Visual Basic, Scripting Edition, is yet another implementation of Microsoft Visual Basic; this version allows developers to write programs—known as scripts—inside an HTML document. Since this is a book about Java, I won't spend any time teaching you how to script with Visual Basic, Scripting Edition.

A Visual Basic, Scripting Edition, program can call any public member of a Java applet. For example, I could create a Java class.

```
public class Alarm extends Applet
{
    private int m_nVolume;

    public void setVolume(int v)
    {
        m_nVolume = v;
    }
}
```

I could then include the applet in an HTML document.

```
<APPLET CODE="Alarm.class" IS=ringer>
```

Then I could call *setVolume* from a script.

```
<SCRIPT language="VBScript">
<!--
Sub setLowVolume
    document.ringer.setVolume 10
End Sub

Sub setHighVolume
    document.ringer.setVolume 100
End Sub
-->
</SCRIPT>
```

The term *document* identifies the location of the *ringer* object, which is part of the web page. What I've done above *isn't* COM programming; I'm simply using Visual Basic, Scripting Edition, to communicate between the web page and the applet. But as you'll see, this mechanism is quite useful in connecting Java applets to ActiveX controls.

Using a COM Object from Java

When you want to use a COM object from within a Java applet, you must first create a set of *.class* files that describe the component's interfaces. Microsoft Developer Studio provides a tool that simplifies this task. Go to the Tools menu and select Java Type Library Wizard. The dialog box that appears displays a list of the COM objects registered on your system; an example of this is shown in Figure 5-1.

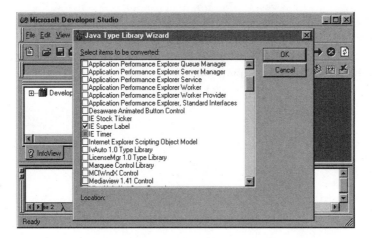

Figure 5-1. *The Java Type Library Wizard.*

In the figure, the box next to the IE Super Label component is checked. Super Label is an ActiveX control provided in Microsoft Internet Explorer; it allows the rotation and curving of text within a boundary box. Later in this chapter, I'll use Super Label from a Java application. So I click the OK button, and the output window displays the information shown in Figure 5-2.

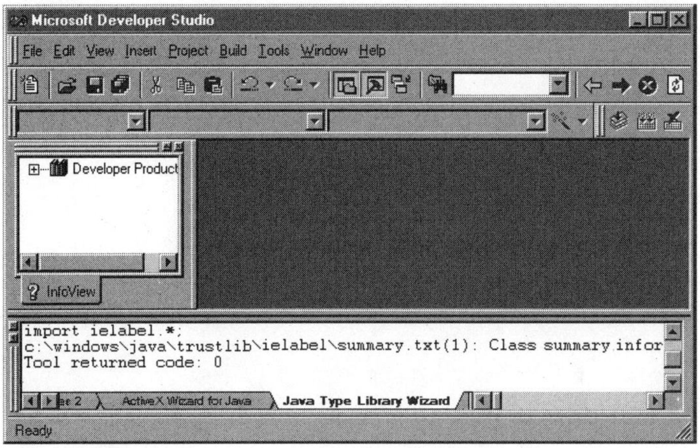

Figure 5-2. *Output from the Java Type Library Wizard.*

The Java Type Library Wizard creates a class for each of the COM interfaces exposed by Super Label. The wizard assumes that all registered COM objects can be trusted (trust is a concept I'll discuss later in this book), so it creates the classes as a Java package named *ielabel* under the directory \windows\java\trustlib. In the output window, you can see the statement

```
import ielabel.*;
```

which will link your Java code to these COM interface classes. Also in that directory is a file that describes the interfaces created; if you were to double-click on the line about "summary.txt," a file like this one would appear.

```
public class ielabel/IeLabel extends java.lang.Object
{
}

public interface ielabel/DIeLabelEvents
    extends com.ms.com.IUnknown
{
    public abstract void Change();
    public abstract void MouseUp(short, short, int, int);
    public abstract void Click();
```

(continued)

```
        public abstract void MouseDown(short, short, int, int);
        public abstract void DblClick();
        public abstract void MouseMove(short, short, int, int);
}

public interface ielabel/IIeLabel extends com.ms.com.IUnknown
{
        public abstract java.lang.String getBotXY();
        public abstract void putBotXY(java.lang.String);
        public abstract int getFontUnderline();
        public abstract void putFontUnderline(int);
        public abstract int getFontItalic();
        public abstract void putFontItalic(int);
        public abstract int getBotIndex();
        public abstract void putBotIndex(int);
        public abstract java.lang.String getFontName();
        public abstract void putFontName(java.lang.String);
        public abstract void AboutBox();
        public abstract int getFontStrikeout();
        public abstract void putFontStrikeout(int);
        public abstract int getBackColor();
        public abstract void putBackColor(int);
        public abstract int getTopIndex();
        public abstract void putTopIndex(int);
        public abstract int getFillStyle();
        public abstract int getFontBold();
        public abstract void putFontBold(int);
        public abstract void putFillStyle(int);
        public abstract java.lang.String getCaption();
        public abstract void putCaption(java.lang.String);
        public abstract java.lang.String getTopXY();
        public abstract void putTopXY(java.lang.String);
        public abstract int getMode();
        public abstract void putMode(int);
        public abstract int getForeColor();
        public abstract void putForeColor(int);
        public abstract int getTopPoints();
        public abstract int getFontSize();
        public abstract void putFontSize(int);
        public abstract void putTopPoints(int);
        public abstract int getAngle();
        public abstract void putAngle(int);
        public abstract int getBackStyle();
        public abstract void putBackStyle(int);
        public abstract int getBotPoints();
        public abstract void putBotPoints(int);
        public abstract int getAlignment();
        public abstract void putAlignment(int);
}
```

```java
public interface ielabel/enumBoolType
    extends com.ms.com.IUnknown
{
    public static final int ValFalse;
    public static final int ValTrue;
}

public interface ielabel/enumBackStyleType
    extends com.ms.com.IUnknown
{
    public static final int BackStyleTransparent;
    public static final int BackStyleOpaque;
}

public interface ielabel/enumFillStyleType
    extends com.ms.com.IUnknown
{
    public static final int FillStyleSolid;
    public static final int FillStyleOutline;
}

public interface ielabel/enumModeType
    extends com.ms.com.IUnknown
{
    public static final int ModeSimpleNoRotation;
    public static final int ModeDefault;
    public static final int ModeUserDefinedNoRotation;
    public static final int ModeUserDefinedRotation;
}

public interface ielabel/enumAlignType
    extends com.ms.com.IUnknown
{
    public static final int AlignLeftTop;
    public static final int AlignCenteredTop;
    public static final int AlignRightTop;
    public static final int AlignLeftCentered;
    public static final int AlignCentered;
    public static final int AlignRightCentered;
    public static final int AlignLeftBottom;
    public static final int AlignCenteredBottom;
    public static final int AlignRightBottom;
}
```

These Java interfaces define the events, methods, and return types exposed by the Super Label COM interfaces. Using classes created by the Java Type Library Wizard, I can begin talking to a COM object from my Java code.

A COM component need not be an ActiveX control, or even an OLE control. You can create a dynamic-link library in C++, for example, that exposes a COM interface, and thus can use that DLL from a Java applet.

ActiveX Controls and Java

A Java application cannot create an ActiveX component itself, nor can it reference a COM object directly. You must create the ActiveX control within the HTML document and then pass a reference to that object's interface to your Java code. Java can talk to an ActiveX control *only* through one of the control's COM interfaces. This is different from the way Java creates and manages the visual controls from the Abstract Window Toolkit, and it may take some getting used to. Here's an example.

Let's say I have created a Super Label object on my web page with the following piece of HTML.

```
<OBJECT ID="AXLabel" WIDTH=137 HEIGHT=137
 CLASSID="CLSID:99B42120-6EC7-11CF-A6C7-00AA00A47DD2">
    <PARAM NAME="_ExtentX" VALUE="3625">
    <PARAM NAME="_ExtentY" VALUE="3625">
    <PARAM NAME="Caption" VALUE="Rotate!">
    <PARAM NAME="Angle" VALUE="0">
    <PARAM NAME="Alignment" VALUE="4">
    <PARAM NAME="Mode" VALUE="1">
    <PARAM NAME="FillStyle" VALUE="0">
    <PARAM NAME="ForeColor" VALUE="#000000">
    <PARAM NAME="BackColor" VALUE="#B0C4C8">
    <PARAM NAME="FontName" VALUE="Arial">
    <PARAM NAME="FontSize" VALUE="24">
    <PARAM NAME="FontItalic" VALUE="0">
    <PARAM NAME="FontBold" VALUE="1">
    <PARAM NAME="FontUnderline" VALUE="0">
    <PARAM NAME="FontStrikeout" VALUE="0">
    <PARAM NAME="TopPoints" VALUE="0">
    <PARAM NAME="BotPoints" VALUE="0">
</OBJECT>
```

In my Java class, I define a reference to an *IIeLabel* interface, which I set via the public *setLabel* method.

```
public class LabelHandler extends Applet
{
    IIeLabel m_label;

    public void setLabel(Object ctl)
    {
        m_label = (IIeLabel)ctl;
    }
}
```

Then, back in the HTML document, I add a piece of script that calls *setLabel* with a reference to the Super Label control.

```
<SCRIPT language="VBScript">
<!--
sub window_onLoad
    document.LabelHandler.setLabel AXLabel
end sub
-->
</SCRIPT>
```

Now the Java program can communicate with the ActiveX label through the COM interface. The only problem with this technique is that you could, by mistake, pass the wrong reference to the *setLabel* method since the Object type can't perform any type checking.

An Example

Linking a Java applet to your active content isn't very complicated; in fact, Java is easier to use with ActiveX controls than C++ is. To demonstrate this connectivity, I've written a small applet that interacts with a pair of ActiveX controls embedded in a web page.

The Controls

Internet Explorer 3.0 comes with a set of built-in ActiveX controls. I'll be using two of these, Timer and Super Label, in my application. The Timer control is an invisible control that generates an event periodically. The Super Label control displays text at various angles or positions within a boundary box. My applet will do the following with a Timer control and a Super Label control located on a web page:

◆ With every *Timer* event, the application will rotate the text in the Super Label control by 5 degrees.

◆ Two buttons will allow the user to increase and decrease the interval at which *Timer* events occur.

◆ A list box will display the events processed by the applet.

The applet is named AXGlue since it "glues" together a pair of ActiveX controls. Using the Java Applet Wizard in Visual Studio, I create a new applet. It doesn't need to be multithreaded, and it won't support animation. After Visual Studio has built a skeleton application for AXGlue, I'm ready to begin filling in the details. (You can find the completed project in the \\ActiveVJ\chapter05\AXGlue directory on the companion disc.)

The Web Page

First I edit the AXGlue web page using Microsoft's ActiveX Control Pad application. This is a wonderful piece of software that Microsoft distributes for free on the Internet (http://www.microsoft.com/workshop/author/cpad); it does most of the work needed to add ActiveX controls to an HTML document. Here's the edited HTML for the web page.

```html
<html>
<head>
<title>AXGlue Applet</title>
</head>
<body>
<H1>AXGlue Applet</H1>
<P>
This application shows how ActiveX components can be linked
via Visual Basic, Scripting Edition, and Java applets
</P>
<P>
<hr>
<OBJECT ID="AXTimer" WIDTH=39 HEIGHT=39
 CLASSID="CLSID:59CCB4A0-727D-11CF-AC36-00AA00A47DD2">
    <PARAM NAME="_ExtentX" VALUE="1005">
    <PARAM NAME="_ExtentY" VALUE="1005">
    <PARAM NAME="Interval" VALUE="0">
</OBJECT>
<OBJECT ID="AXLabel" WIDTH=100 HEIGHT=100
 CLASSID="CLSID:99B42120-6EC7-11CF-A6C7-00AA00A47DD2">
    <PARAM NAME="_ExtentX" VALUE="3625">
    <PARAM NAME="_ExtentY" VALUE="3625">
    <PARAM NAME="Caption" VALUE="Rotate!">
    <PARAM NAME="Angle" VALUE="0">
    <PARAM NAME="Alignment" VALUE="4">
    <PARAM NAME="Mode" VALUE="1">
    <PARAM NAME="FillStyle" VALUE="0">
    <PARAM NAME="ForeColor" VALUE="#000000">
    <PARAM NAME="BackColor" VALUE="#B0C4C8">
    <PARAM NAME="FontName" VALUE="Arial">
    <PARAM NAME="FontSize" VALUE="20">
    <PARAM NAME="FontItalic" VALUE="0">
    <PARAM NAME="FontBold" VALUE="1">
    <PARAM NAME="FontUnderline" VALUE="0">
    <PARAM NAME="FontStrikeout" VALUE="0">
    <PARAM NAME="TopPoints" VALUE="0">
    <PARAM NAME="BotPoints" VALUE="0">
</OBJECT>
```

```
<P>
<hr>
<applet
    code=AXGlue.class
    name=AXGlue
    width=320
    height=240 >
</applet>
<hr>
<a href="AXGlue.java">The source.</a>
<SCRIPT language="VBScript">
<!--
sub window_onLoad
    document.AXGlue.setLabelCtl AXLabel
    document.AXGlue.setTimerCtl AXTimer
    /AXTimer.Interval = 1000
end sub

sub AXTimer_Timer
    document.AXGlue.changeLabel
end sub
-->
</SCRIPT>
</body>
</html>
```

After some quick explanatory headers, I insert a Timer control named AXTimer and a Super Label control named AXLabel. The ActiveX Control Pad automatically includes the appropriate IDs and parameters for each control, based on their registered definitions. Visual Studio adds the instructions for loading the AXGlue applet. The script performs two tasks:

◆ The *window_onLoad* subroutine executes when the web page is loaded, passing references to the ActiveX controls to the applet and initializing the Timer control's interval. I'll describe the *setLabelCtl* and *setTimerCtl* methods in a moment.

◆ When AXTimer generates an event, a call goes out to the *AXTimer_Timer* subroutine, which then passes along the event to the applet via the *changeLabel* method.

That's the only code needed to link the ActiveX controls to the Java applet! Now let's look at the Java code and see what's going on there.

The Java Applet

A Java program communicates with an ActiveX component through a group of interfaces. I used the Java Type Library Wizard, following the procedure outlined in the section titled "Using a COM Object from Java" on page 128, to generate interfaces for the Super Label and Timer controls. The following interfaces were generated for the Timer control.

```
public class ietimer/IeTimer extends java.lang.Object
{
}

public interface ietimer/DIeTimerEvents
    extends com.ms.com.IUnknown
{
    public abstract void Timer();
}

public interface ietimer/IIeTimer
    extends com.ms.com.IUnknown
{
    public abstract void AboutBox();
    public abstract int getInterval();
    public abstract void putInterval(int);
    public abstract int getEnabled();
    public abstract void putEnabled(int);
}

public interface ietimer/enumBoolType
    extends com.ms.com.IUnknown
{
    public static final int ValFalse;
    public static final int ValTrue;
}
```

Taking the framework applet generated by Developer Studio, I added some constants and some references for Abstract Window Toolkit (AWT) controls. The *SPEED* constants define the range of settings for the Timer control; the event interval will be between 0.5 and 5 seconds, and the applet will change the interval in increments of 0.1 second.

```
// Import Java packages
import java.applet.*;
import java.awt.*;

// Import Timer and Super Label ActiveX control packages
import ietimer.*;
import ielabel.*;
```

```
public class AXGlue extends Applet
{
    //-----------------------
    // Constants
    //-----------------------
    static final int SPEED_MIN =  500; // 0.5 second
    static final int SPEED_MAX = 5000; // 5 seconds
    static final int SPEED_INC =  100; // tenths of seconds


    //-----------------------
    // Fields
    //-----------------------

    // ActiveX controls
    IIeLabel m_AXLabel;
    IIeTimer m_AXTimer;

    // AWT components
    Button    m_btnFaster;
    Button    m_btnSlower;
    List      m_lstOutput;
    ⋮
```

Two references, *m_AXTimer* and *m_AXLabel*, will refer to the web page's
ActiveX controls. I've also defined three controls as part of the Java applet. These
controls will be referenced by the *m_btnFaster*, *m_btnSlower*, and *m_lstOutput* fields.

The constructor doesn't have anything to do; the *destroy, paint, start,* and *stop*
methods are also empty. All initialization takes place in the *init* method. I create
the three AWT controls and position them in the applet window.

```
    ⋮
    //-----------------------
    // Methods
    //-----------------------
    public AXGlue()
    {
        // Nothing to do
    }

    public String getAppletInfo()
    {
        return "Name: AXGlue\r\n" +
                "Author: Scott Robert Ladd\r\n" +
                "Created with Microsoft Visual J++ " +
                "Version 1.1";
    }
```

(continued)

```
public void init()
{
    // Prepare display
    setLayout(null);
    resize(320, 240);

    // Create controls
    m_btnFaster = new Button("Faster");
    add(m_btnFaster);
    m_btnFaster.reshape(10, 10, 80, 23);

    m_btnSlower = new Button("Slower");
    add(m_btnSlower);
    m_btnSlower.reshape(10, 40, 80, 23);

    m_lstOutput = new List();
    add(m_lstOutput);
    m_lstOutput.reshape(100, 10, 200, 200);
}

public void destroy()
{
    // Nothing to do
}

public void paint(Graphics g)
{
    // Nothing to do
}

public void start()
{
    // Nothing to do
}

public void stop()
{
    // Nothing to do
}

    ⋮
```

When the web page is loaded, the *window_onLoad* subroutine in the script calls two AXGlue methods to identify the ActiveX controls it will be working with. Both of these methods cast their *Object* arguments to the appropriate interface type before storing the reference.

```
    ⋮

// Set reference to AXLabel control
public void setLabelCtl(Object ctl)
{
    m_AXLabel = (IIeLabel)ctl;
}
```

```
// Set reference to AXTimer control
public void setTimerCtl(Object ctl)
{
    m_AXTimer = (IIeTimer)ctl;
}
    ⋮
```

I created a private utility method, *addOutput*, which adds a string to the end of the *m_lstOutput* list and then scrolls the list down to display the new information. Essentially, *m_lstOutput* is a history of what has happened inside the applet in relation to the ActiveX controls.

When *AXTimer* generates an event, the script passes it along to the applet's *changeLabel* method. That method reads the current angle of the *AXLabel* text and increments it by 5 degrees. Then the new angle is displayed in the output list.

```
    ⋮
public void changeLabel()
{
    // Get the current angle
    int angle = m_AXLabel.getAngle();

    // Compute new angle
    angle = (angle + 5) % 360;

    // Adjust angle
    m_AXLabel.putAngle(angle);

    // Display new angle
    addOutput("Tick - new angle " + angle);
}
    ⋮
```

The final AXGlue method is *action*, which processes clicks of the Faster and Slower buttons. The interval is adjusted by *SPEED_INC* milliseconds, within the bounds set by *SPEED_MIN* and *SPEED_MAX*. Like *changeLabel*, *action* adds a string to the output list to announce the new event interval, as the following code shows.

```
    ⋮
public boolean action(Event event, Object obj)
{
    // Exit if this isn't one of the two buttons
    if ((event.target != m_btnFaster)
    && (event.target != m_btnSlower))
        return false;

    // Get the current timer delay
    int delay = m_AXTimer.getInterval();

    // Change delay within bounds
    if (event.target == m_btnFaster)
    {
```

(continued)

```
        // Decrement delay
        if (delay > SPEED_MIN)
            delay -= SPEED_INC;
    }
    else // m_btnSlower
    {
        // Increment delay
        if (delay < SPEED_MAX)
            delay += SPEED_INC;
    }

    // Set the new delay
    m_AXTimer.putInterval(delay);

    // Display what has been done
    addOutput("Set delay: " + delay);

    // Done!
    return true;
}
```

The screen display of the final application, when run, should resemble the screen shot shown in Figure 5-3. There you have it: a web page built from Visual Basic, Scripting Edition; Java; and ActiveX components; all working together to make an interactive document.

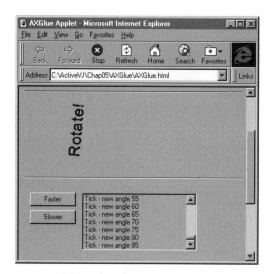

Figure 5-3. *AXGlue in action.*

Onward

Using Java and Visual Basic, Scripting Edition, you can link the active content of your web page, mixing applets, controls, and scripts to create an interactive environment. But you can do more than just use Java to talk to ActiveX components; you can also define a COM interface for a Java class. That is the subject of the next chapter.

6 Understanding COM and Java

n Chapter 5, I demonstrated a simple application that linked a Java applet to an ActiveX control via COM, the Component Object Model. COM is the basis for several Microsoft technologies, including OLE and ActiveX. Chapter 5 provided a basic introduction to COM programming; now I take a closer look at this technology and how you can use it with your Java applications.

The Fundamentals of COM

A modem follows a standard—such as v.32bis—when communicating with another modem. The standard defines a protocol for the conversation between the two modems. Any modem that supports a given communications standard will be able to talk to another modem that supports the same standard. This communication standard defines the behavior of a compliant modem, but it doesn't specify *how* a given modem is to generate that behavior. COM is a standard that defines the behavior of software components.

In 1996, Microsoft added support for COM to Java, through its own Microsoft Internet Explorer and via add-ins for products produced by other vendors. Java vastly simplifies COM programming by handling many details internally. Support for COM is implemented within the virtual machine, not in the language itself, so many of the details are hidden from the Java developer. Not only does this make your job as a Java programmer easier, but also it allows you to avoid some of the more confusing and error-prone aspects of using COM. If you've worked with COM in C++, you'll find that working with it in Java requires a bit of rethinking and adjusting, since you won't be handling many of COM's intricacies.

COM became part of Windows-based programming with the introduction of OLE in the early 1990s, but it became a common term only when the Internet spawned ActiveX in 1996. COM, the underlying foundation of OLE and ActiveX, is a standard that allows independent software objects to communicate with one another. Whereas OLE focuses on building complex documents from objects that are linked to various components, ActiveX is aimed at developing small, downloadable program components for the Internet. ActiveX is not a subset of OLE; rather, it is a different way of using COM technology to build software components. Another name for COM components is *Automation objects*, which refers to their use in automating tasks inside documents and on web pages.

A software component uses COM to declare one or more interfaces; you can think of an interface as a contract presented by a *server* and accepted by a *client*. Server and client might be—and probably are—separate processes, and they might even be located on different machines. However, a single process can be both a server and a client, exposing functions through interfaces and using other components simultaneously. A COM object can be an application, a dynamic-link library (DLL), a visual control, or any other piece of executable code that supports the COM standard.

COM describes the format servers must follow to express their interfaces and how clients locate and communicate with available servers. Think of COM as another way of implementing the object-oriented principles I presented in previous chapters. COM embodies a central principle of object-oriented programming, *encapsulation:* A COM component is accessible only through the methods that are declared in the interfaces it exports. The mechanism a given component uses to implement those methods internally is immaterial; COM concerns itself only with expressing interfaces in a standard fashion so that all compliant components can interact.

In terms of COM, the word interface refers to a set of related methods that are exposed by a component. An exposed method is a method that an object makes available for calling by an outside agent; you can think of an exposed COM method as similar in principle to a public method in a Java class. In fact, a COM interface is much like a Java interface. When a component supports a given COM interface, it supports all methods defined by that interface. The interface definition declares the terms of a contract between a server and a client, but it doesn't say how those terms will be executed. That's the job of the interface implementation, which is completely hidden from all client applications. An interface implementation can be written in any language, using any algorithms; the details of the implementation are hidden from the client. An interface is not an object; it is a pointer to a table of method pointers. A component will provide a table of method pointers for each interface it supports; all communication with the component takes place through these method pointers. The methods exposed via an interface are strongly typed, that is, a call to a COM method will generate a compile-time error if the call parameters and return value don't strictly match the interface definition.

A table of interface method pointers is much like a C++ virtual function table. Such a table is also used by Java to implement all of its methods. This is one reason why Java is eminently suited to writing COM applications: many features of COM correspond to features of Java classes. But don't confuse a COM interface with a Java interface; the former defines a contract between COM components, and the latter declares a set of methods and fields to be implemented by subinterfaces. Nor should you confuse a *COM class* with a *Java class*. The sidebar "How a COM Object Differs from a Java Class" outlines their differences.

How a COM Object Differs from a Java Class

- Whereas a Java class defines a specific type of object, a COM class defines a group of interfaces that are available when a program interacts with a given COM object.

- COM interfaces do not expose any fields, whereas Java interfaces can define constants.

- Whereas a Java class can create several objects within a single program, a COM class defines a specific server object that can be used by multiple clients.

- A Java class defines the attributes of objects that are created at execution time; a COM class defines the interfaces that are supported by an extant dynamic-link library (.dll) file or application (.exe) file.

Interface and Class IDs

Every COM class has a unique Class Identifier, or *CLSID*, that is an instance of a 128-bit Globally Unique Identifier (*GUID*). The CLSID associates a COM class with the executable code that implements it. When you register your component with an operating system, you create a link between the CLSID and its associated .dll or .exe file. An application uses a CLSID to request the services of a COM object, obtaining a pointer to a class object that links interfaces to executable code. In a similar fashion, a client requests a pointer to a given interface by using a GUID known as the Interface Identifier, or *IID*.

A text-based component identification system can easily produce conflicts—for example, when two developers use the same name for different components or interfaces—but with GUIDs, two COM classes that have the same name will be identified by different CLSIDs. CLSIDs are also compact, using only 16 bytes, whereas text-based names can get rather long, confusing, and unwieldy.

The Windows API function *CoCreateGUID* generates what is guaranteed to be a globally unique GUID; this means you don't need to worry that you might duplicate an identifier used by someone else. As a Java developer, though, you probably won't be calling *CoCreateGUID* directly; Microsoft's wizards will obtain and assign CLSIDs and IIDs for you. And because there are more than 3.4×10^{38} possible GUIDs, this function could theoretically identify more unique software components than could be implemented in the lifetime of the known universe!

When you register a COM object, you tell the operating system which CLSID is associated with which .dll or .exe file. Microsoft Windows maintains this information in its registry database, under the HKEY_CLASSES_ROOT hierarchy. In Chapter 7, when I produce a COM-compliant Java class, you'll see how a component makes the operating system aware of its existence.

Java Access to COM Objects

In Chapter 5, I demonstrated how the Java Type Library Wizard creates a set of Java classes for an ActiveX control. But that's only part of the story; the wizard can, in fact, prepare any COM-compliant class for use in Java. Remember, COM is a basic communications standard that applies to a wide variety of software components. It applies not only to ActiveX but also to other software components. A dynamic-link library, for example, might expose some or all of its functionality through COM interfaces.

Here's an example: Let's say that you have a dynamic-link library named *UtilityCOM.dll*, which supports two interfaces, *IMath* and *IUseStates*. Assuming that *UtilityCOM* was registered during its installation, you'll be able to use the Java Type Library Wizard to extract interface information and build Java classes. The *summary.txt* output from the wizard might look like the following.

```
public class utilitycom/CUtilityCOM extends java.lang.Object
{
}

public interface utilitycom/IMath extends
    com.ms.com.IUnknown
{
    public abstract int addInts(int, int);
    public abstract int powInt(int, int);
}

public interface utilitycom/IUseStates extends
    com.ms.com.IUnknown
{
    public abstract int getState();
    public abstract void setState(int);
}
```

The first class listed, *CUtilityCOM*, is the one you use to create objects of this class. But notice that the implementation of *CUtilityCOM* is empty. This should remind you of an important distinction of COM programming in Java: You never directly access COM objects. All interaction with a COM object takes place through an interface, as I'll show you in a moment.

To import the *UtilityCOM* classes, you'll need to include this statement at the beginning of your Java source file.

```
import UtilityCOM.*;
```

You can also import specific interfaces and classes using statements such as these.

```
import UtilityCOM.CUtilityCOM;
import UtilityCOM.IMath;
```

To create a *UtilityCOM* object, you use the standard Java syntax for allocating a class object, casting the result to an appropriate interface.

```
IMath util = (IMath)new CUtilityCOM();

int n = util.addInts(2, 2);
```

If you've done any COM programming in C++, you'll see an immediate advantage to Java: It hides complexities, such as the CLSIDs that are used when *CoCreateObject* is called to build a new COM object. For the most part, using a COM object is just like using any Java object; the important difference is that you *always* communicate with the COM object through a reference to an interface, never through direct reference to the object itself. The following piece of code, for instance, would cause a run-time exception.

```
CUtilityCOM util = new CUtilityCOM();
```

IUnknown

Simple COM objects support at least one interface; very complex COM components, such as embeddable OLE objects, support several interfaces. Each interface describes a different contract between server and client; the number of interfaces you define depends on the number of faces your server shows to the system.

Every COM interface is a subclass of *IUnknown,* which is implemented internally by the JVM. As you learned in Chapter 5, an interface inherits three methods from *IUnknown: QueryInterface*, *AddRef*, and *Release*; these methods provide the core functionality of COM. Java hides many of the details of COM programming; for example, you will almost never call the *IUnknown* methods directly. But you should nevertheless be aware of what those functions do and why they exist, particularly when you are developing your own COM classes in Java. I'll discuss *QueryInterface* here; *AddRef* and *Release* will be discussed later in this chapter, in the section about reference counting.

QueryInterface

As mentioned above, Java communicates with COM objects only through interfaces. When you create a COM object, you don't access it directly, as you would a Java object; instead, you use one of the object's defined interfaces. Through *IUnknown's QueryInterface* method (known as *QI* to many developers), you can request any interface supported by a COM component. Since all COM interfaces derive from *IUnknown,* you can reach any supported interface through any other by calling *QI*.

In C++, you must use the correct IID to request an interface pointer through *QI*. Java, however, simplifies the use of *QI* immensely; in fact, your Java code will probably never call *QueryInterface* directly, nor is it likely to use a single IID. Instead, Java allows you to cast one interface pointer to another, while it handles the details of calling *QI* with IIDs. The following code shows how this works.

```
// Obtain a pointer to an interface
IMath util = (IMath)new CUtilityCOM();
```

```
// Now cast that pointer to a new interface type
IUseStates ius = (IUseStates)util;
```

IDispatch

When you base an interface on *IUnknown,* all calls to the interface's methods occur through pointers that are stored in a virtual table that the operating system initializes with references when the object is loaded. Although Java and C++ include support for tables of function pointers, languages such as Microsoft Visual Basic, Scripting Edition, do not. To make COM objects accessible without pointers, COM provides an additional standard interface, *IDispatch,* which provides a further level of indirection. *IDispatch,* which derives from *IUnknown,* adds a method named *Invoke.* Instead of calling an interface method directly via a pointer, a Visual Basic, Scripting Edition, program calls *IDispatch::Invoke,* which in turn looks up the pointer required for calling the desired function. If an interface supports both pointer-based and indirect calls to its methods, it is known as a *dual interface.*

The use of *IDispatch* and *IUnknown* is transparent in Java programs. In many cases, COM objects support only the indirect method invocation of *IDispatch* because this facility can be used by any programming language. However, when you are designing your own components, consider implementing a dual interface; this will allow languages such as Java to use the most efficient technique by directly calling methods through their pointers.

Interface Definitions

IDL, the Interface Definition Language, is a superset of the Object Definition Language (ODL) used to develop OLE controls. For COM and ActiveX, IDL describes the interfaces and properties supported by a given automation object.

Type Libraries

From an IDL text file, you generate a type library that contains the following information about a COM object:

◆ Declarations of the object's data types, including structures, unions, constants, and aliases

◆ Descriptions of the object's interfaces and its exposed methods

Type libraries can be individual (*.tlb*) files, or they can be embedded within dynamic-link libraries, control libraries, or executable programs. *IDispatch::Invoke* uses the information provided by a type library to select function pointers. When a COM component is registered with Microsoft Windows, an entry is created under HKEY_CLASSES_ROOT\TypeLib in the registry, associating a GUID with its type library data. From within the Microsoft Visual J++ development environment, the Java Type Library Wizard will search the registry entries for components from which it can generate *.class* files for Java.

IDL Files

An IDL source file, which looks somewhat like a Java class definition, describes the functions and constants that are exported by the interfaces supported by a COM object. You probably won't write many IDL files when you are working with Visual J++; the ActiveX Wizard for Java handles that task for you by creating an IDL file that defines a single interface to expose the public methods for all your COM-compliant classes. But you might want to remove some public functions from the generated interface definition, or you might want to distribute methods among two or more interfaces. A basic understanding of IDL syntax is essential if you're going to do such fine-tuning. What follows is an explanation of the type of IDL file that you'll be using with Visual J++; if you work with COM components defined in other languages, you'll need to study the full IDL specification, which you can find on the Microsoft Developer Network.

For the purposes of Java, an IDL file has the following general format.

```
// Declare the library
[
    uuid(nnnnnnnn-nnnn-nnnn-nnnn-nnnnnnnnnnnn),
    helpstring("tname Type Library"),
    version(n.n)
]
library name
{
    // Import standard COM/OLE type library
    importlib("stdole32.tlb");

    // Declare an IDispatch interface
    [
        uuid(nnnnnnnn-nnnn-nnnn-nnnn-nnnnnnnnnnnn),
        helpstring("iname Interface")
    ]
    dispinterface iname
    {
        properties:
            property-def
        methods:
            method-def
    }

    // Declare a dual (IDispatch/vtable) interface
    [
        object,
        uuid(nnnnnnnn-nnnn-nnnn-nnnn-nnnnnnnnnnnn),
        dual,
        pointer_default(unique),
        helpstring("diname Interface")
    ]
    interface diname : IDispatch
    {
        di-method-def
    }
```

```
// Declare a COM class
[
    uuid(nnnnnnnn-nnnn-nnnn-nnnn-nnnnnnnnnnnn),
    helpstring("cname Object")
]
coclass cname
{
    [ default ]
    dispinterface iname;
    interface diname;
};

};
```

Each *uuid* entry must be unique so that each component of the type library can be correctly identified. The *helpstring* text provides documentation through certain COM facilities and should describe the definition entry immediately following it.

For the sake of example, let's assume we're converting a Java class named *Ticker* to a class that supports COM. The type library name, *tname*, is often the name of the Java class with the suffix "Lib" or "TLB" added; in this case, *tname* will be replaced by *TickerLib*.

The *coclass* statement defines a COM component and lists the interfaces that it supports. In the case of the *Ticker* class, our *coclass* name will be *CTicker*, in keeping with COM naming standards. The *coclass* statement is listed last in the library definition because the interfaces must be defined before they can be assigned to a COM class.

INTERFACES IN IDL

The *dispinterface* statement defines an interface derived from *IDispatch*; the interface's *iname* would be *ITicker*. (The "I" prefix designates an interface.) Since Java classes do not, in general, expose data members, there will be no items listed under the *properties* keyword. Under *methods*, each of the public Java methods will be given an entry. For example, if the Java function is declared like this,

```
public String formatComma(int n);
```

the IDL file will contain an entry like this,

```
[ helpstring("formatComma Method") ]
BSTR formatComma([in] long p1);
```

The *helpstring* declaration defines text that can be automatically displayed in a graphic development tool, describing a component's exposed methods and properties.

Some types, such as *String,* will be translated from Java types into IDL-compatible types. Table 6-1 shows how Java types and IDL types correspond. The correspondences are relatively straightforward, and all of these types should be familiar to you. The possible exception might be the *VARIANT* class, a sort of "stores anything" object that is often found in Visual Basic; Microsoft Visual Basic, Scripting Edition; and Visual Basic for Applications programs.

TABLE 6-1
Java-to-IDL Type Correspondences

Classification	Java Type	IDL Type
Simple types	*boolean*	*boolean*
	char	*char*
	double	*double*
	float	*float*
	int	*int*
	long	*int64*
	int	*long*
	single-element array of *type*	pointer to *type*
	short	*short*
	byte	*unsigned char*
	void	*void*
Compound types	class *java.lang.String*	*BTSR*
	long (divide by 10,000 to get original fixed-point number)	*CURRENCY*
	double	*DATE*
	int (see text)	*HRESULT*
	class *com.ms.com.SafeArray*	*SAFEARRAY*
	int (same as HRESULT)	*SCODE*
	class *com.ms.com.Variant*	*VARIANT*
Interfaces	interface *com.ms.com.IUnknown*	*IUnknown*
	class *java.lang.Object*	*IDispatch*

IDL specifies the nature of each method parameter by including qualifiers inside square brackets. The *[in]* designation declares an input value that is read by the method; *[out]* declares a value that can be changed by the method and that is assumed to be a pointer. Again, the *IDispatch::Invoke* method will perform any necessary reference manipulations.

Unlike C and C++, Java does not support pointers. When you are writing code that calls a COM interface that requires a *type* * pointer parameter, you must use a one-element array of *type* instead. Since Java passes array parameters by reference, this piece of programming legerdemain simulates a pointer. For example, if a COM method defines its parameters as follows,

```
void SomeMethod([in] long p1, [out] long * p2);
```

you call it in Java using the following syntax,

```
int x = new int[1];
SomeMethod(23, x);
```

If you don't declare a *dispinterface,* the *interface* statement will define *ITicker* as a dual interface. The dual interface requires more code, and the definition of methods for it is different. Whereas an *IDispatch* method is declared much like a Java method, with a return type, a method in a dual interface must declare its return value as a value of type HRESULT. The actual return value (if not *void)* is added to the parameter list with the qualifier *[out, retval].*

```
[ helpstring("formatComma Method") ]
HRESULT formatComma([in] long p1, [out, retval] BSTR * rtn);
```

An *HRESULT* is an integer value that can indicate whether or not an error has occurred during a method call. The only success value returned by *HRESULT* is the COM constant *S_OK;* all other possible *HRESULTs* are error indications. Since COM does not support the "thrown" exception model, a C++ program needs to check the *HRESULT* of a called COM function and throw an exception if the value is not *S_OK.* The Java virtual machine, however, once again provides a simpler model by throwing a *ComFailException* exception whenever a COM call returns an error value. The JVM stores the value of the *HRESULT* in the *ComFailException* object. And since *ComFailException* is extended from *RuntimeException,* you don't need to declare it in a *throws* statement for functions that call COM methods.

An *HRESULT* is also returned for a *dispinterface* method, even though the function definition will not be written in IDL to indicate this.

EXAMPLES

I'll borrow a bit of code from the next chapter to show you an IDL file generated for a class by the ActiveX Wizard for Java. This class, *FormatNumbers,* supports only the universal *IDispatch* interface.

```
[
    uuid(3a82ef02-9276-11d0-be9b-0020afd208b9),
    helpstring("FormatNumbersLib Type Library"),
    version(1.0)
]
library FormatNumbersLib
{
    importlib("stdole32.tlb");

    [
        uuid(3a82ef01-9276-11d0-be9b-0020afd208b9),
        helpstring("IFormatNumbers Interface")
    ]
    dispinterface IFormatNumbers
    {
        properties:
        methods:
        [ helpstring("setSeparatorSymbol Method"), id(1) ]
        void setSeparatorSymbol([in] char p1);

        [ helpstring("getSeparatorSymbol Method"), id(2) ]
        char getSeparatorSymbol();
```

(continued)

```
        [ helpstring("setGroupLen Method"), id(3) ]
        void setGroupLen([in] long p1);

        [ helpstring("getGroupLen Method"), id(4) ]
        long getGroupLen();

        [ helpstring("formatComma Method"), id(5) ]
        BSTR formatComma([in] long p1);

        [ helpstring("setCurrencySymbol Method"), id(6) ]
        void setCurrencySymbol([in] char p1);

        [ helpstring("getCurrencySymbol Method"), id(7) ]
        char getCurrencySymbol();

        [ helpstring("formatText Method"), id(8) ]
        BSTR formatText([in] long p1);

    }


    [
        uuid(3a82ef00-9276-11d0-be9b-0020afd208b9),
        helpstring("CFormatNumbers Object")
    ]
    coclass CFormatNumbers
    {
        [ default ]
        dispinterface IFormatNumbers;
    };

};
```

For the same Java class, an IDL file for a dual interface looks like this:

```
[
    uuid(7371a240-2e51-11d0-b4c1-444553540000),
    helpstring("FormatNumbersLib Type Library"),
    version(1.0)
]
library FormatNumbersLib
{
    importlib("stdole32.tlb");

    [
        object,
        uuid(7371a240-2e51-11d0-b4c1-444553540000),
        dual,
        pointer_default(unique),
        helpstring("IFormatNumbers Interface")
    ]
```

```
interface IFormatNumbers : IDispatch
{
    [ helpstring("setSeparatorSymbol Method") ]
    HRESULT setSeparatorSymbol([in] char p1);

    [ helpstring("getSeparatorSymbol Method") ]
    HRESULT getSeparatorSymbol(
        [out, retval] char * rtn);

    [ helpstring("setGroupLen Method") ]
    HRESULT setGroupLen([in] long p1);

    [ helpstring("getGroupLen Method") ]
    HRESULT getGroupLen([out, retval] long * rtn);

    [ helpstring("formatComma Method") ]
    HRESULT formatComma([in] long p1,
        [out, retval] BSTR * rtn);

    [ helpstring("setCurrencySymbol Method") ]
    HRESULT setCurrencySymbol([in] char p1);

    [ helpstring("getCurrencySymbol Method") ]
    HRESULT getCurrencySymbol([out, retval] char * rtn);

    [ helpstring("formatText Method") ]
    HRESULT formatText([in] long p1,
        [out, retval] BSTR * rtn);

}

[
    uuid(7371a240-2e51-11d0-b4c1-444553540000),
    helpstring("CFormatNumbers Object")
]
coclass CFormatNumbers
{
    interface IFormatNumbers;
};

};
```

If you use Visual J++'s COM Automation features, your Java classes will have either one *dispinterface* or one dual interface; if you want to divide your methods into two or more interfaces, you'll need to do so manually by changing the generated IDL file.

More About Interfaces

What, there's more? Yes, indeed. COM programming, although not terribly complicated, involves several details, many of which are hidden by the Java language or the virtual machine. The rest of this chapter describes a few of those details you should know about.

Reference Counting

Even if you expect your code to be run only on the most modern, high-powered computer systems, you should try to keep unnecessary pieces of code from cluttering up main memory. COM employs a system of reference counting to determine whether a COM component should remain resident in memory. *IUnknown* implements two functions that manage reference counts: *AddRef* and *Release*. In general, whenever a pointer to an interface is provided, *AddRef* should be called to increment a reference counter; when that interface pointer is no longer needed or in use, *Release* should be called to decrement the counter. When the reference counter reaches 0, the COM component can remove itself from memory. In some cases, the reference count will refer to the sum total of all pointers—whatever their interface type—that refer to a given COM object; in other cases, individual interfaces will track individual reference counts. The latter approach will be used, for example, when different interfaces implement discrete pieces of code. The *Release* method will usually remove a COM object from memory when all reference counts reach 0.

In Java, reference counting is handled internally by the virtual machine; the built-in *IUnknown* interface implements general versions of *AddRef* and *Release* that are automatically called by your Java code. The JVM manages COM objects in much the same way that it handles regular Java objects, performing automatic garbage collection when an object is no longer referenced by an application.

Object Identity

COM defines object identity in terms of pointers to *IUnknown* interfaces; two objects are the same if their *IUnknown* interface pointers are equal. A C++ program would need to do some pretty complicated coding to compare COM objects.

```
// Comparison of two COM objects referenced through
// interfaces c1 and c2
IUnknown *i1, *i2;

c1->QueryInterface(IID_IUnknown, (void **)&i1);
c2->QueryInterface(IID_IUnknown, (void **)&i2);

if (i1 == i2)
    printf("It's the same object");
```

In Java, the equivalent code would look like this:

```
// Comparison of drawable and printable
if (c1 == c2)
    System.out.println("It's the same object");
```

As you can see, this is the same Java syntax you'd use to compare two object references. Again, Java has hidden many of the complexities of COM programming, making your code more readable and saving you from having to get the little details right.

Properties

A COM object's interface will often define *property* values that control its nature. A property named *X* will be written and read using methods named *putX* (or *setX*) and *getX*, respectively. If you've developed ActiveX or OLE controls in Visual Basic, you've worked with property-setting methods such as these. No COM interface allows member values to be directly assigned or read; every access to a COM object must be through a method of some kind. The only exceptions to this rule are the constants that are exposed by some interfaces; such a constant value can be read and usually defines a set of values, such as *true* and *false*, that are returned by a method.

Aggregation

The COM concept of *aggregation* allows an object class to use and enhance the services provided by another object type. In other words, aggregation is the same concept as Java's *inheritance,* which is implemented through the *extends* keyword. Indeed, Java supports aggregation through the standard inheritance model; you simply extend an existing COM class to incorporate its functionality. Java's ability to implement COM aggregation is limited, however. For instance, Java does not support multiple inheritance, whereas COM allows an aggregated class to have more than one parent. In addition, Java cannot create COM and ActiveX objects in the same way other applications do. And a COM object must explicitly be declared "aggregatable" if your Java code is going to declare it in an *extends* clause of a class definition.

Java can extend an existing COM class, even if the class was not written in Java. For example, consider an aggregatable ActiveX component named *Ticker*, which is a timer. Using the Java Type Library Wizard (see Chapter 7), I would generate a set of Java *.class* files for *Ticker*. Then, to add methods to *Ticker*, I would create a class named *ScottTicker*. Assuming that *Ticker* has already been registered by the Java ActiveX Wizard, I'd begin by creating the following class.

```
import Ticker.*;

public class ScottTicker
    extends Ticker.Ticker
{

    void halveInterval()
    {
        putInterval(getInterval() / 2);
    }
}
```

(continued)

```
    void doubleInterval()
    {
        putInterval(getInterval() * 2);
    }

}
```

With my completed class in hand, I use the ActiveX Component Wizard for Java (which is explained more thoroughly in Chapter 7) to implement *ScottTicker* as a COM component. The wizard creates an interface definition from my class, imports it to my *ScottTicker.java* file, and adds a CLSID for my new component.

```
import Ticker.*;
import ScottTickerLib.*;

public class ScottTicker
    extends Ticker.Ticker
    implements ScottTickerLib.IScottTicker
{
    private static final String CLSID =
        "7371a240-2e51-11d0-b4c1-444553540003";


    void halveInterval()
    {
        putInterval(getInterval() / 2);
    }

    void doubleInterval()
    {
        putInterval(getInterval() * 2);
    }

}
```

The wizard also generates an IDL file that describes the interface exposed by *ScottTicker*.

```
[
    uuid(7371a240-2e51-11d0-b4c1-444553540001),
    helpstring("ScottTickerLib Type Library"),
    version(1.0)
]
library ScottTickerLib
{
    importlib("stdole32.tlb");
```

```
    [
        uuid(7371a240-2e51-11d0-b4c1-444553540002),
        helpstring("IScottTicker Interface")
    ]
    dispinterface IScottTicker
    {
        properties:
        methods:
    }


    [
        uuid(7371a240-2e51-11d0-b4c1-444553540003),
        helpstring("CScottTicker Object")
    ]
    coclass CScottTicker
    {
        [ default ]
        dispinterface IScottTicker;
    };

};
```

When I create a *ScottTicker* object, I also create a *Ticker* object; all interfaces defined by *Ticker* can be used with *ScottTicker*.

Now, here's the sticking point: Java can extend only a COM class that declares itself aggregatable in its type library. This means that the COM class, when developed, must have had the *aggregatable* keyword included in its definition. If *aggregatable* was *not* declared, the COM class will be treated as if it were declared *final* in Java.

NOTE

The ActiveX Component Wizard for Java does not always translate types correctly when generating an IDL file from a Java class. For example, if I define the following method inside a Java class,

```
void doWithLong(long n);
```

the wizard will complain that *long* is a type incompatible with IDL. In fact, as Table 6-1 shows, a Java *long* is equivalent to an IDL *int64*. When such problems occur, you'll need to edit the IDL file created by the wizard, adding any functions that the wizard couldn't translate. When you finish adding the untranslated methods, run the wizard again, this time specifying that it use the edited IDL file rather than creating a new one.

What's the Difference Between OLE and ActiveX Controls?

Both OLE and ActiveX are extensions of the underlying COM technology. OLE controls are expected to expose several interfaces; ActiveX controls are only required to expose the *IUnknown* interface. Also, an ActiveX control self-registers by exposing the *DllRegisterServer* and *DllUnregisterServer* methods. In essence, an ActiveX class is a self-registering COM component.

The ActiveX Component Wizard for Java creates a COM component, not a true ActiveX control, since the exposed interfaces do not support self-registration. In Java, you'll need to implement your own versions of the *DllRegisterServer* and *DllUnregisterServer* methods and alter the IDL and registration files to make your class available as an ActiveX component.

Onward

COM programming introduces a lot of new terms and ideas to the developer; fortunately, Microsoft's extensions to the Java virtual machine—and the tools provided by Visual J++—simplify the creation of COM components. Now that you have a firm understanding of COM, you're ready to learn how to develop COM classes in Java. In the next chapter, I demonstrate how to take a Java class and convert it to a universal software component.

7

Creating COM Objects in Java

As you learned in Chapter 6, Java can easily access COM objects. So you should not be surprised to find that you can also expose a Java class through a COM interface. Microsoft Developer Studio automates the process, allowing you to take an existing class and convert it for use as a COM server. In this chapter, I show you how to provide a COM interface for a Java class, making the class's methods available to other applications.

A COM Candidate

Number formatting is a refinement that many programming languages do not automatically provide. For instance, I've often come across applications and web pages that display large numbers in a rather ugly and unreadable form:

Total profits for 1997 were $1673824183.

If only the program would add a few commas, this number would be much more readable. And sometimes—for example, when I want my programs to write checks or other legal documents—I need a mechanism that will allow me to output numbers in text form:

We recorded five thousand, seven hundred, and eighteen people at the conference.

Java, like many other programming languages, lacks tools that produce comma-delimited or textual numbers. Such number formatting isn't terribly difficult to implement, though, and I've provided a pretty good solution with my *FormatNumbers* class.

```
package coyote.math;

//
//
// FormatNumbers
//
//
public class FormatNumbers
{
    //-----------------------
    // Constants
    //-----------------------

    static final char [] DIGIT =
    {
        '0', '1', '2', '3', '4', '5', '6', '7', '8', '9'
    };
```

```java
static final String [] ONES =
{
    "", "one", "two", "three", "four", "five", "six",
    "seven", "eight", "nine", "ten", "eleven",
    "twelve", "thirteen", "fourteen", "fifteen",
    "sixteen", "seventeen", "eighteen", "nineteen"
};

static final String [] TENS =
{
    "twenty", "thirty", "forty", "fifty",
    "sixty", "seventy", "eighty", "ninety"
};

static final String [] POWERS =
{
    "thousand", "million", "billion", "trillion",
    "quadrillion", "quintillion"
};

//----------------------
// Fields
//----------------------

private char m_cSeparator;
private char m_cCurrency;
private int  m_nGroupLen;

//----------------------
// Class methods
//----------------------

// Return 10 raised to the power p
private static int pow10(int p)
{
    int res;
    for (res = 1; --p >= 0; res *= 10);
    return res;
}

// Integer logarithm (determines magnitude of an int)
private static int log10(int l)
{
    int p;
    for (p = 9; 0 == (l / pow10(p)); --p);
    return p;
}
```

(continued)

```
//----------------------
// Methods
//----------------------

// Default U.S. values
public FormatNumbers()
{
    m_cSeparator = ',';
    m_cCurrency  = '$';
    m_nGroupLen  = 3;
}

// Copy constuctor
public FormatNumbers(char dec, char sep, char cur,
                     int len)
{
    m_cSeparator = sep;
    m_cCurrency  = cur;
    m_nGroupLen  = len;
}

// Change the group separator symbol
public void setSeparatorSymbol(char c)
{
    m_cSeparator = c;
}

// Interrogate for the current separator symbol
public char getSeparatorSymbol()
{
    return m_cSeparator;
}

// Set the currency symbol
public void setCurrencySymbol(char c)
{
    m_cCurrency = c;
}

// Interrogate for the current currency symbol
public char getCurrencySymbol()
{
    return m_cCurrency;
}

// Set the number of digits in a grouping
public void setGroupLen(int n)
{
    if ((n < 1) || (n > 4))
        n == 1;
```

```
        m_nGroupLen = n;
}

// Interrogate for the current group length
public int getGroupLen()
{
    return m_nGroupLen;
}

// Integer conversion to comma-delimited format
public String formatComma(int n)
{
    // If n is 0, the format is fixed
    if (n == 0)
        return "0";

    // Local values
    StringBuffer result = new StringBuffer();
    int x, p;
    int t;

    // If n < 0, put a negative sign in the result
    if (n < 0)
    {
        result.append('-');
        n = -n;
    }

    // Add currency sign
    if (m_cCurrency != ' ')
        result.append(m_cCurrency);

    // Loop through each decimal place in n
    for (p = log10(n); p >= 0; --p)
    {
        // Get power for this digit
        x = pow10(p);

        // Get the value of the current digit
        t = (n / x);

        // Remove the digit being displayed from n
        n -= t * x;

        // Insert the proper digit
        result.append(DIGIT[t]);

        // Place a comma after every m_nGroupLen digits
        if ((p % m_nGroupLen == 0) && (p != 0))
            result.append(m_cSeparator);
    }
```

(continued)

```
            return result.toString();
        }

        // Integer conversion to text
        public String formatText(int n)
        {
            // If n is 0, the format is fixed
            if (n == 0)
                return "zero";

            // Local values
            StringBuffer result = new StringBuffer();

            int temp,       // Value used to hold temporary values
                place,      // Current place
                hundreds;   // Amount in the current place

            // If n < 0, say so and then get n's positive value
            if (n < 0)
            {
                result.append("negative ");
                n = -n;
            }

            // Find the highest place in the number
            place = log10(n) / 3;

            while (place >= 0)
            {
                // Find the hundreds amount of the current place
                temp = pow10(place * 3);
                hundreds = n / temp;

                // If it's not 0
                if (hundreds != 0)
                {
                    // Subtract the place amount from n
                    n -= temp * hundreds;

                    // Get the digits in the hundreds place
                    temp = hundreds / 100;

                    // If there are hundreds, add their test to
                    // the result
                    if (temp != 0)
                    {
                        hundreds -= temp * 100;
                        result.append(ONES[temp]);
                        result.append(" hundred");
                    }
```

```java
            // If hundreds still has a value
            if (hundreds != 0)
            {
                if (temp != 0)
                    result.append(' ');

                if (hundreds < 20)
                    // Use specific names such as "one"
                    // or "eleven"
                    result.append(ONES[hundreds]);
                else
                {
                    temp = hundreds / 10;

                    // If there is a number in the tens
                    // spot
                    if (temp != 0)
                    {
                        hundreds -= temp * 10;
                        result.append(TENS[temp-2]);
                    }

                    // If there is a number in the ones
                    // spot
                    if (hundreds != 0)
                    {
                        result.append('-');
                        result.append(ONES[hundreds]);
                    }
                }
            }

            // If the number is one thousand or more,
            // display the place name
            if (place != 0)
            {
                result.append(' ');
                result.append(POWERS[place-1]);

                // If n still has value, add a comma
                if (n != 0) result.append(", ");
            }
        }

        // Go to the next place
        --place;
    }

    return result.toString();
    }
}
```

The *FormatNumbers* class exports two public methods:

- The **formatComma** method creates a string from the given *int* value. The string will contain the digits of the number separated by the *m_cSeparator* character before even *m_nGroupLen* digits. If *m_cCurrency* is not the space character, the method prepends that character to indicate a monetary type. By default, I have set these parameters to the standard values used in the United States: *m_cSeparator* is the comma, *m_cCurrency* is the dollar sign, and *m_nGroupLen* is 3.

- The **formatText** method converts an *int* value to a string of text, using a set of constant arrays to generate the output string. The terminology I've used is that of the United States; to support another magnitude naming system (such as the British system, in which the U.S. "billions" place becomes the British "milliards" place), you could add a user-settable switch and another set of string constants.

I created a basic applet, FormatTest, to test *FormatNumbers*. FormatTest essentially displays a few numbers in a Java panel, in both comma-delimited and text formats. FormatTest is a very short piece of code; most of it was generated by the Java Applet Wizard. I filled in *paint* to allow the applet to use tools provided by the *formatText* and *formatComma* methods from *FormatNumbers* to display a set of values. (You can find the *FormatTest* sample program in the \ActiveVJ\Chap07\ FormatTest directory on the companion disc.)

```java
import java.applet.*;
import java.awt.*;
import coyote.math.*;

//
//
// FormatTest
//
//
public class FormatTest extends Applet
{

    public FormatTest()
    {
    }

    public String getAppletInfo()
    {
        return "Name: FormatTest\r\n" +
               "Author: Scott Robert Ladd\r\n" +
               "Created with Microsoft Visual J++ " +
               "Version 1.1";
    }

    public void init()
    {
        resize(700, 250);
    }
```

```
public void destroy()
{
}

public void paint(Graphics g)
{
    FormatNumbers fm = new FormatNumbers();

    String s1 = fm.formatComma(1234567890);
    String s2 = fm.formatText(1230567001);
    fm.setCurrencySymbol(' ');
    String s3 = fm.formatComma(1);
    String s4 = fm.formatText(1000014081);
    String s5 = fm.formatText(-10000);

    g.drawString(s1, 10, 20);
    g.drawString(s2, 10, 40);
    g.drawString(s3, 10, 60);
    g.drawString(s4, 10, 80);
    g.drawString(s5, 10, 100);
}

public void start()
{
}

public void stop()
{
}
}
```

The applet will display the following strings.

```
$1,234,567,890
one billion, two hundred thirty million, five hundred sixty-
  seven thousand, one
1
one billion, fourteen thousand, eighty-one
negative ten thousand
```

FormatNumbers is a generic tool that formats numbers in two popular styles. Since such a facility might be useful for software written in languages other than Java—Microsoft Visual Basic, Scripting Edition, and C++, for example—*FormatNumbers* is an excellent candidate for conversion to an ActiveX COM object. The first task I must perform to make this conversion is to provide an ActiveX interface to *FormatNumbers*, which I will do using Developer Studio's built-in tools.

Converting a Java Applet to COM

I can make *FormatNumbers* available to other applications through COM without making any changes to the source code; Developer Studio provides a wizard that automatically generates the required interface definitions, registration entries, and identifiers. Figure 7-1 shows the FormatTest application as it appears when it is loaded into the development environment, from which the ActiveX Component For Java Wizard is started.

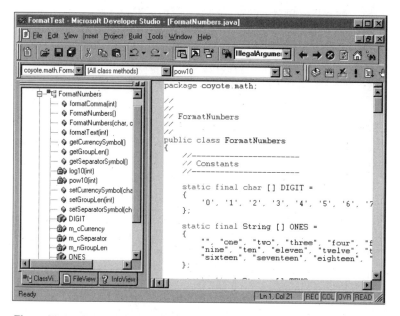

Figure 7-1. *FormatTest in Developer Studio.*

From the Tools menu, I select the ActiveX Wizard For Java item. The Input Files dialog box, shown in Figure 7-2, will appear. In the first text box, I have filled in the name of the class that I want to expose. Note that this should be the name of a *.class* object file, not a *.java* source file; I compiled my Java code before invoking the wizard.

The next field in this dialog box allows me to decide whether to use an existing Interface Definition Language (IDL) file or to have the wizard generate one for me. As I discussed in Chapter 6, an IDL file describes the interfaces exposed by a COM component. For complex classes that export several interfaces, I usually ask the wizard to generate an initial IDL file that I later customize for my own purposes. For this example, I'll have the wizard create a new IDL file based on the methods exported by my *FormatNumbers* class.

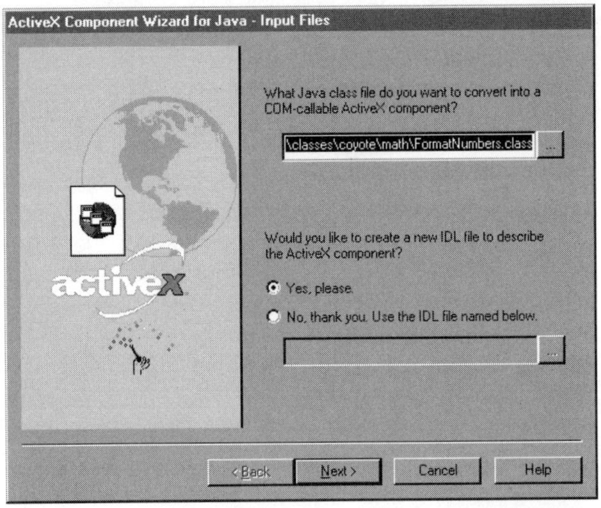

Figure 7-2. *The ActiveX Component Wizard Input Files dialog box.*

The next ActiveX Component Wizard dialog box is shown in Figure 7-3. In this box, I need to determine the CLSID for my ActiveX class; if I had already created a unique identifier, I could enter it in the provided text field; otherwise (and in most cases), I want the wizard to generate a CLSID for me. This value is guaranteed to be unique for my class; for each subsequent release or version of my component, I'll use a new CLSID to differentiate the new code from the old.

At the bottom of the CLSID dialog box is a pair of radio buttons that tell the wizard whether or not I want it to automatically register the new ActiveX component. In this case, I want the wizard to perform the registration for me.

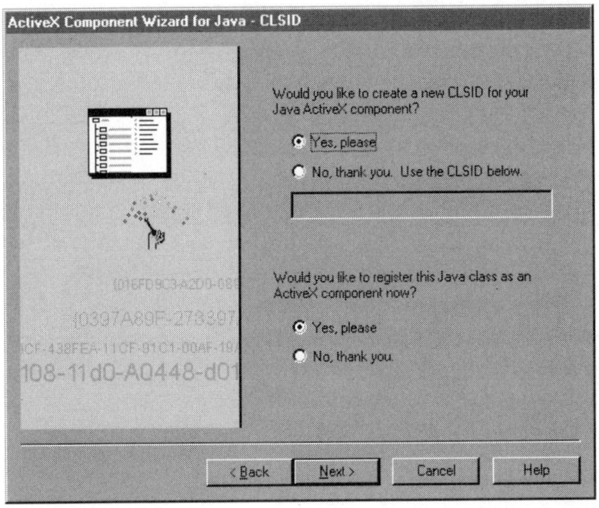

Figure 7-3. *The ActiveX Component Wizard CLSID dialog box.*

The next dialog box, shown in Figure 7-4, asks for information about the type of interface to be supported by the new ActiveX component. Remember, a COM object can support either a dispinterface or a dual interface (for indirect access); the first pair of radio buttons allows me to select one of these options. *FormatNumbers* is a pretty simple class, with only eight exported methods; I decided to have the wizard construct a dispinterface interface.

The second set of radio buttons lets me create a type library from the IDL file; I've done this for *FormatNumbers*. A type library provides information about the types, methods, and interfaces exposed by a COM object; in most cases, you'll want the wizard to generate a *.tlb* file for you.

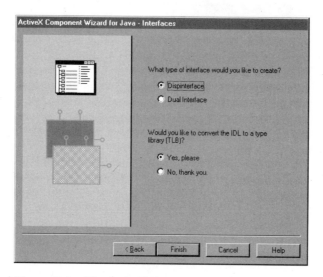

Figure 7-4. *The ActiveX Component Wizard Interfaces dialog box.*

The ActiveX Component Wizard doesn't do everything for me, however. The next dialog box, shown in Figure 7-5, lists the steps I must take to complete the conversion process.

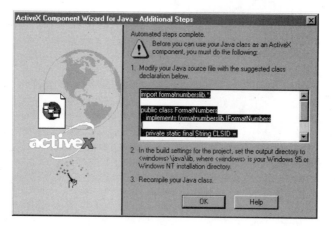

Figure 7-5. *The ActiveX Component Wizard Additional Steps dialog box.*

ACTIVE VISUAL J++

The first item is a list box containing a set of statements that should replace the *class* statement in my source file. For *FormatNumbers*, the wizard used the information from the previous dialog boxes to generate a new import statement, an additional *implements* clause for the *FormatNumbers* class definition, and an exposed constant containing the CLSID for the new COM component. I'll do the following to add this code to my program.

1. Select the code in the list box.

2. Copy the code to the clipboard (using Ctrl-Ins or Ctrl-C).

3. Move to the window that contains the Java source code for my class (in this case, *FormatNumbers.java*).

4. Insert the text from the clipboard in place of the *public class FormatNumbers* header.

5. Save the source file with the new code.

6. Return to the wizard's dialog box.

Figure 7-6 shows how the *FormatNumbers* class will look after the class header has been changed.

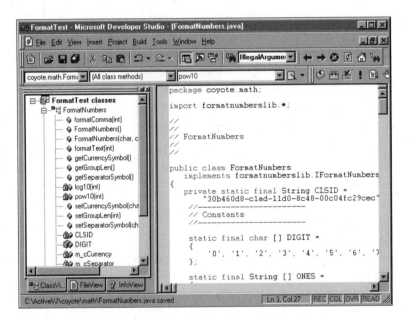

Figure 7-6. FormatNumbers *with the new class header.*

The next step is to verify that the component's output will be stored in the appropriate directory, usually *C:\Windows\java\lib*. You can set the output directory in the Project Settings window, as shown in Figure 7-7 on the following page.

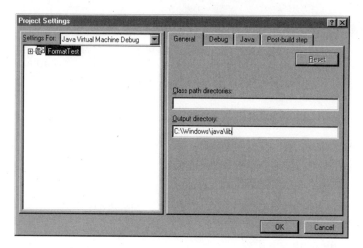

Figure 7-7. *The build settings window for FormatTest.*

Finally, I will recompile my *FormatNumbers* Java class by making it the current text window and pressing Ctrl-F7. I could also have done this by choosing the Compile item from the Build menu or by clicking the Compile button on the toolbar.

In Figure 7-8 (on page 176), I've maximized the output window in Developer Studio so that you can see the output from the various compilers and tools. After it has compiled the Java source file, the MIDL (Microsoft IDL) compiler is invoked for the IDL file I specified earlier. In this example, I asked the ActiveX Wizard to generate an IDL file for me; it creates the following text file.

```
[
    uuid(30b460da-c1ad-11d0-8c48-00c04fc29cec),
    helpstring("FormatNumbersLib Type Library"),
    version(1.0)
]
library FormatNumbersLib
{
    importlib("stdole32.tlb");

    [
        uuid(30b460d9-c1ad-11d0-8c48-00c04fc29cec),
        helpstring("IFormatNumbers Interface")
    ]
    dispinterface IFormatNumbers
    {
        properties:
        methods:
```

```
    [ helpstring("setSeparatorSymbol Method"), id(1) ]
    void setSeparatorSymbol([in] char p1);

    [ helpstring("getSeparatorSymbol Method"), id(2) ]
    char getSeparatorSymbol();

    [ helpstring("setGroupLen Method"), id(3) ]
    void setGroupLen([in] long p1);

    [ helpstring("getGroupLen Method"), id(4) ]
    long getGroupLen();

    [ helpstring("formatComma Method"), id(5) ]
    BSTR formatComma([in] long p1);

    [ helpstring("setCurrencySymbol Method"), id(6) ]
    void setCurrencySymbol([in] char p1);

    [ helpstring("getCurrencySymbol Method"), id(7) ]
    char getCurrencySymbol();

    [ helpstring("formatText Method"), id(8) ]
    BSTR formatText([in] long p1);

}


[
    uuid(30b460d8-c1ad-11d0-8c48-00c04fc29cec),
    helpstring("CFormatNumbers Object")
]
coclass CFormatNumbers
{
    [ default ]
    dispinterface IFormatNumbers;
};

};
```

When the MIDL compiler is finished, Developer Studio runs the Java Type Library Wizard to create a *.tlb* file from your interface definitions. The last output line tells you that a file named *summary.txt* has been generated to describe the interfaces for your class. Double-click on this line to see a Java-like text file that lists the interfaces and exposed methods for the new COM class.

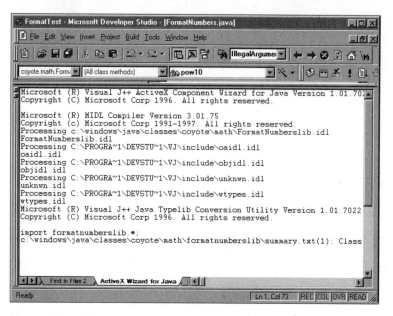

Microsoft (R) Visual J++ ActiveX Component Wizard for Java Version 1.01.702
Copyright (C) Microsoft Corp 1996. All rights reserved.

Microsoft (R) MIDL Compiler Version 3.01.75
Copyright (c) Microsoft Corp 1991-1997. All rights reserved.
Processing c:\windows\java\classes\coyote\math\FormatNumberslib.idl
FormatNumberslib.idl
Processing C:\PROGRÀ~1\DEVSTU~1\VJ\include\oaidl.idl
oaidl.idl
Processing C:\PROGRÀ~1\DEVSTU~1\VJ\include\objidl.idl
objidl.idl
Processing C:\PROGRÀ~1\DEVSTU~1\VJ\include\unknwn.idl
unknwn.idl
Processing C:\PROGRÀ~1\DEVSTU~1\VJ\include\wtypes.idl
wtypes.idl
Microsoft (R) Visual J++ Java Typelib Conversion Utility Version 1.01.7022
Copyright (C) Microsoft Corp 1996. All rights reserved.

import formatnumberslib.*;
c:\windows\java\classes\coyote\math\formatnumberslib\summary.txt(1): Class

Figure 7-8. *The output messages generated by the ActiveX Component Wizard.*

Using a Java COM Class

If I wanted to use *FormatNumbers* in a Java program, I would use it just as I did before I made it available as an ActiveX component. The *FormatTest* program from the beginning of this chapter will work correctly, whether *FormatNumbers* is a plain Java class or a class extended by the ActiveX Component Wizard. However, a Java program can also access *FormatNumbers* via its ActiveX interface, as shown in this example program, *FMTest* (which you can find in the \ActiveVJ\Chap07\FMTest directory on the companion disc).

```java
import java.applet.*;
import java.awt.*;
import formatnumberslib.*;

//
//
// FMTest
//
//
public class FMTest extends Applet
{
    public FMTest()
    {
    }
```

```java
public String getAppletInfo()
{
    return "Name: FMTest\r\n" +
            "Author: Scott Robert Ladd\r\n" +
            "Created with Microsoft Visual J++ " +
            "Version 1.1";
}

public void init()
{
    resize(700, 250);
}

public void destroy()
{
}

public void paint(Graphics g)
{
    IFormatNumbers fm =
        (IFormatNumbers)new CFormatNumbers();

    String s1 = fm.formatComma(1234567890);
    String s2 = fm.formatText(1230567001);
    fm.setCurrencySymbol(' ');
    String s3 = fm.formatComma(1);
    String s4 = fm.formatText(1000014081);
    String s5 = fm.formatText(-10000);

    g.drawString(s1, 10, 20);
    g.drawString(s2, 10, 40);
    g.drawString(s3, 10, 60);
    g.drawString(s4, 10, 80);
    g.drawString(s5, 10, 100);
}

public void start()
{
}

public void stop()
{
}
```

In *FMTest*, I include the interface information for the *FormatNumbers* component; then I create a *CFormatNumbers* object, cast the returned pointer to an *IFormatNumbers* interface, and then proceed to use the interface object as if it were a normal Java object. A C++ program should be able to do the same thing, using the CLSID for *FormatNumbers* to create an object and access it via its interfaces.

Onward

ActiveX is the most recent outgrowth of Microsoft's COM technology. In early 1997, a new feature of the Java language, "Beans," was invented by Sun Microsystems and its partners; a Bean is very much like a Java class in that it allows programmers to create a universal software component. Fortunately, the Java Bean specification is very compatible with ActiveX, and in the next chapter, I'll show you how these two related technologies work together.

8 Java Beans

Whereas Microsoft's ActiveX component technology is based on a binary standard for interobject communication, Java's Bean component technology is defined in terms of the Java virtual machine: the former technology focuses on language independence; the latter, platform independence. In many ways, ActiveX controls and Java Beans are compatible; each can be defined in terms of the other, although the two standards provide slightly different views of component communication and development.

Beans Defined

Like ActiveX controls and COM components, Java Beans can be scaled to a variety of tasks. Some Beans will be components of visual interfaces—buttons and switches, for example. Other Beans will be "invisible" components, such as timers and parsers. And complex Beans can define embeddable applications, such as spreadsheets and calculators. In many cases, a Bean will itself contain or extend other Beans—a practice that is at the core of object-oriented programming.

So what exactly is a Java Bean? In the simplest sense, a Bean is a Java class that adheres to specific coding conventions so that the class's properties and methods can be discovered by other software components. A Bean allows itself to be customized in appearance and behavior; it supports events that communicate its actions, and it can support a persistence mechanism to save its state for later restoration. But in its simplest form, a Java Bean need be nothing more than a Java class that is made available to other components through a special packaging mechanism. A Bean-aware builder tool or development environment can identify Beans and make them available for visual placement into an application. Thus you can add Java Beans to an application in the same way that you insert ActiveX and OLE controls into a Microsoft Visual Basic form, by selecting them from a list and "drawing" them.

A Basic Bean

I've put together a very simple Bean, *SimpleBean*.

```
package coyote.bean;

import java.awt.*;

//
//
// SimpleBean
//
//
```

```
public class SimpleBean extends Canvas
{

    public SimpleBean()
    {
        setBackground(Color.blue);
    }

    public Dimension getMinSize()
    {
        return new Dimension(64, 64);
    }


}
```

SimpleBean looks no different from any other Java class; what makes it a Bean is the way that it is packaged and accessed by other software components. You store Java Beans in a JAR—not the glass kind, but a *Java ar*chive file. A JAR uses the familiar ZIP file format to store a related collection of classes and interfaces. The components of an Internet applet—its *.class* files, graphics images, sounds, and so forth—can be stored as a group in a single JAR file. The client can then quickly download this single compressed file, which the Java virtual machine unpacks and uses. A *manifest* tells the JVM how to use each item in a JAR. You need a basic understanding of JARs if you are to correctly implement Java Beans. The rest of this section will give you sufficient information about JARs to allow you to use them with Beans. The "More about JARs" sidebar explains the non-Bean aspects of using JARs.

More About JARs

A JAR file combines several files into one, using a variation on the popular ZIP format. One of the key benefits of JARs is that they can deliver applets efficiently: a client can download a complete applet—including code, images, and other components—in a single HTTP transaction. Also, the components of a JAR file can be compressed, further shortening the download time. As Java applications grow larger, JAR files become increasingly important in speeding up applet delivery over the Internet.

To add a JARed applet to your web page, use the *archive* parameter of the *APPLET* tag.

```
<applet code=MyApplet.class
    archive="jars/MyApplet.jar"
    width=320 height=240>
    <param name=bounce value="high">
</applet>
```

The *code* parameter identifies the *Applet* class, just as it does for a non-JARed applet; the additional *archive* parameter tells the virtual machine that MyApplet.class is found in MyApplet.jar.

(continued)

The first file in a JAR can be a manifest that describes the other JAR components; Java makes special use of the manifest to identify Beans. The manifest can also declare a "signature" value to identify the origin of an applet component. Without a manifest, the virtual machine cannot identify Java Beans components. See Chapter 11 for more information on signing applets using a JAR or with Microsoft's Authenticode technology and CAB files.

A JAR file can be edited and manipulated with any ZIP-compatible archive manager, including the original PKZip from PKWare. You can create a JAR file with the jar program available from Sun Microsystems, or by using a standard ZIP-compatible utility; in the latter case, simply rename the output file from .zip to .jar. However, the manifest is stored in a compiled format generated by jar; thus you cannot include a manifest when creating a JAR with a general-purpose archive manager.

Creating a JAR

The jar program creates JAR files; it is part of the Java Development Kit freeware distributed by JavaSoft. To define *SimpleBean* as a Java Bean, I place it in a JAR by using the following command.

```
jar cfm SimpleBean.jar SimpleBean.man coyote\bean\SimpleBean.class
```

The *cfm* parameter tells jar to create a new file with a specific name and manifest. Issued at an MS-DOS prompt, the command above will create a new JAR file named *SimpleBean.jar* that contains the manifest *SimpleBean.man* that, in turn, describes the class *coyote.bean.SimpleBean*. The *SimpleBean* manifest is a text file that contains the following information.

```
Manifest-Version: 1.0

Name: coyote/bean/SimpleBean.class
Java-Bean: true
```

That's it! The class is now packaged and ready for use. But how is a Java Bean used? When a Java application executes, the Java virtual machine begins searching for the required classes in the directories defined by the CLASSPATH. In this search, a Bean is treated like any other Java class; it resides in a specific directory and is located and loaded through the usual mechanisms. So why go through all the rigmarole of putting the Bean into a JAR? Wouldn't it be easier to make *SimpleBean* a plain old class?

The Makings of a Good Bean

Yes, if you look at it from this limited point of view, it would be easier to make *SimpleBean* an ordinary Java class. If I do so, however, I must incorporate *SimpleBean* into my program manually, by writing source code. But because I have declared *SimpleBean* to be a Bean, I can access it via a Bean-aware application builder, and I can visually insert it into my application and configure it.

The best candidates for "beanification" are those classes that have a strong visual element that can be customized at interface design time. A purely computational class would probably make a poor Bean, but an animated button and a spin control would be prime candidates because they can be inserted into an application visually.

NOTE

In my description of the programmatic requirements for Beans, I introduce a number of topics—bound properties and event delegation, for example—that can apply to non-Bean classes as well. However, Beans must implement these features according to a standard practice, whereas non-Bean classes have no such restriction.

Events

An *event* is something that happens to an object—the click of a mouse button within its bounds, or the tick of a timer, for example. Java 1.1 introduced a new event model based on *delegation*. In essence, an object's class definition declares that it fires a certain event; other objects in the program can then make known their interest in listening to that event. This focuses the management of events on what is happening and who wants to do something about it, allowing program flow to be structured in a very object-oriented fashion. Beans depend on the Java 1.1 event delegation model. The following example demonstrates this model.

An Event Example

Under Java 1.0, every *Component* class defined an *action* method that captured all events fired by its *Component* subclasses. This meant that every event fired by every *Component* class was handled by an *action* method. In Chapter 4, for example, the GATest applet declared an *action* function to process events generated by the Go button.

```
public boolean action(Event event, Object obj)
{
    if (event.target == ctlGo)
    {
        // Do whatever the Go button is supposed to do
    }
}
```

When the *add* method adds a child *Component* class to a parent, the parent automatically receives notification of all child events via its *action* method, even if the parent has no interest in those events.

In the *delegation* event model introduced in Java 1.1, an event is linked to a set of listener objects; only those objects that declare their interest in an event will be notified when the event fires. Under the delegation model, GATest would declare itself as a listener to specific "action" events by implementing the

ActionListener interface. For instance, the applet would be a listener to *ctlGo*'s events if it included code such as the following.

```
// Create controls
ctlGo = new Button("Go");
add(ctlGo);
ctlGo.addActionListener(this);
```

The *ActionListener* interface declares a method named *actionPerformed*, which has a single parameter of type *ActionEvent*. Notice how the similarity in naming links the *ActionEvent* parameter to an *ActionListener* and to the *actionPerformed* method; this convention is followed for all predefined event types. The following code shows how *actionPerformed* would be implemented in SATest.

```
public void actionPerformed(ActionEvent event)
{
    // Do whatever the Go button is supposed to do
}
```

The *actionPerformed* method will "hear" all events fired by objects that GATest listens to; in this case, GATest registers itself as a listener only for *ctlGo* events. The *actionPerformed* method can safely assume that it will be invoked only when the user clicks the Go button.

> **NOTE**
>
> A powerful technique is to define inner classes as listeners to events from different *Component* classes. For example, if your class contains a pair of buttons, Stop and Go, you can define two inner class objects (such as *HandleStop* and *HandleGo*) to encapsulate event handling for each button.

A Comparison of Event Models

In the Java 1.0 event model, you use inheritance to customize event handling; essentially, you handle an event in a Component subclass by overriding the *action* method inherited from the class's superclass. This is a philosophical break with purely object-oriented design; subclasses should be used to *extend* (not *change*) the features derived from a superclass. And, as I discussed above, the *action*-based event model assumes that all parent containers want to listen to all events fired by all of their child components, which violates the object-oriented concept of encapsulating a function only where it is needed. If nothing else, the Java 1.0 event model is simply inefficient.

Java 1.1 cleanly separates application code, which processes events, from interface code, which generates events. Furthermore, delegation allows programmers to take a structured approach to event handling, an approach that can group related events into hierarchies through the class mechanism. The handling of an event can be targeted to the most appropriate handler, which allows applications to be structured efficiently.

The two event handling models should not be mixed within an application. In general, new programs should conform to the Java 1.1 delegation model, and older code can continue to use the Java 1.0 conventions. The *action*-based event system will not be removed from Java in the foreseeable future, but the delegation model provides better tools for event encapsulation.

Properties

A *property* is a named attribute of a Bean. Nearly every class has properties—size, color, and font, for example. The usual Java coding convention is to manipulate properties via a pair of methods, *set* and *get*. For example, all *Component* classes have a *Foreground* property; you can obtain the current foreground color with the *getForeground* method and change it with the *setForeground* method. Although this coding convention (using *getX* and *setX* methods for property *X*) is strongly suggested for all Java classes, Java Beans *must* follow this style of coding so that a Bean container can easily identify properties by examining method names. The process of identifying a Bean's properties is known as *introspection*. Introspection automatically determines the characteristics of a Bean by examining the bean's definition.

Not every property supports both *get* and *set* methods; some properties are read-only values and have only *get* methods. Properties also come in two basic types:

A *simple property* represents a single value; the name of the property can be derived from its methods. For example, the *getStyle* and *setStyle* methods imply the existence of a property named *Style*. If a simple property is read-only, it will have only a *get* method; a few properties are write-only and support only *set* methods.

An *indexed property* represents an array of values; like a simple property, an indexed property is manipulated with *set* and *get* methods. Some indexed property methods require the specification of an array index and allow changes to only one element; other indexed properties allow you to *set* or *get* the entire array.

Simple and indexed properties can also be bound or constrained, as described in the next two sections.

Bound Properties

Beans use event delegation to manage properties. Components don't exist in a vacuum; for instance, a change in the size property of a component might require other components to adjust their position. Or the setting of a certain state in a control might change another part of an application's interface. A *bound property* notifies interested objects that it has undergone a change.

A bound property has a *set* function that fires a *PropertyChangeSupport* event; other components then declare themselves as listeners for that event. For example, I could modify the *SimpleBean* component to fire notification events when its background color changes.

```
public class SimpleBean extends Canvas
{
    // New field to identify property change
    private PropertyChangeSupport changes =
        new PropertyChangeSupport(this);

    public Color getColor()
    {
        return getBackground();
    }

    public void setColor(Color new_color)
    {
        Color old_color = getBackground();
        setBackground(new_color);

        // Send change event to listeners
        changes.firePropertyChange("New color", old_color,
            new_color);
    }

    // Methods to manage listeners
    public void addPropertyChangeListener(
        PropertyChangeListener l)
    {
        changes.addPropertyChangeListener(l);
    }

    public void removePropertyChangeListener(
        PropertyChangeListener l)
    {
        changes.removePropertyChangeListener(l);
    }

}
```

Notification granularity is per Bean, not per property; in other words, the Bean fires an event that identifies the property change. The implementation of bound properties is simply another use for the delegation event model.

Constrained Properties

A bound property informs interested components that a change has taken place; a *constrained property* gives listeners the opportunity to reject, or *veto*, the change. You can use constrained properties to prevent components from changing their abilities; for example, you can make sure that a timer component will never have its delay changed to an unacceptably short (or long) value. For example, if I wanted to allow other components to veto changes in the color of a *SimpleBean*, I could implement the following process.

```
public class SimpleBean extends Canvas
{
    // New field for vetoable changes
    private VetoableChangeSupport vetoes =
        new VetoableChangeSupport(this);

    private PropertyChangeSupport changes =
        new PropertyChangeSupport(this);

    public Color getColor()
    {
        return getBackground();
    }

    public void setColor(Color new_color)
        throws PropertyVetoException
    {
        Color old_color = getBackground();

        // Inform listeners of the pending change.
        // The exception thrown will be sent to whoever
        // called setColor.
        vetoes.fireVetoableChange("New color", old_color,
            new_color);

        // Now make the change
        setBackground(new_color);

        // Send change event to listeners
        changes.firePropertyChange("New color", old_color,
            new_color);
    }

    // Methods to manage veto listeners
    public void addVetoableChangeListener(
        VetoableChangeListener l)
    {
        vetos.addVetoableChangeListener(l);
    }

    public void removeVetoableChangeListener(
        VetoableChangeListener l)
    {
        vetos.removeVetoableChangeListener(l);
    }
```

(continued)

```
// Methods to manage change listeners
public void addPropertyChangeListener(
    PropertyChangeListener l)
{
    changes.addPropertyChangeListener(l);
}

public void removePropertyChangeListener(
    PropertyChangeListener l)
{
    changes.removePropertyChangeListener(l);
}

}
```

Now a *SimpleBean* checks for a veto before altering its color; each listener that implements the *VetoableChangeListener* interface can throw a *PropertyVetoException* if it objects to the property change. Since *setColor* does not implement an exception handler, the veto will pass back up through the call chain to whichever component tried to change the color.

In general, you should define bound and constrained properties when changes to your component affect other components. This will provide the necessary communication between related objects, improving the reliability of your application by preventing (or at least managing) incompatible changes in components.

A Slideshow Bean

Chapter 1 included a simple applet named Slideshow, which implemented the timed sequential display of several images. In this section, I convert Slideshow into a Java Bean, first changing its design to make it more generic:

- Slideshow is now a subclass of *Canvas*, since it is no longer an independent applet. (A Canvas object represents a rectangular region on which you can print graphics and text.)

- As an applet, the original class allowed the timer delay to be set as a parameter in the APPLET tag. Now that Slideshow is a Bean, the timing is managed as a property via the *setDelay* and *getDelay* methods.

- Whereas the Slideshow applet loaded a predetermined set of images, *SlideshowBean* has an indexed property that can assign a set of *Image*s for display, either through a constructor or via the *setImages* property method.

- *SlideshowBean* has a new read-only property that retrieves the number of *Image*s.

- A *SlideshowBean* fires a *SlideshowEvent* object to designated *SlideshowListener*s whenever the image changes (either because of a mouse click or a timer tick).

The *SlideshowEvent* class is defined by the following code.

```
package coyote.bean;

import java.util.*;
import java.awt.*;

//
//
// SlideshowEvent
//
//
public class SlideshowEvent extends EventObject
{

    //------------------------
    // Fields
    //------------------------
    private Image m_image;

    //------------------------
    // Constructors
    //------------------------
    public SlideshowEvent(Object obj, Image img)
    {
        super(obj);
        m_image = img;
    }

    //------------------------
    // Properties
    //------------------------
    public Image getEventImage()
    {
        return m_image;
    }

}
```

And a *SlideshowListener* class will implement this interface.

```
package coyote.bean;

//
//
// SlideshowListener
//
//
public interface SlideshowListener
{

    void handleSlideshowEvent(SlideshowEvent event);

}
```

The new class, *SlideshowBean*, follows.

```
package coyote.bean;

// Import class packages
import java.applet.*;
import java.awt.*;
import java.beans.*;
import java.util.*;

public class SlideshowBean
    extends Canvas
    implements Runnable
{
    //------------------------
    // Fields
    //------------------------

    // Properties
    private long     m_delay = 5000;
    private int      m_nImages;
    private Image    m_Images[];
    private int      m_nCurImage;
    private int      m_nImgWidth;
    private int      m_nImgHeight;
    private Vector   m_listeners;

    // Thread support
    Thread m_Slideshow = null;

    //------------------------
    // Constructors
    //------------------------
    public SlideshowBean()
    {
        m_nImages     = 0;
        m_nImgWidth   = 0;
        m_nImgHeight  = 0;
        m_nCurImage   = 0;
        m_listeners   = new Vector();

        start();
    }

    public SlideshowBean(Image [] imgs)
    {
        m_listeners   = new Vector();
        setImages(imgs);

        start();
    }
```

```java
protected void finalize()
{
    stop();
}


//------------------------
// Thread methods
//------------------------
private void start()
{
    m_Slideshow = new Thread(this);
    m_Slideshow.start();
}

public void stop()
{
    if (m_Slideshow != null)
    {
        m_Slideshow.stop();
        m_Slideshow = null;
    }
}


//------------------------
// Properties
//------------------------
public long getDelay()
{
    return m_delay / 1000L;
}

public void setDelay(long sec)
{
    m_delay = sec * 1000L;
}

public Image [] getImages()
{
    return m_Images;
}

public void setImages(Image [] imgs)
{
    m_Images      = imgs;
    m_nImages     = imgs.length;
    m_nImgWidth   = m_Images[0].getWidth(this);
    m_nImgHeight  = m_Images[0].getHeight(this);
    m_nCurImage   = 0;
```

(continued)

```java
        setSize(m_nImgWidth, m_nImgHeight);
        repaint();
    }

    public int getImageCount()
    {
        return m_nImages;
    }

    //------------------------
    // Methods
    //------------------------
    public synchronized void addSlideshowListener(
        SlideshowListener sl)
    {
        m_listeners.addElement(sl);
    }

    public synchronized void removeSlideshowListener(
        SlideshowListener sl)
    {
        m_listeners.removeElement(sl);
    }

    public void displayImage(Graphics g)
    {
        if (m_nImages != 0)
        {
            // Display current image
            g.drawImage(m_Images[m_nCurImage],
                    (size().width - m_nImgWidth)  / 2,
                    (size().height - m_nImgHeight) / 2,
                    null);

            // Notify listeners of picture change
            SlideshowEvent event =
                new SlideshowEvent(this,
                    m_Images[m_nCurImage]);

            // Avoid thread conflicts by duplicating vector
            // of listeners
            Vector l;

            synchronized(this)
            {
                l = (Vector)m_listeners.clone();
            }
```

```
            // Call each listener with event
            for (int i = 0; i < l.size(); ++i)
            {
                SlideshowListener sl =
                    (SlideshowListener)l.elementAt(i);
                sl.handleSlideshowEvent(event);
            }
        }
    }

    public void drawNext()
    {
        if (m_nImages != 0)
        {
            // Increment image index
            m_nCurImage++;

            if (m_nCurImage == m_nImages)
                m_nCurImage = 0;

            // Display new image
            displayImage(getGraphics());
        }
    }

    public void paint(Graphics g)
    {
        // Clear the rectangle
         Rectangle r = g.getClipRect();
         g.clearRect(r.x, r.y, r.width, r.height);
         displayImage(g);
    }

    //-------------------------
    // Events
    //-------------------------
    public boolean mouseDown(Event evt, int x, int y)
    {
        // Skip to next image
        drawNext();
        return true;
    }
```

(continued)

```
//-------------------------
// Runnable methods
//-------------------------
public void run()
{
    // Timer loop draws next image every
    // m_delay_ms milliseconds
    while (true)
    {
        try
        {
            Thread.sleep(m_delay);
            drawNext();
        }
        catch (Exception e) {}
    }
}
}
```

After I compiled these classes, I stored them in a JAR file by using the following command.

```
jar cfm SlideshowBean.jar SlideshowBean.man
 coyote\bean\SlideshowBean.class
 coyote\bean\SlideshowEvent.class
 coyote\bean\SlideshowListener.class
```

The following text is the manifest for *SlideshowBean*.

```
Manifest-Version: 1.0

Name: coyote/bean/SlideshowBean.class
Java-Bean: True

Name: coyote/bean/SlideshowEvent.class
Java-Bean: False

Name: coyote/bean/SlideshowListener.class
Java-Bean: False
```

Using a Bean is no more difficult than using a class. In the SSBTester applet, I create a *SlideshowBean* object, load it with images, and set a method to capture and count *SlideshowEvent*s.

```
import java.applet.*;
import java.awt.*;
import coyote.bean.*;

//
//
// SSBTester
//
//
```

```java
public class SSBTester
    extends Applet
    implements Runnable, SlideshowListener
{
    private Thread    m_SSBTester = null;
    private int       m_count;
    private Label      m_label;

    private SlideshowBean m_bean;

    public SSBTester()
    {
        m_count = 0;
    }

    public String getAppletInfo()
    {
        return "Name: SSBTester\r\n" +
               "Author: Scott Robert Ladd\r\n" +
               "Created with Microsoft Visual J++ " +
               "Version 1.1";
    }


    public void init()
    {
        resize(320, 240);
        setLayout(null);

        Image [] imgs = new Image[6];

        MediaTracker tracker = new MediaTracker(this);
        String imageName;

        for (int i = 0; i < 6; i++)
        {
            imageName = "image"
                        + "/"
                        + "slide"
                        + ((i < 10) ? "0" : "")
                        + i
                        + ".gif";

            imgs[i] = getImage(getDocumentBase(),
                imageName);

            tracker.addImage(imgs[i], 0);
        }
```

(continued)

```
        try
        {
            tracker.waitForAll();
        }
        catch(InterruptedException e) {}

        m_bean = new SlideshowBean(imgs);
        add(m_bean);
        m_bean.addSlideshowListener(this);
        m_bean.setLocation(10, 10);

        m_label = new Label();
        add(m_label);
        m_label.setBounds(10, 100, 100, 23);
    }

    public void destroy()
    {
    }

    public void paint(Graphics g)
    {
    }

    public void start()
    {
        if (m_SSBTester == null)
        {
            m_SSBTester = new Thread(this);
            m_SSBTester.start();
        }
    }

    public void stop()
    {
        if (m_SSBTester != null)
        {
            m_SSBTester.stop();
            m_SSBTester = null;
        }
    }

    public void run()
    {
        while (true)
        {
            try
            {
                repaint();
                Thread.sleep(50);
            }
```

```
        catch(InterruptedException e)
        {
            stop();
        }
    }
}

public void handleSlideshowEvent(SlideshowEvent event)
{
    ++m_count;
    m_label.setText("Change: " + m_count);
    repaint();
}

}
```

Some visual tools, such as Sun Microsystems' *BeanBox*, will not be able to completely configure *SlideshowBean* objects because they do not support indexed properties such as *Images*.

Beans as ActiveX Controls

By design, the Bean standard is compatible with binary component standards, including OpenDoc and ActiveX. Microsoft provides a command-line utility, regbean, that generates type library information and registers a Bean as an ActiveX control. To make *SlideshowBean* compatible with ActiveX, I use the following command.

```
regbean coyote\bean\SlideshowBean.class new
```

The *new* parameter tells regbean to generate a new CLSID for *SlideshowBean*; I could have replaced *new* with a CLSID in braces to identify the component with a CLSID of my own choice. The regbean utility would then have produced the following output.

```
Microsoft (R) Java(tm) Beans Registration Utility
Copyright (C) Microsoft Corp 1997. All rights reserved.

Setting code base to
 file:C:\WINDOWS\JAVA\CLASSES\coyote\bean\
loading object...
saving type library...

Java class coyote.bean.SlideshowBean.class successfully registered.
Using CLSID {a996dac0-bf4c-11d0-be9b-ad92d0e6814a}
```

When I run the Java Type Library Wizard on the resulting *.tlb* file, the wizard shows that regbean created the following interfaces by analyzing *SlideshowBean.class*.

```
public class slideshowbean/SlideshowBean extends
    java.lang.Object
```

(continued)

```
        {
        }

        public interface slideshowbean/SlideshowBean_Events
            extends com.ms.com.IUnknown
        {
            public abstract void componentShown(java.lang.Object);
            public abstract void mouseClicked(java.lang.Object);
            public abstract void mouseDragged(java.lang.Object);
            public abstract void componentResized(java.lang.Object);
            public abstract void mousePressed(java.lang.Object);
            public abstract void componentHidden(java.lang.Object);
            public abstract void mouseMoved(java.lang.Object);
            public abstract void keyPressed(java.lang.Object);
            public abstract void keyTyped(java.lang.Object);
            public abstract void mouseReleased(java.lang.Object);
            public abstract void focusLost(java.lang.Object);
            public abstract void keyReleased(java.lang.Object);
            public abstract void mouseExited(java.lang.Object);
            public abstract void mouseEntered(java.lang.Object);
            public abstract void focusGained(java.lang.Object);
            public abstract void componentMoved(java.lang.Object);
        }

        public interface slideshowbean/SlideshowBean_Dispatch
            extends com.ms.com.IUnknown
        {
            public abstract boolean gotFocus(java.lang.Object,
                java.lang.Object);
            public abstract boolean lostFocus(java.lang.Object,
                java.lang.Object);
            public abstract java.lang.Object createImage(int, int);
            public abstract void setBounds2(java.lang.Object);
            public abstract void hide();
            public abstract float getAlignmentY();
            public abstract int getbackground();
            public abstract void putbackground(int);
            public abstract void repaint4(int, int, int, int);
            public abstract void enable(boolean);
            public abstract boolean isVisible();
            public abstract void disable();
            public abstract void list5(java.lang.Object, int);
            public abstract void doLayout();
            public abstract void layout();
            public abstract java.lang.Object getClass();
            public abstract java.lang.Object
                getComponentAt(java.lang.Object);
            public abstract boolean isValid();
            public abstract boolean isShowing();
            public abstract void addNotify();
            public abstract boolean mouseUp(java.lang.Object, int,
                int);
```

```
public abstract void displayImage(java.lang.Object);
public abstract void toFront();
public abstract java.lang.Object getComponentAt2(int,
    int);
public abstract boolean keyUp(java.lang.Object, int);
public abstract java.lang.Object
    getFontMetrics(java.lang.Object);
public abstract java.lang.Object getGraphics();
public abstract void
    removeSlideshowListener(java.lang.Object);
public abstract void
    addComponentListener(java.lang.Object);
public abstract void addKeyListener(java.lang.Object);
public abstract java.lang.Object getTreeLock();
public abstract void
    addMouseMotionListener(java.lang.Object);
public abstract void run();
public abstract void repaint2();
public abstract void wait2(long);
public abstract java.lang.Object location();
public abstract java.lang.Object getLocation();
public abstract void stop();
public abstract void setLocation(java.lang.Object);
public abstract void add(java.lang.Object);
public abstract void drawNext();
public abstract void repaint3(long);
public abstract void wait3();
public abstract boolean contains2(int, int);
public abstract void resize2(int, int);
public abstract java.lang.String getName();
public abstract void setName(java.lang.String);
public abstract java.lang.Object getPeer();
public abstract boolean keyDown(java.lang.Object, int);
public abstract void notifyAll();
public abstract void requestFocus();
public abstract int getBackground();
public abstract void setBackground(int);
public abstract void dispatchEvent(java.lang.Object);
public abstract void wait(long, int);
public abstract void paint(java.lang.Object);
public abstract java.lang.Object getParent();
public abstract void repaint(long, int, int, int, int);
public abstract int getImageCount();
public abstract void setVisible(boolean);
public abstract int getimageCount();
public abstract void resize(java.lang.Object);
public abstract java.lang.Object size();
public abstract void show(boolean);
public abstract void show2();
public abstract long getDelay();
public abstract void setDelay(long);
```

(continued)

```
public abstract long getdelay();
public abstract void putdelay(long);
public abstract boolean mouseDrag(java.lang.Object, int,
    int);
public abstract void
    removeMouseListener(java.lang.Object);
public abstract boolean mouseEnter(java.lang.Object,
    int, int);
public abstract void addFocusListener(java.lang.Object);
public abstract java.lang.Object bounds();
public abstract void invalidate();
public abstract java.lang.Object getToolkit();
public abstract java.lang.String getname();
public abstract void putname(java.lang.String);
public abstract void transferFocus();
public abstract boolean prepareImage(Object, int, int,
    Object);
public abstract int checkImage(java.lang.Object,
    java.lang.Object);
public abstract void list(java.lang.Object);
public abstract boolean equals(java.lang.Object);
public abstract void printAll(java.lang.Object);
public abstract void setSize(int, int);
public abstract java.lang.Object getSize();
public abstract float getAlignmentX();
public abstract java.lang.Object preferredSize();
public abstract java.lang.Object getMaximumSize();
public abstract void notify();
public abstract java.lang.Object getCursor();
public abstract void setCursor(java.lang.Object);
public abstract void removeNotify();
public abstract void move(int, int);
public abstract void remove(java.lang.Object);
public abstract void reshape(int, int, int, int);
public abstract void setLocation2(int, int);
public abstract boolean mouseExit(java.lang.Object,
    int, int);
public abstract boolean isEnabled();
public abstract java.lang.Object
    createImage2(java.lang.Object);
public abstract boolean getenabled();
public abstract java.lang.String toString();
public abstract void putenabled(boolean);
public abstract boolean inside(int, int);
public abstract void list4(java.lang.Object);
public abstract void setLocale(java.lang.Object);
public abstract java.lang.Object getLocale();
public abstract void
    removeComponentListener(java.lang.Object);
public abstract void
    removeMouseMotionListener(java.lang.Object);
public abstract boolean contains(java.lang.Object);
```

```
public abstract void addMouseListener(java.lang.Object);
public abstract void
    removeKeyListener(java.lang.Object);
public abstract void setFont(java.lang.Object);
public abstract java.lang.Object getFont();
public abstract java.lang.Object getfont();
public abstract void putfont(java.lang.Object);
public abstract void nextFocus();
public abstract boolean mouseDown(java.lang.Object, int,
    int);
public abstract boolean action(java.lang.Object,
    java.lang.Object);
public abstract void print(java.lang.Object);
public abstract void setForeground(int);
public abstract java.lang.Object getColorModel();
public abstract boolean handleEvent(java.lang.Object);
public abstract int getforeground();
public abstract void putforeground(int);
public abstract int getForeground();
public abstract boolean postEvent(java.lang.Object);
public abstract boolean getvisible();
public abstract boolean mouseMove(java.lang.Object, int,
    int);
public abstract void putvisible(boolean);
public abstract void deliverEvent(java.lang.Object);
public abstract java.lang.Object getLocationOnScreen();
public abstract int hashCode();
public abstract boolean imageUpdate(Object, int, int,
    int, int, int);
public abstract void update(java.lang.Object);
public abstract void list2(java.lang.Object, int);
public abstract void validate();
public abstract boolean prepareImage2(Object, Object);
public abstract int checkImage2(Object, int, int,
    Object);
public abstract java.lang.Object locate(int, int);
public abstract void
    addSlideshowListener(java.lang.Object);
public abstract void
    removeFocusListener(java.lang.Object);
public abstract void setBounds(int, int, int, int);
public abstract java.lang.Object getBounds();
public abstract boolean isFocusTraversable();
public abstract void paintAll(java.lang.Object);
public abstract void list3();
public abstract java.lang.Object minimumSize();
public abstract void toBack();
public abstract void enable2();
public abstract java.lang.Object getMinimumSize();
public abstract java.lang.Object getPreferredSize();
public abstract void setImages(java.lang.Object);
```

(continued)

```
public abstract java.lang.Object getimages();
public abstract void putimages(java.lang.Object);
public abstract void setEnabled(boolean);
public abstract java.lang.Object getImages();
public abstract void setSize2(java.lang.Object);
}
```

The interfaces above define many methods not explicitly declared by *SlideshowBean*. The regbean utility finds and makes available all methods defined by or inherited by a Bean; the interfaces above show the superclass methods from *Canvas*. Once regbean is finished, you'll be able to see and use the *SlideshowBean* component from applications such as Visual Basic or the ActiveX Control Pad.

Onward

Java provides a rich set of interface components in its Abstract Window Toolkit (AWT), which is explored in the next chapter.

Part 3

Application Java

Capital ———

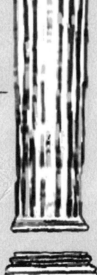

Fluted Shaft ———

Base ———

9 The Abstract Window Toolkit

Y our application might employ a terrific object-oriented design and perform amazing algorithmic tricks, but if your user interface is poorly constructed, users will *not* be pleased. The world will beat a path to your door only if your applications are easy to use and visually interesting. Fortunately, Java provides a powerful package of classes that makes interface development simple.

Those of you who have written programs in C++ that work directly with a graphical user interface—such as Microsoft Windows or the Macintosh system—know how complicated user interface development can be. Programming directly to the operating system can be powerful but time-consuming; even if you use a higher-level object-oriented library, you'll have to spend some time learning a complex collection of classes. And perhaps the worst aspect of interface programming is the likelihood that, when your program must be ported to a new operating system, nearly all of your user interface code will have to be rewritten. Different graphical environments often use conflicting terms and designs; frankly, porting interface code is one of my least favorite tasks.

Java was intended from the outset to be a language for the creation of universal, operating-system–independent software. As such, it comes with a collection of predefined tools for developing user interfaces. The Abstract Window Toolkit (AWT) is a set of packages that is included in every Java installation; the Java virtual machine (JVM) links the various interface components in your applets to the equivalent features of the execution environment. Thus a program written with the AWT will work in any environment that properly implements the JVM.

The AWT is far too extensive to be completely documented here; in this chapter, I discuss the most important elements of the package, touching on its overall design while discussing the features you'll use most often in your applications.

> **NOTE**
>
> The following discussion pertains to the Java 1.1 AWT libraries; see Appendix A for a list of differences between versions 1.0 and 1.1.

The AWT Component Hierarchy

You build an AWT interface by combining components: buttons, list boxes, labels, and other "widgets" that direct an application's actions. Figure 9-1 shows the class hierarchy of the Abstract Window Toolkit packages. The *Component* superclass is the core of the package; it defines the common features of all user interface objects.

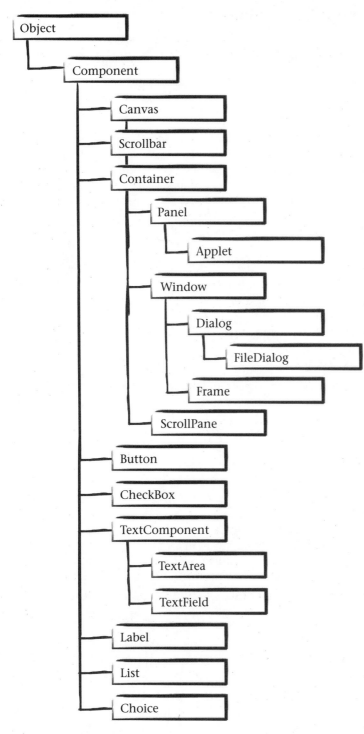

Figure 9-1. *The AWT component hierarchy.*

The *Component* Superclass

Component implements the interfaces *ImageObserver*, *MenuContainer*, and *Serializable*. The class defines the following frequently used methods.

void setBounds(int x, int y, int w, int h)
void setLocation(int x, int y)
void setSize(int w, int h)

These methods set the size and location of a component. A component usually exists within another component—a *Frame*, *Window*, *Canvas*, or *Applet* object—in which it has been included with the *add* method. The width (*w*) and height (*h*) parameters define the size of the component in pixels. The *x* and *y* parameters specify an offset in pixels from the origin of the parent container; Java defines the origin point as the location of the upper left corner of a component. The *setBounds* method combines the actions of *setLocation* and *setSize*.

void paint(Graphics g)

The *paint* method will be called when a component is first drawn or whenever it needs to be "repaired." If only part of the component needs to be redrawn, the *Graphics* object will define a clipping region. You will often override this method to redraw your custom components.

void paintAll(Graphics g)

The *paintAll* method paints a component and all of its subcomponents.

void repaint()
void repaint(int x, int y, int w, int h)
void repaint(long tm)
void repaint(long tm, int x, int y, int w, int h)
void update(Graphics g)

A call to *repaint* causes a call to be made to *Component.update*, either as soon as possible or within *tm* milliseconds. By default, *update* clears the component background before calling *paint*; this practice is safe (because it erases and redraws everything), but it leads to an annoying flicker in animated components. If your component is repainted often, you'll want to override this default behavior by having *update* clear and redraw only the affected portions of the display.

You should consider implementing an efficient form of *update* and then calling it from *paint*. You'll see an example of this technique in the LifeBox application in Chapter 13.

public boolean isEnabled()
public void setEnabled(boolean b)

When a component is enabled, it accepts user input from the keyboard and mouse; a disabled component is, essentially, inert. A component should change its appearance for different states by "graying" its text or otherwise indicating that it has been disabled. A good user interface will de-emphasize any visible but disabled components. These methods are most often used with controls such as buttons.

Image createImage(int w, int h)

This method creates a new, blank image that is compatible with the component and that is *w* pixels wide and *h* pixels high. This method is most useful for creating an off-screen image that will be drawn inside the component.

boolean contains(int x, int y)

This method returns *true* if the specified coordinate is within the bounds of the component.

Font getFont()
synchronized void setFont(Font f)

These methods set and retrieve the current font being used by the component. The *Font* object returned by *getFont* is often used to generate *FontMetrics* to size a component based on the characteristics of its text.

Graphics getGraphics()

This method returns a *Graphics* object that references the context and display area of the component. You use this *Graphics* object to plot lines, display text, and perform other acts of drawing within your component's area.

Toolkit getToolkit()

The *getToolkit* method returns the *Toolkit* object associated with a component. A *Toolkit* object provides a set of tools for loading external images and interrogating the environment in which your component exists. The *Applet* class includes many similar features; in general, you'll use a *Toolkit* object when you are working with standalone Java applications, which do not have access to *Applet*'s features.

void setBackground(Color c)
Color getBackground()
void setForeground(Color c)
Color getForeground()

These methods set or retrieve the background and foreground colors of a component. When you draw within a component via an associated *Graphics* object, text and graphics will appear, by default, in the current foreground color. If you do not set the colors, they default to those of the parent component. For example, if a panel has a gray background and black lettering, a button contained within that panel will have the same color scheme when it is first created.

Component getComponentAt(int x, int y)

This method returns a reference to the child component located at the specified coordinates within a container. If no child is present, it returns a reference to the container itself.

```
void setVisible(boolean b)
boolean isVisible()
boolean isShowing()
```

Calling *setVisible(true)* makes the component visible; *setVisible(false)* hides it. The *isVisible* method returns the current visible state of the component and the *isShowing* method returns *true* or *false* depending on whether the component is displayed on the screen.

```
void addComponentListener(ComponentListener l)
void addFocusListener(FocusListener l)
void addKeyListener(KeyListener l)
void addMouseListener(MouseListener l)
void addMouseMotionListener(MouseMotionListener l)
void removeComponentListener(ComponentListener l)
void removeFocusListener(FocusListener l)
void removeKeyListener(KeyListener l)
void removeMouseListener(MouseListener l)
void removeMouseMotionListener(MouseMotionListener l)
```

These methods add and remove listeners for the specified types of events; see Chapter 10 for more information about event handling.

The *Container* Subclass

A *container* is a component that contains other components (child components). Such a container component is known as a parent; the subcomponents can be called children. A parent can also be a child if it is included in a higher-level container.

A subclass of *Component*, *Container* includes methods that allow you to add new components. Predefined subclasses of *Container* include *Panel*, *Applet*, *Window*, *Frame*, and *Dialog*. A well-organized user interface might link related elements by building containers within other containers. The LifeBox application in Chapter 13 demonstrates this hierarchical system of component management. The *Container* class defines the following methods.

```
public Component add(Component comp)
public Component add(Component comp, int index)
```

These methods add a *component* object to a *Container* object. The first method adds the new object to the end of the container's list of child components. Using the second method, you can specify the ordinal position of the new component within the list.

```
public Component add(Component comp, Object constraints,
    int index)
public Component add(Component comp, Object constraints)
```

Some layout managers—*BorderLayout*, for example—require an additional argument, as shown in these methods, to locate a child component within its parent. See the section on *BorderLayout* later in this chapter for more information.

public void remove(Component comp)
public void remove(int index)

These methods remove a child component, either by reference or by its position within the subcomponent list.

public void removeAll()

This method removes all components previously added to this container.

public void addContainerListener(ContainerListener l)
public void removeContainerListener(ContainerListener l)

These methods add and remove listeners for the *ContainerListener* events; see Chapter 10 for more about event handling.

public Component getComponent(int index)

This method returns a reference to the child component located at position *index* in the subcomponent list of this container.

public Component getComponentAt(int x, int y)
public Component getComponentAt(Point p)

These methods each return a reference to the child component that contains the specified coordinates.

public int getComponentCount()

This method returns the number of child components in this container.

public Component[] getComponents()

This method returns an array of references to the child components resident in this container.

public boolean isAncestorOf(Component comp)

This method returns *true* if this component is a child in the hierarchy of the specified container; otherwise it returns *false*.

public LayoutManager getLayout()
public void setLayout(LayoutManager mgr)

These methods set and retrieve the container's layout. A layout defines a default organization for the child components within a container. See the "Layouts" section later in this chapter for a discussion of the standard layout classes.

public Insets getInsets()

The actual weights of a component's border lines vary depending on the operating system and the selected layout of the component. The *getInsets* method returns an *Insets* object that contains, in its *top*, *left*, *bottom*, and *right* members, the number of pixels that are used for each edge. If your program explicitly places a component by position, you should use *getInsets* to ensure that the component is completely within the valid display area.

public Dimension getMaximumSize()
public Dimension getMinimumSize()
public Dimension getPreferredSize()

These methods each return a *Dimension* argument specifying the maximum, minimum, or preferred size of a container. You may want to override these methods if your custom-designed containers require a certain amount of workspace; these methods are usually called by layout managers to place child components according to a predefined scheme.

public void paintComponents(Graphics g)

This method calls the *paint* method for each child component.

public void invalidate()
public void validate()

Although *validate* and *invalidate* are actually defined in the *Component* superclass, their primary use is within a container. A call to *validate* asks a container to ensure that its child components have been laid out correctly. The *invalidate* method explicitly declares that the layout needs to be reset for this container and all of its parents. This is usually required after a new component has been inserted into the midst of existing children or when a child component changes its size. The *invalidate* method might be called often for dynamic containers and should be written to execute quickly.

Peers

Both *Canvas* and *Container* implement the concept of *peers*, which are platform-specific code blocks, implemented in the background, that allow a virtual machine to link component code directly to an operating system or hardware. In essence, a component defines a platform-independent interface that is defined internally as a connection to platform-specific code.

Although a thorough discussion of peers is outside the scope of this book, you should be aware of their existence, because most virtual machines implement at least some common components—particularly simple ones, such as buttons—via peers. Unless you write your own platform-specific code, the use (or non-use) of peers by a component is largely a matter of internal code that is invisible to your Java application. That, indeed, is the reason for using peers: to facilitate the efficient implementation of a component without making Java code platform-specific.

The *Canvas* Subclass

Canvas is another subclass of *Component*; it is, essentially, a blank object used as a base class for your own noncontainer components. *Canvas* adds little to its parent other than support for peers (see the sidebar) and a version of the *paint* method that redraws the component background in the default color.

The *Button* Subclass

In Java, the *Button* class is a subclass of *Component*; it defines a labeled rectangular image that a user clicks to invoke some action. This class adds a few methods to *Component*.

public Button()
public Button(String text)

The first constructor creates a button without text; the second constructor specifies the button's initial label.

public synchronized void setLabel(String text)
public String getLabel()

A button's label is the text it displays to indicate its function. These methods set and return the label for the button.

public void addActionListener(ActionListener l)
public void removeActionListener(ActionListener l)

These methods add and remove listeners for the *ActionListener* events; see Chapter 10 for more about event handling. Essentially, an *ActionListener* event occurs whenever the user clicks on a button.

The *Checkbox* Subclass

A checkbox is a labeled Boolean state that the user can set to *true* or *false* by clicking a marker box. The marker will be checked or crossed if the Checkbox state is *true*; it will be blank if the state is *false*.

public Checkbox()
public Checkbox(String text)
public Checkbox(String, boolean)

The first constructor creates a checkbox without text; the second constructor specifies the checkbox's initial label. The variant constructors with boolean parameters allow your code to set the initial state of the component.

public Checkbox(String text, CheckboxGroup group,
    boolean state)

This constructor creates a checkbox with the specified label and state as part of the given *CheckboxGroup* object. (See page 214.)

public synchronized void setLabel(String text)
public String getLabel()

A checkbox's label is the text it displays to indicate what is being toggled between *true* and *false*. These methods set and get the label for the component.

public boolean getState()
public void setState(boolean state)

These methods get and set the state of a checkbox, which will be either *true* or *false*.

public void addItemListener(ItemListener l)
public void removeItemListener(ItemListener l)

These methods add and remove listeners for the *ItemListener* events; see Chapter 10 for more about event handling.

THE *CHECKBOXGROUP* OBJECT

public CheckboxGroup()

This method creates an empty *CheckboxGroup* object. A *CheckboxGroup* object defines a set of *Checkbox* components that are mutually exclusive; in other words, only one checkbox in a *CheckboxGroup* object can be selected (*true*) at a time. The selection of one checkbox will deselect the previous *true* choice within a group. A *CheckboxGroup* object does not have a visual representation; you are free to arrange, in an application-relevant format, the member checkboxes within their container.

public Checkbox getSelectedCheckbox()

This method returns a reference to the currently selected checkbox within this group.

public synchronized void setSelectedCheckbox(Checkbox box)

This method sets, by reference, the checkbox that is to be marked *true* (selected).

The *Label* Subclass

Although buttons and checkboxes display text known as labels, the *Label* class defines a text area that is not associated with another control. One of the simpler derivatives of *Component*, the *Label* class adds a few methods to those it inherits.

public Label()
public Label(String text)
public Label(String text, int alignment)

You can use the first two constructors to create a label with or without an initial text value; you can use the third constructor to specify one of three constants— *Label.RIGHT*, *Label.LEFT*, or *Label.CENTER*—to declare the alignment of the text within the label boundaries.

public int getAlignment()
public synchronized void setAlignment(int alignment)

These methods set or retrieve the alignment for a label's text. They use the constants defined above in the discussion of *Label* constructors.

public String getText()
public synchronized void setText(String text)

These methods set or retrieve the current text displayed by a label.

The *TextArea* Subclass

A *Label* object displays a single line of simple text; a *TextArea* object is a multiline component designed for the display of many lines of complex text. Whereas a label's text can be changed only from within an application, a text area can be set to allow editing. In many cases, a text area is a simple single-line component used for data entry of a single line; however, a text area can provide a simple editor for larger blocks of text. Also, a text area can support scrollbars that allow the user to move through text blocks that are larger than the display area. Use the *toString* method to obtain the text currently stored in a *TextArea* object.

A subclass of *Component*, the *TextArea* class defines some additional methods.

public TextArea()

This constructor creates an empty *TextArea* object.

public TextArea(String text)

This constructor creates a *TextArea* object containing the given text.

public TextArea(int rows, int columns)

This constructor creates a *TextArea* object with the given number of rows and columns.

public TextArea(String text, int rows, int columns)

This constructor is the same as the previous one, but it also defines initial content for the text area.

public TextArea(String text, int rows, int columns,
    int scrollbars)

This constructor creates a *TextArea* object with the specified content, rows, and columns; the fourth parameter defines the appearance of scrollbars within the text area, using one of the following constants.

TextArea.SCROLLBARS_NONE

TextArea.SCROLLBARS_HORIZONTAL_ONLY

TextArea.SCROLLBARS_VERTICAL_ONLY

TextArea.SCROLLBARS_BOTH

public synchronized void insert(String text, int index)

This method inserts *text* at index position *index* in the content of the *TextArea* object.

public void appendText(String text)

This method appends *text* at the end of a text area's content.

public synchronized void replaceRange(String text, int start,
   int end)

This method replaces the *TextArea* object's content between the *start* and *end* indexes (inclusive) with the text contained in *text*.

public int getRows()
public void setRows(int rows)
public int getColumns()
public void setColumns(int columns)

These methods change or retrieve the number of columns or rows in a text area.

public int getScrollbarVisibility()

This method returns one of the constants that specify the use of scrollbars in this text area.

The *List* Subclass (List Boxes)

A *List* component provides a scrolling pane within which one or more items can be selected from a list. *List* components are most often used to provide a set of predefined selections. A program can reference items in a list by using a positive integer index. A subclass of *Component*, the *List* class defines the following additional methods.

public List()

This constructor creates an empty *List* object with no visible contents. The *List* object does not allow multiple selection.

public List(int rows)

This constructor creates a new *List* object with the specified number of rows; multiple selections are not allowed.

public List(int rows, boolean multipleMode)

This constructor creates a new *List* component with a given number of rows. The ability to select multiple items is defined by the boolean argument.

public void addItem(String text)
public synchronized void addItem(String text, int index)

The first variant of *addItem* adds a new text item to the end of this *List* object; the second version inserts the new text item at a specific index position within the list.

public synchronized void replaceItem(String newTextValue,
    int index)

This method replaces the item at *index* with *newTextValue*.

public synchronized void removeAll()

This method removes all items from the list.

public synchronized void remove(String text)
public synchronized void remove(int index)
public synchronized void delItem(int index)

The first method removes an item by searching the list for a match to a string; if the item is not found, *remove* throws an *IllegalArgumentException*. The last two methods delete an item based on its index position within the list; they do not throw any exceptions.

public synchronized int getSelectedIndex()
public synchronized int[] getSelectedIndexes()

The first version of this method returns the index of the selected item in a list. If the list allows multiple selections, the first selected item will be returned. A return value of −1 indicates that nothing is selected in this list.

    The second method returns an array of indexes indicating the multiple selected items in a list. It returns *null* if nothing is selected.

public synchronized String getSelectedItem()
public synchronized String[] getSelectedItems()

Similar to the *getSelectedIndex* methods, these methods return the text of the selected items rather than the index values.

public String getItem(int index)
public synchronized String[] getItems()

The first method obtains the value of a single item at a given index position; the second returns an array containing the text of all items in the list.

public synchronized void select(int index)
public synchronized void deselect(int index)

These methods select or deselect an item at a given index position within a list.

public boolean isIndexSelected(int index)

This method returns *true* if the item at the specified index position is selected; the method returns *false* if it is not.

public int getRows()

The value returned from this method is the number of rows in this list.

public boolean isMultipleMode()
public synchronized void setMultipleMode(boolean state)

These methods discover or set the ability to select multiple items in a list.

public synchronized void makeVisible(int index)

This method scrolls the list so that the item at *index* is displayed.

public int getItemCount()

This method returns the number of items in a list.

void addActionListener(ActionListener l)
void removeActionListener(ActionListener l)
void addItemListener(ItemListener l)
void removeItemListener(ItemListener l)

These methods add and remove listeners for the specified types of events; see Chapter 10 for more about event handling.

The *Choice* Subclass (Combo Boxes)

A *Choice* component is what users of Microsoft Windows call a combo box—a combination of a text-entry field and a drop-down list of choices. The user can either enter a value directly into the text area or access the list and select a predefined choice. The *Choice* component is often used in filename selection; the user can elect to type in a new name or use a name provided in the list.

The *Choice* subclass adds the following methods to those it inherits from *Component*.

public Choice()

This constructor creates a new, blank *Choice* component with an empty item list.

public synchronized void addItem(String text)

This method adds a new text item to the end of the items list.

public synchronized void remove(String text)
public synchronized void remove(int index)

The first method deletes an item at an index position within the *Choice* object. The second method removes an item by searching the list for a match to a string; if the object is not found, *remove* throws an *IllegalArgumentException*.

public synchronized void removeAll()

This method removes all items from the list.

public synchronized void select(int index)
public synchronized void select(String text)

These methods select an item in a list, either by index value or by searching for the given string.

public int getSelectedIndex()

This method returns the index of the selected item in a *Choice* object. A return value of −1 indicates that nothing is selected in this *Choice* object.

public synchronized String getSelectedItem()

This method is the same as the previous method with the exception that it returns the String value of the selected item as opposed to its index.

public String getItem(int index)

This method obtains the value of a single item at a given index position.

public int getItemCount()

This method returns the number of items in a *Choice* object.

public synchronized void addItemListener(ItemListener I)
public synchronized void removeItemListener(ItemListener I)

These methods add and remove listeners for the specified types of events; see Chapter 10 for more about event handling.

Layouts

A layout allows you to specify the way in which the child components in a container are arranged. In some cases, you'll want to position your components explicitly; for this purpose, the *setLayout(null)* method call will remove any existing layout manager and allow you to use the *setLocation* and *setBounds* methods to draw child components in specific places. Generally, however, you won't call any methods defined by layout objects; when you add components to a container, the container's currently assigned layout automatically maintains the sizing and position according to its design. The standard layout managers are described here.

BorderLayout

The *BorderLayout* layout manager positions child components according to a system of directions: North, South, East, West, and Center. These directions are specified by a *String* argument in a call to the *add* method for a container. Here's an example:

```
setLayout(new BorderLayout());

add("North", new Button("North"));
add("South", new Button("South"));
add("East", new Button("East"));
add("West", new Button("West"));
add("Center", new Button("Center"));
```

Figure 9-2 shows what the button layout specified by the above code would look like; notice that all of the buttons have been "stretched" to fill their respective locations.

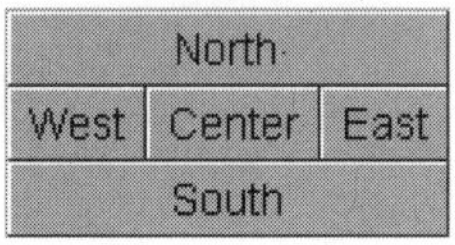

Figure 9-2. *A* BorderLayout *example.*

If you spell the direction names wrong when calling *add*, your child component might not even be displayed. For convenience, the *BorderLayout* class defines the *NORTH*, *SOUTH*, *EAST*, *WEST*, and *CENTER* constants as the appropriate *String* constants.

In the example shown in Figure 9-2, I constructed a *BorderLayout* object with no parameters; such a layout will pack components as tightly as possible. Another *BorderLayout* constructor accepts a pair of *int* values that specify the horizontal and vertical "padding" between children.

FlowLayout

The *FlowLayout* layout manager places components in a row; if it can fit all of the child controls into a single row, it will; otherwise, it creates extra rows as needed.

```
setLayout(new FlowLayout());

add(new Button("Button 1"));
add(new Button("2"));
add(new Button("Button 3"));
add(new Button("Long-Named Button 4"));
add(new Button("Button 5"));
```

Figure 9-3 shows how these five buttons would be placed in a window controlled by a *FlowLayout* layout.

Figure 9-3. *A* FlowLayout *example.*

Like *BorderLayout*, *FlowLayout* has more than one constructor.

public FlowLayout()

This constructor creates a basic *FlowLayout* object. The components in the object have centered alignment and the horizontal and vertical gaps between components are 5 pixels.

public FlowLayout(int alignment)

The *alignment* parameter in this constructor specifies one of the following constants: *FlowLayout.CENTER*, *FlowLayout.LEFT*, and *FlowLayout.RIGHT*. These specify the justification of child components within a row. The default horizontal and vertical gaps between components are 5 pixels.

public FlowLayout(int alignment, int hGap, int vGap)

In addition to alignment, this constructor allows you to declare the horizontal and vertical gaps between child components.

GridLayout

The *GridLayout* layout manager creates a set of evenly spaced rows and columns to contain child components. Components added to a container with *GridLayout* will be stored in row-column order; in other words, the layout will fill the first row, then the second, then the third, and so on.

```
setLayout(new GridLayout(0,2));

add(new Button("Button 1"));
add(new Button("2"));
add(new Button("Button 3"));
add(new Button("Long-Named Button 4"));
add(new Button("Button 5"));
```

Figure 9-4 shows the window generated by the above code. (A zero for either the number of rows or columns means "any number.") Note that the lower right corner is blank; although the grid has six total "slots" (two columns by three rows) in which components can be displayed, the code example adds only five buttons.

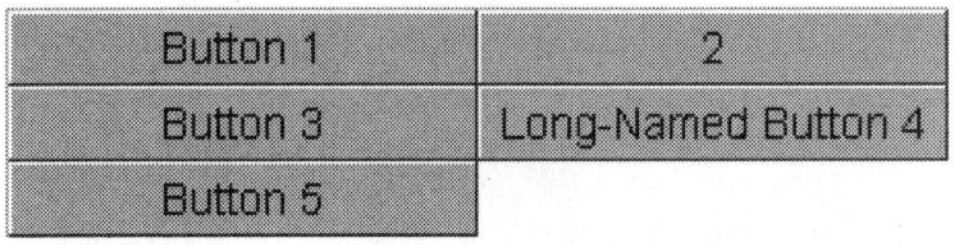

Button 1	2
Button 3	Long-Named Button 4
Button 5	

Figure 9-4. A GridLayout *Example.*

GridLayout has two constructors.

public GridLayout(int rows, int columns)
public GridLayout(int rows, int columns, int hGap, int vGap)

A *GridLayout* object can be created only with a constructor that specifies the number of rows and columns; a variation of the basic constructor allows specification of horizontal and vertical gaps (which are 0 by default).

Utility Types

Some of the method definitions in the first part of this chapter used utility classes, such as *Color* and *Font*. I'll take a quick look at some of those classes here. Many of these utility classes are enhanced or extended by Microsoft's Application Foundation Classes.

Color

The *Color* class encapsulates a platform-independent concept of color, providing constants for common hues and allowing programmers to custom-define colors. Java makes no guarantee as to how a color will appear in an implementation of the virtual machine. Different execution environments might cause some colors to be rendered as dithered; even a standard color such as red is unlikely to be identical on all platforms.

The *Color* class defines the following constructors, methods, and constants.

public Color(int r, int g, int b)
public Color(float r, float g, float b)
public Color(int rgb)

The first constructor creates a color from three integer values, each from 0 through 255, representing the intensity of the red, green, and blue channels. The intensities can also be specified as a set of three *float* values, each from 0.0 through 1.0. The third constructor is used to explicitly assign a combined RGB value.

public int getRed()
public int getGreen()
public int getBlue()
public int getRGB()

These methods return the individual red, green, and blue values or a combined RGB value for a color.

public Color brighter()
public Color darker()

These methods compute a brighter or darker hue of a color. They are frequently used to paint the edges of three-dimensional objects, such as buttons. Java does not specify how much brighter or darker the resulting color will be.

public static Color getHSBColor(float h, float s, float b)

This method computes a *Color* value based on the hue, saturation, and brightness model. The three *float* parameters must have values from 0.0 through 1.0.

public static final Color white
public static final Color lightGray
public static final Color gray
public static final Color darkGray
public static final Color black
public static final Color red
public static final Color pink
public static final Color orange
public static final Color yellow
public static final Color green
public static final Color magenta
public static final Color cyan
public static final Color blue

These are the standard colors defined as static constants by *Color*.

Font

Java's approach to fonts is very generic. The *Font* class provides basic information about a style of text; a component allows you to retrieve its current font via the *getFont* method or assign a new font with *setFont*. By default, all virtual machines support three standard fonts: "Serif" (known as "TimesRoman" in Java 1.0), "SanSerif" (formerly "Helvetica"), and "Monospaced" (formerly "Courier"). Java 1.0 also defined a "ZapfDingbats" font, which is now deprecated because those characters have become part of the Unicode standard.

Font defines one constructor and several methods and constants.

public Font(String name, int style, int size)

The constructor requires a font name, its style (one of the constants *Font.BOLD*, *Font.ITALIC*, or *Font.PLAIN*), and a size in points. (There are 72 points in an inch, or approximately 28.3 points in a centimeter.) Java does not guarantee that you will get the precise font you request, because operating systems vary considerably in their font support. When a new *Font* object is created, Java will match your request with the closest available font in the current execution environment.

public String getFamily()
public String getName()
public boolean isPlain()
public boolean isItalic()
public boolean isBold()
public int getStyle()
public int getSize()

These methods retrieve information about a font, such as its family, style, and size.

The *java.awt.Toolkit.getFontList* method (described in the next chapter) can provide your application with a list of all the fonts installed on a system.

Font Metrics

Font metrics measure the characteristics of a font, such as the height of letters or the length of descenders. The measurement of a font is specific to the environment it is drawn in. When you want to obtain the metrics for a given font, you cannot simply create a *FontMetrics* object; you must request a *FontMetrics* object through the *getFontMetrics* method of *Component*, *Graphics*, or *Toolkit*. Because fonts may differ from platform to platform—even fonts with the same point size and face name—a well-designed interface will size components according to the metrics of the font being displayed.

The *FontMetrics* class defines the following methods. All measurements are in pixels.

public Font getFont()

This method returns a reference for the *Font* referenced by this metric.

public int getLeading()

This method returns the standard line spacing for a font. This measurement is used to ensure that the descenders and ascenders do not overlap.

public int getAscent()
public int getMaxAscent()

These methods return the distance from the baseline of a font to the top of most alphanumeric characters; some characters might extend above this limit.

public int getDescent()
public int getMaxDescent()

These methods return the distance from the baseline of a font to the bottom of most alphanumeric characters; some characters might extend below this limit.

public int getHeight()

This method returns the distance between the baseline of two contiguous lines of text in this font. The height represents the amount of vertical space needed to display text in this font without cutting off or overlapping the characters.

public int charWidth(int ch)
public int charWidth(char ch)

These methods return the width of the given character.

public int stringWidth(String str)

This method returns the length of a character string in pixels; it is useful for sizing the horizontal extent of text areas and labels.

public int[] getWidths()

This method returns the pixel widths of the first 256 characters (the ASCII set) in the font.

In later chapters, you'll see how I use font metrics to size controls and customize the look of an application.

Onward

A solid understanding of components is vital. But in and of themselves, user interface controls are simply the tools with which we build applications. In the next chapter, I look at how components come together and communicate with each other.

10

The Elements
of User Interface
Design

n the previous chapter, I examined the user interface components defined by the Abstract Window Toolkit. In this chapter, I show you how these components come together to make a complete application. I begin with an explanation of Java's coordinate system, followed by an introduction to the standard window types that are the foundations of most applications.

Coordinate Conventions

Java's coordinate conventions are different from those of some other graphics systems. In Java, the upper left corner of a component, panel, or window is the origin point (0,0); the *x* value increases to the right of the origin, and the *y* value increases below the origin. Figure 10-1 shows the Java coordinate system.

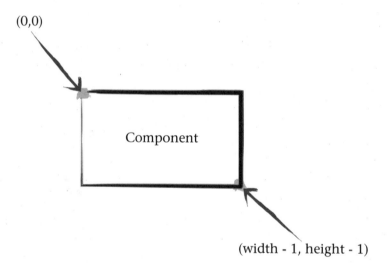

(0,0)

Component

(width - 1, height - 1)

Figure 10-1. *Java coordinates.*

Java measures the dimensions of a component in pixels. A 320-by-240-pixel component will have an *x* coordinate space ranging from 0 through 319 and a *y* coordinate space ranging from 0 through 239.

Coordinate Space Objects

A *Point* object represents an *x, y* coordinate within a component's drawing space. It has two public members, *x* and *y*, and it can be constructed from a pair of values with the constructor *Point(int x, int y)*; the default constructor, *Point()*, assigns the value (0,0). You can change the coordinates of a point by making direct assignment to its *x* and *y* fields or through the *setLocation(int x, int y)* and *setLocation(Point p)* methods.

The *translate(int xinc, int yinc)* method computes:

```
x += xinc;
y += yinc;
```

A *Dimension* object is a simple encapsulation of height and width elements, with two public *int* members providing the size of some object in pixels. *Component* defines a *getSize* method that returns a *Dimension* object.

Borders, menus, and title bars all use space inside a container's area. You determine the thicknesses of these window elements by calling the *getInsets()* method defined by *Container*, which returns an *Insets* object that contains four public integer fields: *top*, *bottom*, *left*, and *right*. These values represent the distance you must "inset" a child control from the edge of the parent; for example, a frame with a 5-pixel-wide border and a 20-pixel-high title bar would have a *top* inset of 25 and *left*, *right*, and *bottom* insets each equal to 5.

Panels, Windows, and Frames

The AWT defines a set of ready-made components derived from *Container* that allow you to combine child components in an application. The three most useful types of containers are panels, windows, and frames.

Panels

A *Panel* object is nothing more than a container that supports peers (see the sidebar "Peers" in Chapter 9) and that has a constructor that allows a layout manager to be specified when the panel is created. Like the *Canvas* class, the *Panel* class is essentially a foundation for component classes of your own design; in Chapter 13, I use panels extensively to create my own combinations of interface tools.

Windows

Every applet runs in a panel embedded in an HTML document, but you will often want to display an independent window that "floats" on the screen. The *Window* class defines a borderless, menuless window as the basis for more complex window types such as *Frame*. The *Window* class includes the following methods.

Window(Frame)

This constructor creates a window that is owned by the specified frame (all windows must be owned by a frame). The newly constructed window will be invisible and will operate in a modal fashion, blocking all user input to other windows belonging to its owner frame.

public void show()
public void hide()

These methods, inherited from *Container*, allow you to specify whether the window is displayed or hidden.

public void dispose()

The *dispose* method destroys the window; it must be called to dispose of any resources used by the window.

public void toFront()
public void toBack()

These methods move the window either to the front or the back of the "stack" of windows owned by a particular frame.

public synchronized void addWindowListener(WindowListener I)
public synchronized void
   removeWindowListener(WindowListener I)

These methods add and remove listeners for the specified types of events; event handling is discussed later in this chapter.

public boolean isShowing()

This method returns *true* if the window is currently visible (in other words, if it has not been hidden), and *false* if it is not.

Frames

A frame is a top-level window with all the bells and whistles you've come to expect—menus, title bars, and so on. Figure 10-2 shows a typical *frame* object, as displayed by Microsoft Windows 95 and Microsoft Internet Explorer version 3.01.

Figure 10-2. *An example of a frame.*

A Java program that is to be run as an independent application, not as an *Applet* object, must use a frame. A subclass of the *Window* class, *Frame* extends the methods it inherits with the following additions.

public Frame()
public Frame(String title)

These each construct a *Frame* object; the second method includes a parameter to set the title of the new window.

public String getTitle()
public synchronized void setTitle(String title)

These methods get and set the *Title* property, which names the frame in a title bar or some other prominent location.

public Image getIconImage()
public synchronized void setIconImage(Image image)

Some systems allow the user to minimize an application; you can load or construct an icon image to perform this task and assign it to a frame via *setIconImage*; however, Java doesn't guarantee that the host operating system will actually use the icon. The *getIconImage* method returns the icon that is currently assigned to the frame.

public MenuBar getMenuBar()
public synchronized void setMenuBar(MenuBar mb)

I discuss menus later in this chapter.

public boolean isResizable()
public synchronized void setResizable(boolean resizable)

If you set the *Resizable* property to *false*, you prevent the user from changing the size of the frame. This property is operating-system-dependent and might not work the same way in all environments.

Standard Events

In Chapter 8, I introduced the Java 1.1 event delegation model, wherein an object implements an event-related interface and then declares itself a "listener" for events of that type. The event interfaces define methods that are called when an event occurs; an event could be the clicking of a button, the closing of a window, or any other such occurrence. Java 1.1 defines several event types, all of which are part of the *java.awt.event* package.

Each event consists of the following program components:

◆ An event type, derived from *AWTEvent*, that contains information about the event and the object that generated it. The *ActionEvent* type is an example of such a type.

◆ An interface, derived from *EventListener*, that defines the methods that can be called for this type of event. For example, a button might generate an *ActionEvent* that will be handled by a listener implementing the *ActionListener* interface. The *ActionListener* interface, in turn, defines an *actionPerformed* method that will receive notification of any *ActionEvent*s generated by objects the listener is interested in.

♦ A pair of methods, *addXXXListener* and *removeXXXListener*, in which *XXX* is the name of the event type. These methods will be defined by any class implementing the listener interface for the event in question. For example, the *ActionListener* interface declares two methods, *addActionListener* and *removeActionListener*.

Each object that creates events also maintains internal lists of listeners for those events. Only those objects that explicitly declare their interest in an event will be notified of the event's occurrence; this is far superior to the older and less efficient model employed in Java 1.0, in which a container heard all events generated by all of its child components, even if it did nothing about those events.

The *EventObject* class, in the *java.util* package, is the basis for all event types. The *EventObject* constructor takes a single *Object* parameter that should reference the object generating the event. *EventObject*'s *getSource* method returns this stored *Object* reference. You'll probably use *EventObject* directly only when subclassing it for the purposes of your own event types.

Action Events

Java 1.1 defines several standard event types in the *java.awt.event* package. One of these is *ActionEvent*, which indicates that the user did something. An *ActionEvent* can be reported by a *MenuItem*, *Button*, or *List* object; in addition to an *Object* reference (inherited from *EventObject*), the constructor takes an *int* value containing information about modifier keys (Ctrl, Alt, and Shift) and a string containing the name of the command that caused the event. *ActionEvent*'s vital statistics are presented here:

Event Class	*ActionEvent*
Listener Interface	*ActionListener*
Listener Methods	*void actionPerformed(ActionEvent event)*
Add/Remove Methods	*void addActionListener(ActionListener x)* *void removeActionListener(ActionListener x)*
Implementing Classes	*Button* *MenuItem* *CheckedMenuItem* *List*

In general, *ActionEvent* is broadcast by an object when a selection is made or a button is clicked; the listener can use the *getSource* method to find the source of the action. (See the FrameApp example later in this chapter.)

Component Events

A *ComponentEvent* indicates that a *Component* object has been hidden, moved, resized, or shown (displayed). All classes derived from *Component* can assign listeners for this event. Here are *ComponentEvent*'s details:

Event Class	*ComponentEvent*
Listener Interface	*ComponentListener*
Listener Methods	*void componentResized(ComponentEvent event)*
	void componentMoved(ComponentEvent event)
	void componentHidden(ComponentEvent event)
	void componentShown(ComponentEvent event)
Add/Remove Methods	*void addComponentListener(ComponentListener x)*
	void removeComponentListener(ComponentListener x)
Implementing Classes	*Component*
	All *Component* subclasses

ComponentListener is best used for managing a dynamic interface, in which a control or a window might be moved or resized, affecting the arrangement of visual components.

Container Events

ContainerListener watches for changes in its list of new child components, such as the addition or deletion of a user interface element. All classes that extend *Container* can implement *ContainerListener*s.

Event Class	*ContainerEvent*
Listener Interface	*ContainerListener*
Listener Methods	*void componentAdded(ContainerEvent event)*
	void componentRemoved(ContainerEvent event)
Add/Remove Methods	*void addContainerListener(ContainerListener x)*
	void removeContainerListener(ContainerListener x)
Implementing Classes	*Container*
	All *Container* subclasses

I've used *ContainerListener* when developing custom container types; sometimes a container has a fixed capacity, so I must throw an exception when too many child components have been added. In other situations, I've used *ContainerListeners* to catch inadvertent deletions from a custom container.

Item Events

An *ItemEvent* occurs when a component's state is changed, such as when the user changes the selection in a list or when the state of a checkbox is toggled.

Event Class	*ItemEvent*
Listener Interface	*ItemListener*
Listener Methods	*void itemStateChanged(ItemEvent event)*
Add/Remove Methods	*void addItemListener(ItemListener x)*
	void removeItemListener(ItemListener x)
Implementing Classes	*Checkbox*
	Choice
	List

I sometimes use a checkbox to turn an "expert mode" on and off on applet displays. When the checkbox state changes, I either add or remove interface elements as appropriate by catching an *ItemEvent*.

Key Events

Any component can process keyboard entries while it has the input focus. When a keyboard entry is processed, a *KeyEvent* containing a value that identifies the key is broadcast to all registered *KeyListeners*.

Event Class	*KeyEvent*
Listener Interface	*KeyListener*
Listener Methods	*void keyPressed(KeyEvent event)*
	void keyReleased(KeyEvent event)
	void keyTyped(KeyEvent event)
Add/Remove Methods	*void addKeyListener(KeyListener x)*
	void removeKeyListener(KeyListener x)
Implementing Classes	*Component*
	All *Component* subclasses

To discover the key involved, you can call the *KeyEvent* methods *getKeyCode* and *getKeyChar*. The former returns a virtual key code, whereas the latter returns the character associated with that key. (See the sidebar on pages 234–35 for a list of common virtual key codes.) The *getKeyModifiers* method returns a string containing text such as "Shift" or "Ctrl+Alt"; call the *getKeyName* method to obtain a text description, such as "Home" or "F5".

Each keystroke generates three events—one when the key is first pressed, one when it is released, and then a final event when the keypress is complete, informing listeners that the key was typed. Here's an example: If you press and hold Shift, a call to *keyPressed* will be generated with a *KeyEvent* object containing the virtual key code *VK_Shift*. Then if you press the *z* key, a *keyPressed* call for *VK_z* will be generated. Now if you release the *z* key, the listener will receive a call to *keyReleased* with a key code of *VK_z*. This will be followed by a call to *keyTyped*, with the character content Z. Finally, releasing the Shift key generates a set of *keyReleased* and *keyTyped* calls to the listeners.

You can use this system to implement toggle keys for which a state remains in effect while a control key—Shift, perhaps—is being held. Listen for the control key in *keyPressed*, toggling the program state until a *KeyEvent* for the key arrives in your *keyReleased* method.

Mouse Events

There are two kinds of mouse events: *MouseEvents* and *MouseMotionEvents*. *MouseEvent* notifies listeners that the mouse has been clicked or that the mouse pointer has moved either into or out of a component's domain.

Event Class	*MouseEvent*
Listener Interface	*MouseListener*
Listener Methods	*void mousePressed(MouseEvent event)*
	void mouseReleased(MouseEvent event)
	void mouseClicked(MouseEvent event)
	void mouseEntered(MouseEvent event)
	void mouseExited(MouseEvent event)
Add/Remove Methods	*void addMouseListener(MouseListener x)*
	void removeMouseListener(MouseListener x)
Implementing Classes	*Component*
	All *Component* subclasses

The *mousePressed*, *mouseReleased*, and *mouseClicked* listener methods correspond in purpose to the *keyPressed*, *keyReleased*, and *keyTyped* methods for keyboard events.

MouseMotionEvent notifies listeners that the mouse has moved while within the boundaries of a component.

Event Class	*MouseMotionEvent*
Listener Interface	*MouseMotionListener*
Listener Methods	*void mouseDragged(MouseMotionEvent event)*
	void mouseMoved(MouseMotionEvent event)
Add/Remove Methods	*void addMouseMotionListener(MouseMotionListener x)*
	void removeMouseMotionListener(MouseMotionListener x)
Implementing Classes	*Component*
	All *Component* subclasses

A call to *mouseDragged* is made when the mouse pointer moves inside a component while one of the mouse buttons is pressed; mouse movement with no buttons pressed will result in a call to *mouseMoved*.

Virtual Codes

All of the virtual key codes are *int* constants defined by the *KeyEvent* class.

Key Code(s)	Comment
VK_0 through VK_9	Digits 0 through 9
VK_A through VK_Z	Alphabetic keys
VK_ACCEPT	
VK_ADD	
VK_ALT	
VK_BACK_QUOTE	
VK_BACK_SLASH	
VK_BACK_SPACE	
VK_CANCEL	
VK_CAPS_LOCK	
VK_CLEAR	
VK_CLOSE_BRACKET	
VK_COMMA	
VK_CONTROL	
VK_CONVERT	
VK_DECIMAL	
VK_DELETE	
VK_DIVIDE	
VK_DOWN	Down arrow
VK_END	
VK_ENTER	
VK_EQUALS	
VK_ESCAPE	
VK_F1 through VK_F12	Function keys
VK_FINAL	
VK_HELP	
VK_HOME	
VK_INSERT	
VK_KANA	Used for toggling Asian character sets
VK_KANJI	Used for toggling Asian character sets
VK_LEFT	Left arrow
VK_META	
VK_MODECHANGE	
VK_MULTIPLY	
VK_NONCONVERT	
VK_NUM_LOCK	

Key Code(s)	Comment
VK_NUMPAD0 through VK_NUMPAD9	Numeric keys on entry pad
VK_OPEN_BRACKET	
VK_PAGE_DOWN	
VK_PAGE_UP	
VK_PAUSE	
VK_PERIOD	
VK_PRINTSCREEN	
VK_QUOTE	
VK_RIGHT	Right arrow
VK_SCROLL_LOCK	
VK_SEMICOLON	
VK_SEPARATER	
VK_SHIFT	
VK_SLASH	
VK_SPACE	
VK_SUBTRACT	
VK_TAB	
VK_UNDEFINED	Not used with *keyTyped* events
VK_UP	Up arrow

Window Events

The *Window* class and its subclasses define the *WindowEvent* type to announce changes in a window's appearance or status.

Event Class	*WindowEvent*
Listener Interface	*WindowListener*
Listener Methods	*void windowActivated(WindowEvent event)*
	void windowDeactivated(WindowEvent event)
	void windowOpened(WindowEvent event)
	void windowClosing(WindowEvent event)
	void windowClosed(WindowEvent event)
	void windowIconified(WindowEvent event)
	void windowDeiconified(WindowEvent event)
Add/Remove Methods	*void addWindowListener(WindowListener x)*
	void removeWindowListener(WindowListener x)
Implementing Classes	*Window*
	Frame
	Dialog
	FileDialog

Programs based on Java 1.0 handle window events in a *handleEvent* method. Deprecated under Java 1.1, *handleEvent* has been replaced by *WindowListener* interfaces. For example, when Visual J++'s Applet Wizard generates a *Frame*-based application class, it uses *handleEvent*.

```java
class ProgTestFrame extends Frame
{
    public ProgTestFrame(String str)
    {
        super (str);
    }

    public boolean handleEvent(Event evt)
    {
        switch (evt.id)
        {
            case Event.WINDOW_DESTROY:
                // TODO: Place additional clean up code here
                dispose();
                System.exit(0);
                return true;

            default:
                return super.handleEvent(evt);
        }
    }
}
```

Although the code above will work in the foreseeable future, a better technique is to replace the *handleEvent* method with a *WindowListener*.

```java
class ProgTestFrame extends Frame implements WindowListener
{
    public ProgTestFrame(String str)
    {
        super (str);
    }

    public void windowActivated(WindowEvent e) {}
    public void windowClosed(WindowEvent e) {}
    public void windowDeactivated(WindowEvent e) {}
    public void windowDeiconified(WindowEvent e) {}
    public void windowIconified(WindowEvent e) {}
    public void windowOpened(WindowEvent e) {}
    public void windowClosing(WindowEvent e)
    {
        dispose();
        System.exit(0);
    }
}
```

The empty event methods are merely placeholders that are included to satisfy the requirement for implementations of methods defined in the *WindowListener* interface.

Event Adapters

In this chapter's *WindowListener* example, I handle only one type of event in the *FrameAppFrame* class, so I implement one *WindowListener* method (*windowClosing*) and override the six other methods with empty implementations. Because *FrameAppFrame* implements the *Window-Listener* interface, Java requires it to explicitly override every method defined for a listener, even if it has no need for those methods.

Java 1.1 solves this problem by implementing a set of "adapter" classes. Each adapter implements a listener interface and defines empty implementations of all inherited methods. For example, instead of using this initial declaration,

```
class MyClass implements WindowListener
```

I could declare

```
class MyClass extends WindowAdapter
```

in my program.

Since Java does not support multiple inheritance (extension of more than one base class), you can use an adapter only with a class that does not already require a superclass. For example, I can't redefine *FrameAppFrame* to use *WindowAdapter*, because it already extends *Frame*. I could, however, define another inner class and use it to process *WindowListener* events.

```
class FrameAppFrame extends Frame
{
    private class WindowEventHandler
        extends WindowAdapter
    {
    // Class code
    }
}
```

The standard adapter classes are:

- *ComponentAdapter*
- *KeyAdapter*
- *MouseAdapter*
- *MouseMotionAdapter*
- *WindowAdapter*

The *ActionListener* and *ItemListener* interfaces do not need adapters because they each define only one event method.

Menus

Java defines drop-down and pop-up menus that provide the same functionality you've seen in Microsoft Windows and other operating systems. An AWT menu is an object of the *Menu* class, which is a container for *MenuItem* and *CheckboxMenuItem* objects; *Menu* itself is a subclass of *MenuItem*, which allows the easy creation of submenus. The standard menu format is that of a pop-up menu; to create the typical application menus that reside along the top of a window, you would use a *MenuBar* object containing a series of *Menu* or *MenuItem* objects. Only *Frame* objects can contain menu bars.

The easiest way for me to show you how menus work in Java is with an example program. (You will find the example program in the \ActiveVJ\Chap10\ FrameAppFrame directory on the companion CD.) I'll create a *Frame* subclass, *FrameAppFrame*, that defines three menus on a menu bar. In the constructor, I define a menu bar and three drop-down menus. The first menu contains five items; the third item opens a submenu and the last two items are disabled. The second menu contains a pair of checked items, and the third menu has two entries that are divided by a separator. I display a message in a label control each time the user selects a menu item.

In my first design, the *FrameAppFrame* class was a *WindowListener* that processed its own *windowClosing* event to terminate the application.

```java
import java.awt.*;
import java.awt.event.*;

class FrameAppFrame
    extends Frame
    implements ActionListener, WindowListener
{

    private Label m_label;

    public FrameAppFrame(String str)
    {
        super(str);

        // Make this object its own listener
        addWindowListener(this);

        // Set background color
        setBackground(Color.gray);

        // Add a menu bar
        MenuBar mBar = new MenuBar();
        setMenuBar(mBar);

        // Create menu 1
        Menu menu1 = new Menu("File");

        // Create a submenu
        Menu submenu = new Menu("Save...");

        MenuItem submenu_item1 = new MenuItem("Save");
        MenuItem submenu_item2 = new MenuItem("Save As...");

        submenu.add(submenu_item1);
        submenu.add(submenu_item2);

        // Create additional menu items
        MenuItem menu1_item0 = new MenuItem("Open");
        MenuItem menu1_item1 = new MenuItem("New");
        MenuItem menu1_item3 = new MenuItem("Close");
        MenuItem menu1_item4 = new MenuItem("Exit");
```

```
// Add items to menu
menu1.add(menu1_item0);
menu1.add(menu1_item1);
menu1.add(submenu);
menu1.add(menu1_item3);
menu1.add(menu1_item4);

// Disable one menu item via explicit reference
menu1_item3.setEnabled(false);

// Disable the other menu item via position in menu
menu1.getItem(4).setEnabled(false);

// Create menu 2
Menu menu2 = new Menu("Option");

// Make checkbox items
CheckboxMenuItem chkItem1 =
    new CheckboxMenuItem("Autosave");
CheckboxMenuItem chkItem2 =
    new CheckboxMenuItem("Optimize");

// Add checkbox items to menu
menu2.add(chkItem1);
menu2.add(chkItem2);

// Create menu 3
Menu menu3 = new Menu("Help");

// Add menu items explicitly
menu3.add("Help Topics");
menu3.addSeparator();
menu3.add("About FrameApp...");

// Add menus to menu bar
mBar.add(menu1);
mBar.add(menu2);
mBar.add(menu3);

// Make this frame the listener
menu1_item0.addActionListener(this);
menu1_item1.addActionListener(this);
submenu_item1.addActionListener(this);
submenu_item2.addActionListener(this);
menu1_item3.addActionListener(this);
menu1_item4.addActionListener(this);

chkItem1.addActionListener(this);
chkItem2.addActionListener(this);

menu3.addActionListener(this);
```

(continued)

```java
        // Create a control to display the status
        m_label = new Label();
        setLayout(new BorderLayout());
        add("Center", m_label);
        m_label.setBackground(Color.white);
        m_label.setForeground(Color.black);
    }

    public void actionPerformed(ActionEvent event)
    {
        // Process menu items
        if (event.getSource() instanceof MenuItem)
        {
            MenuItem item = (MenuItem)event.getSource();

            String out = "You selected "
                        + item.getLabel();

            if (item instanceof CheckboxMenuItem)
            {
                CheckboxMenuItem chk =
                    (CheckboxMenuItem)item;

                // Toggle check state
                chk.setState(!chk.getState());

                out += ", new state = " + chk.getState();
            }

            m_label.setText(out);
        }
    }

    public void windowActivated(WindowEvent e) {}
    public void windowClosed(WindowEvent e) {}
    public void windowDeactivated(WindowEvent e) {}
    public void windowDeiconified(WindowEvent e) {}
    public void windowIconified(WindowEvent e) {}
    public void windowOpened(WindowEvent e) {}

    public void windowClosing(WindowEvent e)
    {
        dispose();
        System.exit(0);
    }
}
```

Figure 10-3 shows the frame with the File menu dropped down. Notice that the JVM drew the Close and Exit items as disabled, just as the program requested.

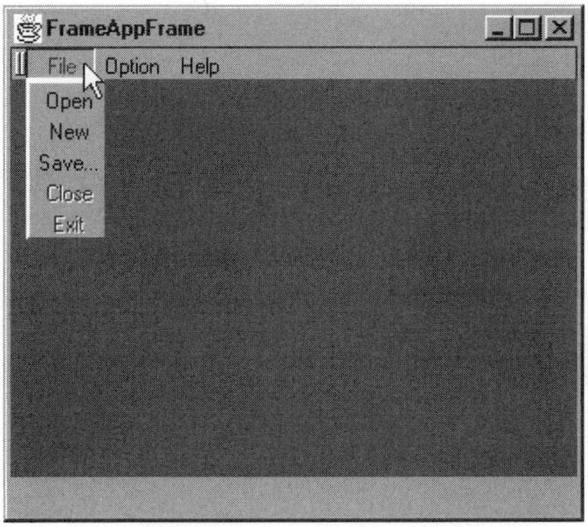

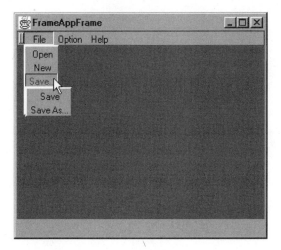

Figure 10-3. *The File menu.*

Save... is a submenu; clicking on it brings up the menu containing the Save and Save As options, as shown in Figure 10-4.

Figure 10-4. *The Save submenu.*

The Option menu (shown in Figure 10-5 on the following page) contains a pair of checked menu items that are set initially (by default) to *false*. When the user clicks on Autosave or Optimize, the associated *CheckedMenuItem* object changes the checkbox to add a check mark, but the actual state of the item, as returned by the *getState* method, does *not* change. This is why I trap the event that announces the selection of these items and set the state manually.

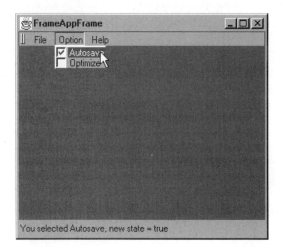

Figure 10-5. *The Option menu and checked items.*

The Help menu contains two menu items divided by a separator, as shown in Figure 10-6.

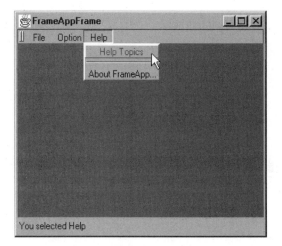

Figure 10-6. *The Help menu with a separator.*

After I finished the initial version of *FrameAppFrame*, I realized that I was handling two different types of events—menu item selections and checked menu item toggles—in the same *actionPerformed* method. I decided to change my event handling to employ a pair of inner classes, each an *ActionListener* for a specific type of event. To accomplish this, I removed *ActionListener* from the list of interfaces implemented by *FrameAppFrame* and then added these two inner classes.

```
private class MenuItemHandler
        implements ActionListener
    {
```

```java
    public void actionPerformed(ActionEvent event)
    {
        MenuItem item = (MenuItem)event.getSource();

        String out = "You selected "
                    + item.getLabel();

        m_label.setText(out);
    }

}


private class CheckedMenuItemHandler
    implements ActionListener
{
    public void actionPerformed(ActionEvent event)
    {
        CheckboxMenuItem chk =
            (CheckboxMenuItem)event.getSource();

        // Toggle check state
        chk.setState(!chk.getState());

        // Display information
        String out = chk.getLabel()
                    + " new state = "
                    + chk.getState();

        m_label.setText(out);
    }

}
```

Instead of using *FrameAppFrame* itself as an *ActionListener*, I created objects
based on the *MenuItemHandler* and *CheckedMenuItemHandler* inner classes and made
these the listeners for events from the different components. You will find the
updated version of the program on the companion CD in the \ActiveVJ\Chap10\
FinalFrameAppFrame directory.

Onward

When working with Java and ActiveX, you need to know how the Internet handles
security. An ActiveX control runs outside the Java sandbox and, therefore, is not
restricted from accessing the local file system and resources. Recognizing this
problem, Microsoft has developed technologies to identify the source of an ActiveX
control. In the next chapter, I examine Microsoft's Authenticode technology and
its ramifications for Visual J++ users.

11

Security and Authenticode

When you buy software from a retail store, you know who wrote the application and who sold you the package. You can trust that no reputable company would put defective software out for sale. If something does go wrong with the software you've purchased, you can confront the companies that developed and sold it to you. But what about software downloaded over the Internet? How can we trust the software or data we're receiving through the modem?

Through interactive web pages, items such as Java applets, Microsoft ActiveX components, scripts, and other live content—as well as viruses and distasteful images—can arrive in your browser from almost anywhere. A seemingly harmless web component could access personal information on your PC. In the Wild West atmosphere of the Internet, we need some way of protecting ourselves from technological terrorists and malicious hackers.

The Java Sandbox

In light of such safety concerns, the designers of Java placed restrictions on any applet downloaded over a network. Web-based Java applets operate within a set of conceptual restrictions commonly known as the "sandbox." Because of the sandbox, a web-based applet must operate within specific limitations in reference to the client system. It cannot:

- read or write to a file,
- check for the existence of a file,
- rename a file,
- create a new file,
- create or remove a directory,
- list or review a directory,
- check a file's type,
- look at a file's time stamp, or
- read a file's size.

Furthermore, the application is limited in the type of information it can obtain about the client through the *System* object. The following System properties cannot be read by a network applet using the *getProperty* method:

- *java.home*
- *java.class.path*
- *user.name*
- *user.home*
- *user.dir*

These restrictions do not apply to applets or Java applications loaded from your local file system; only network-delivered applets run inside the sandbox. In short, when you download a Java applet from the network, it operates within a very restricted universe, unable to interact with your local files in any meaningful way.

At first, this approach to network security might seem excessive. But remember, you know nothing about a Java applet that arrives on your system; you don't even know that a web page contains an applet until it actually begins loading. Without the sandbox, a Java applet could arrive on your system and do incredible damage before you could react. While it would be nice to trust everything we encounter on the Internet, the fact is that someone, somewhere, might try to damage your system and your data.

How tight is Java's sandbox security? Very tight. As I'm writing this, the Java community is buzzing about recent tests performed by researchers at the University of Washington. Using an independently developed security analysis system, these computer scientists found numerous holes in various Java implementations. No known security attack has ever occurred because of these security bugs; in fact, the holes were obscure and already have been addressed by Microsoft, Sun, and other Java developers. The Java sandbox remains one of the tightest network-based security systems; you can use it with the reasonable confidence that your system is safe from the outside world.

ActiveX and Internet Explorer

Through Microsoft's Java virtual machine, Microsoft Internet Explorer enforces the sandbox restrictions on any applet downloaded from anywhere other than the local file system. VBScript and JScript code operate under similar restrictions. Therefore, these kinds of active content pose no threat to the integrity of your computer.

ActiveX controls, however, are another matter entirely because they operate outside the Java virtual machine. An ActiveX control is a piece of native code, which means that it has access to any part of your system—including files, I/O ports, and other sensitive facilities. The JVM has no way of controlling the actions of any ActiveX control, even if it is linked by script to an applet.

Internet Explorer allows you to customize your security. For example, click on View|Option in Explorer's menu, and select the Security tab. You'll see a dialog box similar to the one shown in Figure 11-1. Notice the options available to control active content on your computer.

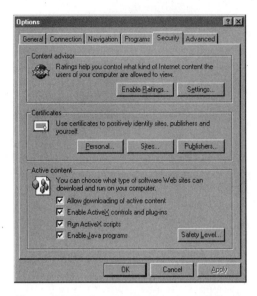

Figure 11-1. *Internet Explorer security options.*

Why is there so much concern about downloading ActiveX components from the web? ActiveX is essentially a refinement of the existing OLE technology that has allowed component linking and embedding within an implicitly trustworthy environment, your PC. Once ActiveX technology is moved to the Internet, you're confronted with unknown ActiveX components, written in native code and executed by your system. Unlike a Java applet, an ActiveX control is not limited by a sandbox. Nothing inherent in COM prevents an ActiveX control from accessing your files or examining your system; in fact, since most ActiveX controls begin as components of desktop software, these are precisely the actions they are designed to perform.

By setting your security in Internet Explorer, you can control the execution of ActiveX controls. For example, you can tell your browser to ignore all incoming active content, a decision that could be very inconvenient, since not every ActiveX control will pose a threat to your system. An ActiveX component might be a simple animated button or marquee. Or you might want a selected applet or ActiveX control to access the client-side file system, if, for example, you're working in a corporate intranet environment where the software is being built and used in-house. Somehow, you need to be able to identify trusted active content—and that's just what Microsoft's Authenticode technology was invented for.

You won't need to provide an Authenticode certificate for your Java applets, even if they are COM components, since all Java code operates within the browser's sandbox. The following discussion applies when your HTML documents link ActiveX components to Java code using VBScript. If a user's security prevents the downloading of an ActiveX component, your Java applet is unlikely to work.

Code Signing

Go back to Figure 11-1 and look at the four checkboxes in the Active content group. By checking these items, you give Internet Explorer permission to download certain types of active components, such as ActiveX controls and Java applets.

In the same group is the Safety Level button. Clicking on it will bring up the dialog box shown in Figure 11-2. When you download a web page containing active content, Internet Explorer reacts to the content according to the safety level setting you have selected.

Figure 11-2. Safety levels in Internet Explorer.

The *None* setting means exactly what it says. The browser trusts everything delivered to your system, loading active content automatically and without warning you. While this setting might be fine on a limited intranet, where all content is known and safe, only a reckless user would browse the web without some sort of security.

Selecting the *Medium* safety level tells Internet Explorer to warn you about unsafe content, using a dialog box like the one in Figure 11-3.

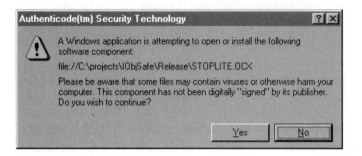

Figure 11-3. *Medium security dialog box.*

Choosing *High* security causes Internet Explorer to reject any content that cannot be verified as safe. When it encounters something it doesn't trust, Internet Explorer will display a dialog box similar to the one in Figure 11-4. If a component is rejected—either explicitly by the user or implicitly by a high safety setting—its place on a web page will be taken by a blank spot.

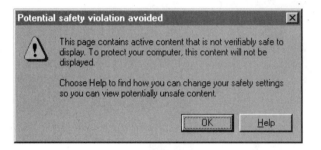

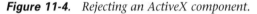

Figure 11-4. *Rejecting an ActiveX component.*

Active content is considered safe when it is accompanied by an *Authenticode certificate* verifying its creator and origin. Authenticode is a technology developed by Microsoft to verify the safety of ActiveX components. Think of a certificate as an electronic signature on a contract. The people who created the active content promise that it is safe to load onto your system, just as a corporate logo and sealed package guarantee that software purchased in a store is reliable.

When your security is set at high and your browser attempts to download an unknown ActiveX control from the web, you will probably see its certificate in a dialog box similar to that in Figure 11-5. If the incoming component lacks a certificate, a high safety level will automatically prevent it from being downloaded; a medium safety level will cause a dialog box to appear, asking whether you're willing to allow the installation of the component.

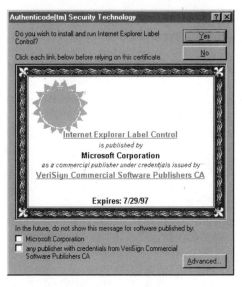

Figure 11-5. *An Authenticode Certificate.*

The fancy background and border are there only to make the certificate look nice; your concern is with the name of the company and the fact that its credentials were issued by a trusted entity. Notice that you can tell Internet Explorer always to trust any active content signed with a certificate from Microsoft Corporation, or that you are willing to trust any signature from a company whose credentials were issued by VeriSign. The browser will store your decision by making an entry in an internal table; you can see this table by selecting the Publishers button in the Security panel of the View|Options menu item. Figure 11-6 shows the dialog box with Microsoft as a trusted software publisher.

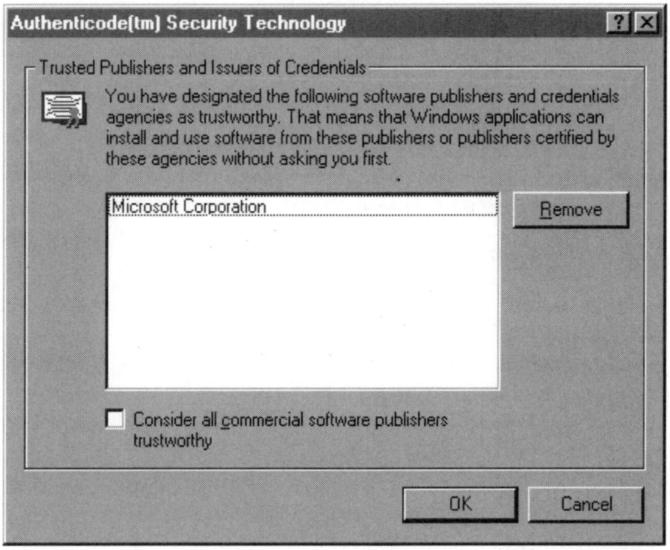

Figure 11-6. *Trusted publisher certificates in Internet Explorer.*

While you can use the dialog box to tell Internet Explorer to trust all commercial software vendors, I strongly recommend against that. It's better to be safe and put up with the occasional certificate display.

The Authenticode certificate contains the following information:

- Identity of the component

- Company or person who published the component

- Entity that provided the certificate and vouches for the integrity of the component publisher

- Public key

- Encrypted digest of the cabinet file's contents

The encrypted digest is a cryptographic value calculated from the file's original contents. Like a checksum or CRC in data communications, the encrypted digest can be compared to a value calculated "on the fly" from the contents of a file received by your browser. The digest is encrypted by the publisher and decoded by Internet Explorer using the provided public key. If a one-way hash of the file content doesn't match the stored encrypted digest, the data has been altered after their creation, either by errors in transmission or malicious human action.

Assuming that the certificate is valid, the user has two options: click the No button to reject the incoming component or select Yes to allow its installation. Once a component has been downloaded and accepted by the user, it is installed in the C:\Windows\OCCache folder, and several entries will be made in the system registry. The next time a web document (or, for that matter, a local program) uses that control, the document or program will execute the already installed copy on the local computer. In other words, once an ActiveX component is accepted as trusted, it becomes a part of the local system.

Certificate Types

Authenticode certificates follow the X.509 standard and come in two types:

- Class 2 certificates, for individuals who publish software, cost $20 per year and require that you provide your name, address, e-mail address, date of birth, and Social Security number. After the certificate provider verifies this information, you will be issued a certificate.

- Class 3 certificates, for commercial software publishers, cost $400 per year and require a Dun and Bradstreet rating in addition to company name, location, and contacts.

Both certificates are considered trustworthy, and there is no way to tell Internet Explorer to accept one type of certificate but not the other.

Remember, Java applets cannot operate outside the confines of the JVM sandbox, and they do not pose the security threat presented by ActiveX controls. As an additional benefit, Authenticode automatically provides version control and checks against vendor conflicts as it installs the applet files.

Cabinet (CAB) Files

When used for Java applets, the cabinet (CAB) file is a single, compressed repository not only for all class files, but also for all audio and image data required by the applet. (CAB does not support other types of data.) One reason Microsoft introduced the concept of CAB files was to provide a way to combine several components into a form that could be downloaded easily and quickly. By default, a browser downloads applets one class at a time, the data isn't compressed, and a communication channel is opened for each file—a process that can be very time-consuming, especially for large Java applets. CAB files can reduce the overall download and applet initialization time by 70 percent over the transfer of individual class and image files.

A second reason for Microsoft's creation of CAB files was to facilitate adding an Authenticode certificate to the complete file. You will not often be signing your Java code, but you can attach an Authenticode certificate if you feel users will want the additional security of seeing it.

Microsoft Visual J++ 1.1 includes the tools you'll need for storing and delivering your applets using CAB files. To install the cabinet file development kit, run the file CABDEVKIT.EXE in the Cab&Sign directory of your Visual J++ CD-ROM.

Internet Wars and Code Signing

The competition over Internet standards has affected both code signing and the archive formats used for storing applets. JAR and CAB are similar, competing technologies, but have different features and abilities. For example, JAR is based on the ZIP file format; CAB files are a technology developed by Microsoft. JAR files cannot contain ActiveX components or Authenticode certificates, and CAB files cannot hold Java Beans. Only CAB files can be signed with Authenticode certificates (although an alternative signing system has been proposed by the Java community for JAR files.)

Even more troublesome is the varying support for different archive formats. While Microsoft supports the JAR format in Internet Explorer, Netscape Navigator does not intrinsically allow applets to be packaged in CAB files. While Microsoft has made available a Netscape add-in that supports the CAB format, future versions of Navigator are not guaranteed to support Microsoft's technology. Furthermore, CAB files may not be supported on other browsers or platforms.

Microsoft also provides a command-line tool (run in an MS-DOS window) called cabarc (*cab*inet *arc*hiver); it comes in the Java SDK or when you install the CAB development kit. If you want to create a cabinet of all the files in a directory, you would use the command

```
cabarc n foo.cab *.*
```

Typing cabarc by itself will display a list of its command-line options.

To use a CAB file from a web page, you need to use the CABBASE parameter in an APPLET tag to point to the cabinet file. If the applet is not already present on the user's system, the CAB is downloaded, the contents extracted, and the applet started:

```
<APPLET CODE="sample.class" WIDTH=100 HEIGHT=100>
<PARAM NAME="cabbase" VALUE="vendor.cab">
</APPLET>
```

Using the CABBASE parameter does not conflict with CODEBASE or any parameters necessary for other browsers. Using CABBASE along with the additional tags allows Internet Explorer and other CAB-supporting browsers to use CAB files without impeding the ability of another browser to download and execute Java applets.

Onward

Security is only a concern when Java code arrives on someone's system through a network connection. While Java is still used primarily for web applets, it is, in fact, a powerful tool for developing complete, standalone applications. In the next two chapters, I build a set of Java classes as the basis for a combination application and applet.

12 Constructing Components

To create my LifeBox application, I needed to build a set of component classes to implement certain desired features. In this chapter, I discuss how I built these support classes and then move on to the main application in Chapter 13.

More Colors

The *Color* class exposes a set of constants, with names such as *Color.red* and *Color.blue*, that predefine common colors. Unfortunately, this list of colors is limited and, in many cases, inaccurate. Even more frustrating is the problem of creating highlighted 3D effects with some of the standard colors. Calling the *brighter* method for *Color.red*, for example, will not produce a brighter red, since *Color.red* is defined with the maximum possible value for its red component. So, I created an interface, *MoreColors*, that declares constants for some colors I like to use.

```java
package coyote.ui;

import java.awt.Color;

//
//
// MoreColors
//
//
public class MoreColors
{
    public static final Color Orange      =
        new Color(255,128,  0);
    public static final Color brightGreen =
        new Color(  0,255,  0);
    public static final Color Green       =
        new Color(  0,192,  0);
    public static final Color darkGreen   =
        new Color(  0,128,  0);
    public static final Color brightBlue  =
        new Color(  0,  0,255);
    public static final Color Blue        =
        new Color(  0,  0,192);
    public static final Color darkBlue    =
        new Color(  0,  0,128);
    public static final Color brightRed   =
        new Color(255,  0,  0);
    public static final Color Red         =
        new Color(192,  0,  0);
```

```
    public static final Color darkRed    =
        new Color(128,  0,  0);
}
```

A set of 256 gray-scale colors can also be helpful, so I defined the *GrayScale* class. I've used *GrayScale* in image conversion programs, for example, where an input color image must be translated into a gray-scale one. The static initializer fills the *Gray* array automatically.

```
package coyote.ui;

import java.awt.Color;

//
//
// GrayScale
//
//
public class GrayScale
{

    public static final Color [] Gray;

    static
    {
        Gray = new Color [256];

        for (int i = 0; i < 256; ++i)
            Gray[i] = new Color(i,i,i);
    }
}
```

Separator Bars

A separator bar is a vertical or horizontal divider in a menu, toolbar, or other collection of tools. I use separator bars to group related controls, to give the user a visual clue. The following code will create a pair of lines that look raised on the display.

```
package coyote.ui;

import java.awt.*;

//
//
// SeparatorBar
//
//
public class SeparatorBar
    extends Panel
{
```

(continued)

```java
//------------------------
// Constants
//------------------------

public static final int VERTICAL = 0;
public static final int HORIZONTAL = 1;

//------------------------
// Fields
//------------------------

private int m_orientation;

//------------------------
// Constructors
//------------------------

public SeparatorBar()
{
    m_orientation = VERTICAL;
}

public SeparatorBar(int orient)
{
    if (orient == HORIZONTAL)
        m_orientation = HORIZONTAL;
    else
        m_orientation = VERTICAL;
}


//------------------------
// Properties
//------------------------

public int getOrientation()
{
    return m_orientation;
}

//------------------------
// Methods
//------------------------

public void update(Graphics g)
{
    paint(g);
}

public void paint(Graphics g)
{
    Dimension dim = getSize();
```

```
// Fill rectangle with background color
g.setColor(getBackground());
g.fillRect(0,0,dim.width - 1,dim.height - 1);

// Draw lines
Color hilite =
    getForeground().brighter().brighter();

if (m_orientation == VERTICAL)
{
    int x = dim.width / 2;

    g.setColor(hilite);
    g.drawLine(x,0,x,dim.height);

    g.setColor(getForeground());
    g.drawLine(x + 1,0,x + 1,dim.height);
}
else // Horizontal line
{
    int y = dim.height / 2;

    g.setColor(hilite);
    g.drawLine(0,y,dim.width,y);

    g.setColor(getForeground());
    g.drawLine(0,y + 1,dim.width,y + 1);
}
}

public Dimension getPreferredSize()
{
    return getSize();
}

}
```

Edged Panels

The standard AWT *Panel* is flat, and most Java applets have all the visual appeal of a gray board. Most users prefer that their applications have a beveled look, in which the edges of frames and windows have been drawn to look angled or raised. For my own applets, I created the *EdgedPanel* type, which draws a raised or lowered border, depending on a property. My program defines the width of the bevel, determines whether it is raised or pushed in, and creates an additional inset from the inside edge of the bevel. I overload the *getInsets* method to return these values so that layout managers know how to organize components without drawing over the edges of the panel.

You can create a double-edged or picture-frame panel using a simple technique. Create an outer *EdgedPanel*, and set its layout manager to *BorderLayout*; then create a second, inner *EdgedPanel*, and add it to the outer panel in the Center location. Finally, add your other components to the inner panel.

Splash Frames

When it starts running, an application produces a splash frame to display a graphic image while the program is loading and initializing. *SplashFrame*, which extends the class *Window*, resizes the display area to accommodate the graphic that is provided when the frame is constructed. *SplashFrame* sets the location of the graphic so that it is centered over the parent frame. The class definition follows.

```java
package coyote.ui;

import java.awt.*;

//
//
// SplashFrame
//
//
public class SplashFrame
    extends Window
{
    //-------------------------
    // Fields
    //-------------------------
    private Image m_splash;

    //-------------------------
    // Constructor
    //-------------------------
    public SplashFrame
        (Frame parent, Image img)
    {
        super(parent);

        m_splash = img;

        Insets i = getInsets();

        setSize(i.left + i.right  + m_splash.getWidth(this),
                i.top  + i.bottom +
                m_splash.getHeight(this));

        if (parent != null)
        {
            Rectangle psize = parent.getBounds();

            setLocation((psize.width  -
                m_splash.getWidth(this))  / 2,
                    (psize.height -
                m_splash.getHeight(this)) / 2);
        }
```

```
        show();
        repaint();
    }


//------------------------
// Methods
//------------------------
public void paint(Graphics g)
{
    Insets i = getInsets();

    g.drawImage(m_splash, i.left, i.top,
        Color.black, this);
    }
}
```

Fixed Stacks

Because they are based on linked lists, the class *java.util.Vector* and its derivatives are too slow for many applications (including LifeBox). I created a fixed stack that has a finite number of elements, which I use to improve the performance of my LifeBox application.

```
package coyote.tools;

//
//
// FixedStack
//
//
public class FixedStack
{
    //==========================
    // Fields
    //==========================

    private Object [] stack;
    private int top;

    //==========================
    // Constructors
    //==========================

    public FixedStack(int capacity)
    {
        stack = new Object [capacity];
        top = 0;
    }
```

(continued)

```
//=========================
// Methods
//=========================

public boolean push(Object x)
{
    if (top < stack.length)
    {
        stack[top] = x;
        ++top;
        return true;
    }
    else
        return false;
}

public Object peek()
{
    if (top > 0)
        return stack[top - 1];
    else
        return null;
}

public Object pop()
{
    if (top > 0)
    {
        --top;
        return stack[top];
    }
    else
        return null;
}

public int getCount()
{
    return top;
}

public boolean empty()
{
    return top == 0;
}

public boolean hasStuff()
{
    return top != 0;
}
}
```

The *FixedStack* class creates an array of *Object* references. FixedStack pushes and pops values and maintains a pointer to the top of its stack. Using this class noticeably increased the speed of some stack-intensive operations.

Checkbox Columns

The checkbox column control is a grid of checkboxes that I developed to allow a user to select the states for the birth and survival rules in LifeBox. I have found it useful in other contexts as well.

The basic constructor creates a grid with a given number of rows and columns; row labels are defined by an array of *String* objects. You can also specify column headings by using another constructor. *CheckboxColumns* is an extension of *Panel*.

```
package coyote.ui;

import java.awt.*;

//
//
// CheckColumns
//
//
public class CheckGrid
    extends Panel
{

    //=========================
    // Fields
    //=========================

    protected int m_nRows;
    protected int m_nCols;

    protected Checkbox [][] m_btn; // [r][c] check buttons

    protected Label [] m_rLabel = null;
    protected Label [] m_cLabel = null;

    protected GridBagLayout m_layout;

    protected IllegalArgumentException err1 =
        new IllegalArgumentException(
            "Mismatch in labels and rows for CheckColumn");

    protected IllegalArgumentException err2 =
        new IllegalArgumentException(
            "CheckColumn in dimension is less than one");
```

(continued)

```
//===========================
// Constructors
//===========================

protected void addComponent
    (Component comp, GridBagConstraints gbc)
{
   m_layout.setConstraints(comp,gbc);
   add(comp);
}

private void setupHelper
    (int rows, int cols,
    String [] labels,
    String [] headings)
{
    // Verify parameters
    if (labels.length != rows)
        throw err1;

    if ((rows < 1) || (cols < 1))
        throw err2;

    // Retain constants
    m_nRows = rows;
    m_nCols = cols;

    m_layout = new GridBagLayout();
    setLayout(m_layout);

    GridBagConstraints gbc = new GridBagConstraints();

    gbc.fill    = GridBagConstraints.BOTH;
    gbc.weightx = 1.0;
    gbc.weighty = 1.0;
    gbc.anchor  = GridBagConstraints.CENTER;

    // Set layout
    if (headings != null)
    {
        m_cLabel = new Label [cols + 1];

        m_cLabel[0] = new Label();
        addComponent(m_cLabel[0],gbc);

        for (int i = 0; i < cols; ++i)
        {
            m_cLabel[i + 1] =
                new Label(headings[i],Label.LEFT);
```

```
                    if (i == (cols - 1))
                        gbc.gridwidth =
                            GridBagConstraints.REMAINDER;

                    addComponent(m_cLabel[i + 1],gbc);
                }
            }


        // Create buttons
        m_btn    = new Checkbox [rows][cols];
        m_rLabel = new Label [rows];

        for (int r = 0; r < rows; ++r)
        {
            gbc.gridwidth = 1; // Reset
            gbc.anchor    = GridBagConstraints.EAST;

            m_rLabel[r] = new Label(labels[r],Label.RIGHT);
            addComponent(m_rLabel[r],gbc);

            gbc.anchor = GridBagConstraints.SOUTHWEST;

            for (int c = 0; c < cols; ++c)
            {
                m_btn[r][c] = new Checkbox();
                m_btn[r][c].setLabel(null);

                if (c == (cols - 1))
                    gbc.gridwidth =
                        GridBagConstraints.REMAINDER;

                addComponent(m_btn[r][c],gbc);
            }
        }

        repaint();
    }

public CheckGrid
    (int rows, int cols,
    String [] labels,
    String [] headings)
{
    setupHelper(rows,cols,labels,headings);
}


public CheckGrid
    (int rows, int cols,
    String [] labels)
```

(continued)

```
{
    setupHelper(rows,cols,labels,null);
}


//===========================
// Properties
//===========================

public boolean isChecked
    (int row, int col)
{
    return m_btn[row][col].getState();
}

public void setChecked
    (int row, int col,
    boolean state)
{
    m_btn[row][col].setState(state);
}

//===========================
// Methods
//===========================

public void setEnabled(boolean b)
{
    for (int r = 0; r < m_nRows; ++r)
    {
        for (int c = 0; c < m_nCols; ++c)
        {
            m_btn[r][c].setEnabled(b);
            m_btn[r][c].repaint();
        }
    }

    super.setEnabled(b);
}
}
```

Column headings should be relatively short, since the *GridLayout* will use the widest item in a column to set the column width, and long labels might cause checkboxes to spread unnecessarily. *GridBagLayout* creates a control in which the row labels use as much space as the longest of them requires.

The *setEnabled* method overrides the *Panel* implementation to ensure that all radio buttons are disabled or enabled in conjunction with the container. *CheckboxColumns* doesn't fire any events; it is designed to hold static data that will be read when needed. The *isChecked(int, int)* method is used to determine the state of a checkbox at a given column and row coordinate.

Cell Panels

CellPanel defines a rectangular panel divided into rows and columns of cells; each cell is painted according to its current state. A *CellPanel* isn't a cellular automaton; it is the superclass for the *Automata* class and provides a tool that can be used effectively in nonautomata applications. *CellPanel* is an example of compartmentalizing a function—taking a general concept (a grid of cells) and making it into a general-purpose tool extended by more specific classes.

CellPanel is a subclass of *Panel* and implements the *MouseListener* interface. I didn't use an inner class as a listener because that would have compromised the ability of the *Automata* class (in Chapter 13) to control user changes in cell values by overloading the *mousePressed* method.

This class is rather lengthy. I'll present the complete class first and provide explanations afterward.

```
package coyote.ui;

import java.awt.*;
import java.awt.event.*;

//
//
// CellPanel
//
//
public class CellPanel
    extends Panel
    implements MouseListener
{
    //=========================
    // Fields
    //=========================

    // Parameters
    protected int m_nRows;
    protected int m_nCols;
    protected int m_nMaxRow;
    protected int m_nMaxCol;
    protected int m_nCellSize;
    protected int m_nWidth;
    protected int m_nHeight;
    protected int m_nMaxState;

    protected boolean  m_b3D;

    protected Color [] m_colorMap;
```

(continued)

```java
// Internal data
protected int [][]  m_nCellState;
protected Image     m_cellImage;
protected Image []  m_cellPics;

// Exception objects
protected IllegalArgumentException err1 =
    new IllegalArgumentException(
        "CellPanel must have at least 2 states");

protected IllegalArgumentException err2 =
    new IllegalArgumentException(
        "Invalid CellPanel dimensions");

protected IllegalArgumentException err3 =
    new IllegalArgumentException(
        "Too few cell states for this automata");

//==========================
// Constructors
//==========================

public CellPanel
    (Component base,
    int cols, int rows,
    int cellSize,
    boolean is3D,
    Color [] map)
{
    // Verify parameters
    if (map.length < 2)
        throw err1;

    if ((rows < 2) || (cols < 2) || (cellSize < 1))
        throw err2;

    if (base == null)
        base = this;

    // Set instance fields
    m_nRows     = rows;
    m_nCols     = cols;
    m_nMaxRow   = rows - 1;
    m_nMaxCol   = cols - 1;
    m_nCellSize = cellSize;
    m_b3D       = is3D;
    m_nMaxState = map.length - 1;
    m_colorMap  = map;
    m_nWidth    = m_nCols * m_nCellSize;
    m_nHeight   = m_nRows * m_nCellSize;
```

```
        // Allocate the state array
        m_nCellState = new int [m_nRows][m_nCols];

        // Create image
        m_cellImage =
            base.createImage(m_nWidth, m_nHeight);

        // Set panel size
        setSize(m_nWidth, m_nHeight);

        // Generate images for cells
        m_cellPics = new Image [m_nMaxState + 1];

        for (int i = 0; i <= m_nMaxState; ++i)
        {
            m_cellPics[i] =
                base.createImage(cellSize, cellSize);
            Graphics g = m_cellPics[i].getGraphics();

            g.setColor(m_colorMap[i]);

            if (m_b3D)
                g.fill3DRect(0, 0, m_nCellSize,
                    m_nCellSize, true);
            else
                g.fillRect(0, 0, m_nCellSize,
                    m_nCellSize);
        }

        // Make this a mouse listener
        addMouseListener(this);

        redraw();
    }


    //==========================
    // Methods
    //==========================
    public void paint
        (Graphics g)
    {
        g.drawImage(m_cellImage, 0, 0, this);
    }

    public synchronized void redraw()
    {
        Graphics g = m_cellImage.getGraphics();

        int y = 0;
```

(continued)

```
        for (int r = 0; r < m_nRows; ++r)
        {
            int x = 0;

            for (int c = 0; c < m_nCols; ++c)
            {
                g.drawImage(
                    m_cellPics[m_nCellState[r][c]],
                    x, y, this);
                x += m_nCellSize;
            }

            y += m_nCellSize;
        }

        repaint();
    }

    public synchronized void fill
        (int state)
    {
        // Change all cells
        for (int r = 0; r < m_nRows; ++r)
        {
            for (int c = 0; c < m_nCols; ++c)
            {
                setCellState(r, c, state);
            }
        }
    }

    public synchronized void setCellState
        (int row, int col, int state)
    {
        // Store new state
        m_nCellState[row][col] = state;

        // Draw new cell
        Graphics g = m_cellImage.getGraphics();

        int y = row * m_nCellSize;
        int x = col * m_nCellSize;

        g.drawImage(m_cellPics[state], x, y, this);
    }

    public int getCellState
        (int row, int col)
    {
        return m_nCellState[row][col];
    }
```

```java
public int getWidth()
{
    return m_nWidth;
}

public int getHeight()
{
    return m_nHeight;
}

public Dimension getPreferredSize()
{
    return new Dimension(m_nWidth, m_nHeight);
}

public Dimension getMinimumSize()
{
    return getPreferredSize();
}

public Dimension getMaximumSize()
{
    return getPreferredSize();
}

//=========================
// Events
//=========================
public void mousePressed
    (MouseEvent evt)
{
    // Change a random cell
    int r = evt.getY() / m_nCellSize;
    int c = evt.getX() / m_nCellSize;
    int s = m_nCellState[r][c];

    if (s == m_nMaxState)
        s = 0;
    else
        ++s;

    setCellState(r, c, s);

    repaint(c * m_nCellSize,
            r * m_nCellSize,
            m_nCellSize,
            m_nCellSize);
}
public void mouseClicked
    (MouseEvent evt)
{
```

(continued)

```
                   // Does nothing
              }

              public void mouseReleased
                   (MouseEvent evt)
              {
                   // Does nothing
              }

              public void mouseEntered
                   (MouseEvent evt)
              {
                   // Does nothing
              }

              public void mouseExited
                   (MouseEvent evt)
              {
                   // Does nothing
              }

         }
```

When creating a *CellPanel* object, the constructor requires that you give parameters specifying the number of rows and columns and the size of each square cell. You must also provide an array of *Color* values representing cell states and indicate whether or not cells should be drawn in 3D.

CellPanel draws its display using a set of bitmap images for each cell state, beginning with a grid in the required size, filled with cells in zero state. The constructor does not, however, build the images; that is left to the *redraw* method. Because an object is incomplete when program flow is in a constructor, a call to *createImage* in a constructor will return *null*. *CellPanel* is a double-buffered component, storing its display image in an off-screen *Image* class for display by the *paint* method. When *paint* is called, it checks to see if the *Image*s are *null*; if they are, *paint* assumes that the panel needs to be redrawn and issues a call to *redraw*. The *redraw* method, in turn, creates new images if necessary. Notice that the overridden *invalidate* method declares the need to redraw the images by setting their references to null.

CellPanel implements *MouseListener* to trap mouse events, allowing the user to edit the grid. When a user clicks on a cell, its state is incremented; if the cell is in the maximum state, it returns to zero state. The state of any cell can be manually set or read through the *setCellState* and *getCellState* methods. The *fill* method sets all cells to the same state.

Onward

A Java program can be built from standard AWT classes combined with a series of custom components, each an extension of an existing AWT class. In Chapter 13, I present a complete Java program, *LifeBox*, for working with some types of cellular automata.

13 Life with Java

U sing Microsoft Visual J++, I'm going to build a complete Java program, a combination applet and application that uses the tools, components, and technologies presented in this book. The program LifeBox allows the user to experiment with cellular automata, a part of artificial life that is revolutionizing computer science.

Artificial Life

Artificial Life (often called ALife) is a branch of computer science that attempts to model the mechanics of biology in a computer. This differs from artificial intelligence (AI), which develops computer-based simulations of mental processes. While AI models logic or psychology, ALife models biology. Although each reaches into the world of real life for archetypes, they have different purposes.

The design of computer programs hasn't changed much in the last few decades. Ideas such as object-oriented programming, while changing the form of our designs, do little to alter the underlying principle of how programs go about their work. A program still begins someplace and follows a restricted path toward some end; while the program may change its operating parameters, it's still limited in how much it can adapt to new situations.

Artificial Life is based on two concepts: bottom-up design and emergent behavior. In writing artificial intelligence software, programmers build underlying software to fit a defined high-level task. A neural network, for example, simulates the interaction of neurons and axons that make up our brains. Like traditional programs, AI applications begin with the goal, and then work on the foundations.

ALife works from the opposite direction by allowing complex behavior to emerge from simple components. Rather than try to predetermine the best way to search a data set, an ALife application will find the best process based on the performance of competing algorithms.

Some programmers may be uncomfortable with emergent behavior. Some people dislike the idea that a piece of inanimate software can develop behaviors that did not exist in its original design; they find it even more disconcerting that a program might develop a behavior that wasn't envisioned by its creator. Yet don't we create software to make our lives easier? If so, shouldn't we let our programs determine the best ways of doing things, instead of doing all the work ourselves? If computers are to move beyond their role as glorified calculators, we need to allow software to mold itself to the task at hand.

ALife is in its formative years. In a way, you can view the ALife field as an evolving ecosystem, in which a wide variety of organisms is narrowed through competition—a modern version of "survival of the fittest." We'll have to wait and see which ALife concepts survive to flourish.

To demonstrate ALife capabilities, I developed the LifeBox application, which focuses on cellular automata. These are some of the oldest and most fascinating tools of the ALife developer, and they exhibit remarkably complex behavior derived from basic principles.

Cellular Automata

A cellular automaton is a one-, two-, or three-dimensional grid of cells, in which each cell reacts independently to the state of its neighbors. An automaton functions as a dynamic system that operates in cycles. In each cycle, every cell in the grid changes its status by reacting to an examination of its neighbors. Starting from an initial condition, the cellular automaton will evolve according to a set of simple rules.

A cellular automaton has three formal characteristics:

1. Parallelism   All cells are updated simultaneously.

2. Locality   The new status of each cell is determined from its position in the grid and by examining the status of its neighboring cells. The new value of a cell is based on the old value of that cell and the old values of the surrounding cells.

3. Homogeneity   All cells of a given type use the same rules for updating their status.

The Game of Life

The most common and popular cellular automaton is Life, a computerized imitation of a colony of living cells. The system was developed by mathematician John Horton Conway of the University of Cambridge (England) in the late 1960s. He built his automaton system on a two-dimensional grid. In it, cells are born, live, and die according to a simple set of rules:

◆ If a cell is on and has either two or three on neighbors, it stays on; otherwise, it turns off.

◆ If a cell is off and has exactly three neighbors, it turns on; otherwise, it stays off.

LIFE IN ACTION

To demonstrate how these rules operate, I'll begin with the six-by-six grid of cells shown in Figure 13-1 on the following page, in which I've marked live cells with a black circle.

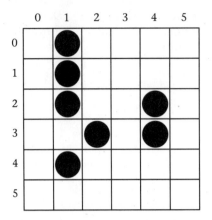

Figure 13-1. *Starting population.*

The grid is addressed in row-column order: the first row, third column is referenced as (0,2), the lower-right corner as (5,5). Let's see what happens when we apply Life's rules to the pattern above. Begin with the cell at row 0, column 0, which, because it has two neighbors, stays dead. The cell at (0,1) is on, but it has only one live neighbor, so it dies. Remember that any changes affect the future state of a cell; thus, turning off the cell at (0,1) occurs only after you count it as a neighbor of its adjacent cells. In general, it's best to write the next state of a cell in a new grid, leaving the original grid intact for counting neighbors.

As we continue, we find that the remaining cells in row 0 have two or fewer neighbors, so they all stay off. Cell (1,0) is off and has three neighbors, so it comes alive. The cell at (1,1), has two neighbors, so its next state will be on. After examining each cell, we end up with a new grid as shown in Figure 13-2.

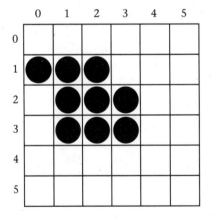

Figure 13-2. *First generation.*

From the original seven live cells, the Life rules create nine. Large blocks of live cells tend to dissipate in Life, since most cells within the block will have more than three neighbors. Applying the rules to Figure 13-2 results in the grid shown in Figure 13-3.

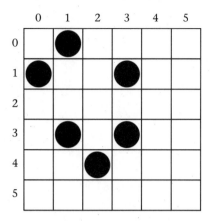

Figure 13-3. *Second generation.*

At the same time, when live cells disperse, they might have so few neighbors that many die out. Application of the rules to Figure 13-3 leaves us with only three cells, in a line, as shown in Figure 13-4. This pattern is a common and classic Life image.

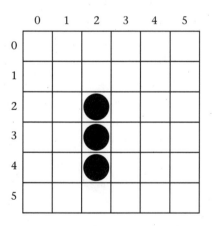

Figure 13-4. *Third generation.*

If we perform another cycle, we get the image shown in Figure 13-5 on the following page.

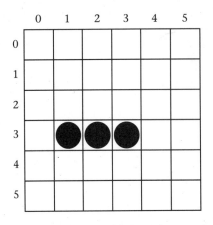

Figure 13-5. Fourth generation.

Another application of the Life rules will change Figure 13-5 back into Figure 13-4. In a never-ending cycle, the line of three cells oscillates from vertical to horizontal and back again. This oscillator is called a *blinker*, and it's just one of many patterns in Life that appear to move. In theory, there is no maximum size or time limit for an oscillator.

GLIDERS

Oscillators produce a set of recurrent patterns, but they stay in one place unless perturbed by other live cells. Some patterns, however, move through the grid by copying themselves. Figure 13-6 shows one of the most interesting Life patterns, a *glider*.

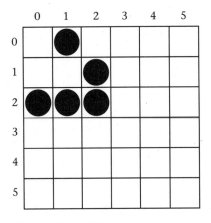

Figure 13-6. Glider pattern.

Four applications of the Life rules transform Figure 13-6 into an offset copy of the same pattern, as shown in Figure 13-7. The glider pattern duplicates itself with a slight offset, appearing to move across the grid. Look closely, and you'll notice that the glider alternates between translations of only two patterns. The orientation of the glider pattern affects the direction in which it crawls.

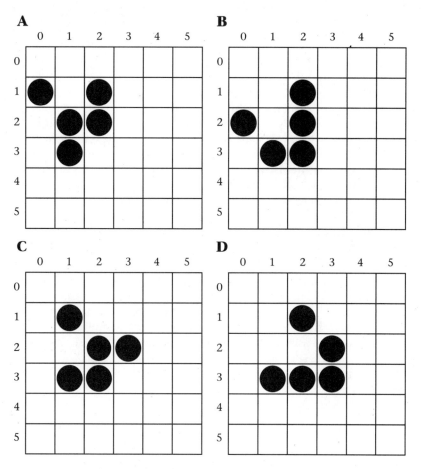

Figure 13-7. *Moving glider.*

Once I've implemented Life in Java, I'll show you some other interesting patterns.

THE MEANING OF LIFE

Conway invented Life using the checkered floor of a hallway in his home. He used dishes to mark live cells, calculated new generations by hand, and experimented with variations on his rules. Conway's goal was to define a set of rules that promoted interesting patterns while avoiding runaway cell growth.

In October 1970 and February 1971, Martin Gardner presented Conway's Life in his "Mathematical Recreations" column in *Scientific American*. Almost overnight, Life became ubiquitous among computer enthusiasts, who still spend hours watching patterns evolve. The effect is almost hypnotic, watching images form and move in a universe defined inside a machine. Life may be the most-often implemented application ever, in part because it exemplifies a basic premise of artificial life: the emergence of complex behavior from simple principles. Embodied in two absolute rules is a pocket universe.

Starting patterns in Life face one of two fates: complete extinction or eternal repetition. The blinker mentioned earlier is an example of the latter fate because it will forever repeat two states. But the glider's oscillations cause it to copy itself along a diagonal line. Given an infinite grid of cells, the glider will travel forever—or until it encounters other live cells that disrupt its form.

In the first *Scientific American* presentation of Life, Conway theorized that no initial arrangement of cells could grow without bound. Even the mobile glider is limited, in that its pattern always contains five live cells. The only way Conway saw to create continuous growth was for someone to find an arrangement that generated new, mobile patterns. Given the limited size of Conway's hallway, he didn't find a glider generator. However, he thought one might exist and offered a fifty dollar reward to the first person who found such a device. The so-called "glider gun" was discovered by Bill Gosper, a researcher at the Massachusetts Institute of Technology. Computer technology was still very primitive, and Gosper used another graphic device to run Life—an oscilloscope. Today researchers know of several glider-producing or glider-affecting programs which, when combined, produce logical gates and other components that could constitute a complete computing device.

Life is the most common cellular automaton, but it is by no means the only one. Conway's Life has four parameters: high and low values for birth and survival. Changing those parameters—perhaps by allowing a cell to survive with three or four neighbors—would create a new automaton with new dynamics. Additional automata could be created using different criteria for determining the number and conditions of cell states. Life's rules could be modified, for example, to state that a dead cell with either two or three neighbors comes alive, and a live cell with anything other than three neighbors will die.

Brain

An interesting automaton, originally named Mutants, was created by Brian Silverman in 1984 on an Apple II, using a program he called The Phantom Fishtank. Silverman decided that cells would have three states: dead, alive, and ghost. A dead cell comes alive when it has two neighbors; a live cell automatically becomes a ghost; a ghost cell automatically dies.

These rules might seem a bit simplistic, but they produce a fascinating variety of colliding gliders. The gliders arise from the asymmetry of the rule, in which the ghost cells block creation of live cells in one direction. When Silverman ran Mutants on a computer dedicated to automata, it was renamed Brian's Brain to reflect an analogy between the interacting gliders and the interactions of signals in the brain.

Generalized Automata

An entire class of cellular automata can be defined by setting three rules:

- ◆ Determine the number of live neighbors required for a dead cell to be born.

- ◆ Determine the number of live neighbors a live cell must have to keep on living.

- ◆ Determine the number of ghost, or *echo*, states.

The application I'll be developing will implement Conway's Life and Brian's Brain, as well as allow the user to define a custom automaton using the preceding rules. But before we begin to write code, one more topic needs to be covered—topography.

Topography

For working with cellular automata, I've defined a two-dimensional window as having one of two different topologies: island or torus. In the island topology, the window is assumed to be surrounded by dead cells. In a torus, the bottom row of cells are assumed to be neighbors to the top row, and the left cell column is treated as if it were adjacent to the right side of the window. In an island world, cell growth and patterns end at the edges of the window. A torus allows patterns to wrap around the screen, top to bottom and left to right. Figure 13-8 shows how a 16-by-16 window would be wrapped onto a torus. (Note how the glider and blinker move on the surface.) For many applications, a toroid world is by far the more interesting of the two topologies.

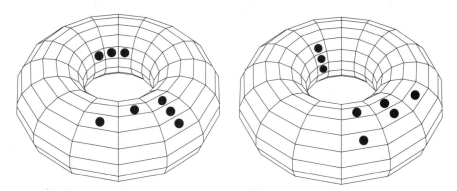

Figure 13-8. Torus topography.

The LifeBox Application

Using these utility classes, I can now build the final application classes for LifeBox. My design is modular and object-oriented, with plug-in objects defining the behavior displayed by a given automaton type.

Automata

The *Automata* class extends the *CellPanel* class to support the cycle mechanism required by cellular automata. *Automata* implements *Runnable* and creates a thread to manage grid updates. In the *run* method, the *Automata* calls *update* to apply a given automata rule to every cell in the grid; for each cell update, the rule returns a *CellChange* object if its state has changed. The *CellChange* object is simply a data structure containing the coordinates and the new state of a changing cell.

```
package coyote.automata;

//
//
// CellChange
//
//
public class CellChange
{

    public int m_nRow;
    public int m_nCol;
    public int m_nState;

    public CellChange(int r,
        int c,int s)
    {
        m_nRow = r;
        m_nCol = c;
        m_nState = s;
    }

    public CellChange(int s)
    {
        m_nRow = 0;
        m_nCol = 0;
        m_nState = s;
    }

}
```

Automata.update builds a *FixedStack* of cell changes, and then unloads the stack in applying the new states. This two-step process allows all cells to report their new state based on the rules; then all new states can be applied simultaneously.

Multithreading causes coordination problems between the main program thread and a running *Automata* object. When the user clicks the Stop button in LifeBox, the program cannot simply terminate the *Automata* thread, which may be in the middle of an update operation. The *update* method is a critical section of code that shouldn't be interrupted when in progress. Java doesn't support a built-in mechanism for marking a section of code as critical, and thereby preventing its interruption, but it isn't difficult to simulate such a mechanism using a flag. The first thing *update* does is set an internal flag, *m_busy*, to *true*; when *update* is finished, it sets *m_busy* back to *false*. The method *isBusy* reports the current value of *m_busy*. In the LifeBox application, the listener for the Stop button will not terminate the *Automata* thread until *isBusy* returns to false.

```
package coyote.automata;

import java.awt.*;
import java.awt.event.*;
import java.util.*;
import coyote.ui.*;
```

```java
import coyote.tools.*;

//
//
// Automata
//
//
public class Automata
    extends CellPanel
    implements Runnable
{
    //-------------------------
    // Fields
    //-------------------------

    // Thread for this automata
    Thread m_thread;

    boolean m_busy;

    // Row and column offsets to neighbors
    // { row_off, col_off, direction from
    // neighbor }
    protected final static int [][] NBR_OFF =
    {
        { -1,  0, 4 }, // North
        { -1, +1, 5 }, // North-east
        {  0, +1, 6 }, // East
        { +1, +1, 7 }, // South-east
        { +1,  0, 0 }, // South
        { +1, -1, 1 }, // South-west
        {  0, -1, 2 }, // West
        { -1, -1, 3 }  // North-west
    };

    protected boolean m_bTorus;

    protected AutomataRule m_rule;

    protected int  [][] m_nNbrFlags;
    protected FixedStack m_ccStack;

    //-------------------------
    // Constructors
    //-------------------------
    public Automata(Component base,
        int rows, int cols, int cellSize,
        boolean is3D, Color [] map,
        boolean isTorus)
    {
```

(continued)

```
        // Call superclass constructor
        super(base, rows, cols, cellSize,
            is3D,map);
        finishAutomata(isTorus);
    }

    protected void finishAutomata
        (boolean isTorus)
    {
        // Set instance variables
        m_busy   = false;
        m_bTorus = isTorus;
        m_rule   = new GameOfLife();

        // Allocate neighbor information
        m_nNbrFlags =
            new int[m_nRows][m_nCols];

        // Create a stack
        m_ccStack = new FixedStack(m_nRows
            * m_nCols);
    }

    //-------------------------
    // Thread methods
    //-------------------------
    public void start()
    {
        if (m_thread == null)
        {
            m_thread = new Thread(this);
            m_thread.start();
        }
    }

    public void stop()
    {
        if (m_thread != null)
        {
            m_thread.stop();
            m_thread = null;
        }
    }

    public void run()
    {
        try
        {
            while (true)
            {
```

```
                update();
                m_thread.sleep(20);
            }
        }
    catch (InterruptedException e)
    {
        stop();
    }
}


//-------------------------
// Methods
//-------------------------

public boolean isBusy()
{
    return m_busy;
}

public synchronized void update()
{
    m_busy = true;

    CellChange cc;

    for (int r = 0; r < m_nRows; ++r)
    {
        for (int c = 0; c < m_nCols; ++c)
        {
            try
            {
                cc =
                    m_rule.rule(m_nCellState[r][c],
                    m_nNbrFlags[r][c]);
            }
            catch (IndexOutOfBoundsException e)
            {
                cc = new CellChange(0);
            }

            if (cc != null)
            {
                cc.m_nRow = r;
                cc.m_nCol = c;
                m_ccStack.push(cc);
            }
        }
    }
```

(continued)

```
        while (m_ccStack.hasStuff())
        {
            cc = (CellChange)m_ccStack.pop();
            setCellState(cc.m_nRow, cc.m_nCol,
                cc.m_nState);
        }

        getGraphics().drawImage(m_cellImage,
            0, 0, this);

        m_busy = false;
    }

    public synchronized void fill
        (int state)
    {
        // Change all cells
        for (int r = 0; r < m_nRows; ++r)
        {
            for (int c = 0; c < m_nCols; ++c)
            {
                m_nCellState[r][c] = state;
                updateNeighbors(r, c);
            }
        }
    }

    public synchronized void setCellState
        (int row, int col, int state)
    {
        // Call overridden superclass method
        super.setCellState(row, col, state);

        // Update surrounding cells
        updateNeighbors(row, col);
    }

    protected synchronized void updateNeighbors
        (int row, int col)
    {
        int rn, cn;

        if (m_bTorus)
        {
            for (int n = 0; n < 8; ++n)
            {
                rn = row + NBR_OFF[n][0];
                cn = col + NBR_OFF[n][1];

                if (rn < 0)
                    rn = m_nMaxRow;
```

```java
            if (rn >= m_nRows)
                rn = 0;
            if (cn < 0)
                cn = m_nMaxCol;
            if (cn >= m_nCols)
                cn = 0;

            // If ((m_nCellState[row][col]
            // & 1) == 1)
            if (m_nCellState[row][col]
                == 1)
                m_nNbrFlags[rn][cn] |= 1
                    << NBR_OFF[n][2];
            else
                m_nNbrFlags[rn][cn] &=
                    ~(1 << NBR_OFF[n][2]);
        }
    }
    else
    {
        for (int n = 0; n < 8; ++n)
        {
            rn = row + NBR_OFF[n][0];
            cn = col + NBR_OFF[n][1];

            if ((rn >= 0) && (rn < m_nRows)
                && (cn >= 0) && (cn < m_nCols))
            {
                // If ((m_nCellState[row][col]
                // & 1) == 1)
                if (m_nCellState[row][col] == 1)
                    m_nNbrFlags[rn][cn] |= 1
                        << NBR_OFF[n][2];
                else
                    m_nNbrFlags[rn][cn] &=
                        ~(1 << NBR_OFF[n][2]);
            }
        }
    }
}


//------------------------
// Properties
//------------------------
public synchronized void setTorus
    (boolean b)
{
    m_bTorus = b;
}
```

(continued)

```
        public boolean isTorus()
        {
            return m_bTorus;
        }

        public synchronized void setRule
            (AutomataRule rule)
        {
            m_rule = rule;
        }

        public AutomataRule getRule()
        {
            return m_rule;
        }

        //-------------------------
        // Events
        //-------------------------
        public void mousePressed
            (MouseEvent evt)
        {
            if (m_thread == null)
                super.mousePressed(evt);
        }
    }
```

The *Automata* constructor adds a parameter to those required for making a *CellPanel*; a boolean value determines whether the grid is mapped as a torus (*true*) or island (*false*). *Automata* overrides the *mousePressed* method, part of the *Mouse-Listener* interface implemented by *CellPanel*, to prevent the user from changing a cell value while the *Automata* thread is active.

Automata also overrides the *fill* and *setCellState* methods inherited from *CellPanel*, adding a call to *updateNeighbors* that tracks neighbor states. I follow neighbor states by using an array of bitmasks. When a cell changes state in the *updateNeighbors* method, a bit is set in the bitmask of each neighboring cell. The bit will be 1 if the cell state is 1; otherwise, the bit will be 0. The *NBR_OFF* array contains grid offsets to locate neighbors within the grid, and an index value stating which "neighbor bit" to update.

Automata Rules

The *AutomataRule* interface defines a single abstract method, *cycle*. This is the method called by *Automata* for each cell during an update. An implementation of the method should examine the state and neighbors of a given cell, and return a new *CellChange* object if it determines that a state change has occurred. If the cell state should not change, *cycle* will return *null*. The following code defines the interface.

```
package coyote.automata;

//
//
// AutomataRule
```

```
//
//
public interface AutomataRule
{
    // Method to implement a rule
    public CellChange rule(int state, int nbrs);
}
```

I define my rule types using tables, in which the bitmask of neighbors' states indexes to the next state of a given cell. In *GameOfLife*, for example, there exist two states: dead and alive. The two dimensional table uses a cell's current state and the bitmask of its neighbors' states as indexes into a 2-by-256 array; the value stored in the array is the new state value. *GameOfLife* indexes into the table and returns a *CellChange* object if the state found differs from the current state.

```
package coyote.automata;

import java.awt.*;

//
//
// GameOfLife
//
//
public class GameOfLife
    implements AutomataRule
{

    //=========================
    // Fields
    //=========================

    private final int [][] Table =
    {
        // Look-up table for dead cells
        {
        0,0,0,0,0,0,0,1,0,0,0,1,0,1,1,0,
        0,0,0,1,0,1,1,0,0,1,1,0,1,0,0,0,
        0,0,0,1,0,1,1,0,0,1,1,0,1,0,0,0,
        0,1,1,0,1,0,0,1,0,0,0,0,0,0,0,0,
        0,0,0,1,0,1,1,0,0,1,1,0,1,0,0,0,
        0,1,1,0,1,0,0,1,0,0,0,0,0,0,0,0,
        0,1,1,0,1,0,0,1,0,0,0,0,0,0,0,0,
        1,0,0,0,0,0,0,0,0,0,0,0,0,0,0,0,
        0,0,0,1,0,1,1,0,0,1,1,0,1,0,0,0,
        0,1,1,0,1,0,0,1,0,0,0,0,0,0,0,0,
        0,1,1,0,1,0,0,1,0,0,0,0,0,0,0,0,
        1,0,0,0,0,0,0,0,0,0,0,0,0,0,0,0,
        0,1,1,0,1,0,0,1,0,0,0,0,0,0,0,0,
        1,0,0,0,0,0,0,0,0,0,0,0,0,0,0,0,
        1,0,0,0,0,0,0,0,0,0,0,0,0,0,0,0,
        0,0,0,0,0,0,0,0,0,0,0,0,0,0,0,0
        },
```

(continued)

```
        // Look-up table for live cells
        {
        0,0,0,1,0,1,1,1,0,1,1,1,1,1,1,0,
        0,1,1,1,1,1,1,0,1,1,1,0,1,0,0,0,
        0,1,1,1,1,1,1,0,1,1,1,0,1,0,0,0,
        1,1,1,0,1,0,0,0,1,0,0,0,0,0,0,0,
        0,1,1,1,1,1,1,0,1,1,1,0,1,0,0,0,
        1,1,1,0,1,0,0,0,1,0,0,0,0,0,0,0,
        1,1,1,0,1,0,0,0,1,0,0,0,0,0,0,0,
        1,0,0,0,0,0,0,0,0,0,0,0,0,0,0,0,
        0,1,1,1,1,1,1,0,1,1,1,0,1,0,0,0,
        1,1,1,0,1,0,0,0,1,0,0,0,0,0,0,0,
        1,1,1,0,1,0,0,0,1,0,0,0,0,0,0,0,
        1,0,0,0,0,0,0,0,0,0,0,0,0,0,0,0,
        1,1,1,0,1,0,0,0,1,0,0,0,0,0,0,0,
        1,0,0,0,0,0,0,0,0,0,0,0,0,0,0,0,
        1,0,0,0,0,0,0,0,0,0,0,0,0,0,0,0,
        0,0,0,0,0,0,0,0,0,0,0,0,0,0,0,0
        },
    };

    //==========================
    // Methods
    //==========================

    public CellChange rule
        (int state,int nbrs)
    {
        int s = Table[state][nbrs];

        if (s != state)
            return new CellChange(s);
        else
            return null;      .
    }
}
```

The implementation of Brian's Brain follows a similar pattern. While I could have simply generated a *CellChange* to state 2 for any state 1 cell, using the table allowed me to simplify the *cycle* method. The following code displays the *Brain* class.

```
package coyote.automata;

import java.awt.*;

//
//
// Brain
//
//
public class Brain implements AutomataRule
{
```

```java
//===========================
// Fields
//===========================

private int [] Table =
{
    // Look-up table for live cells
    0,0,0,1,0,1,1,0,0,1,1,0,1,0,0,0,
    0,1,1,0,1,0,0,0,1,0,0,0,0,0,0,0,
    0,1,1,0,1,0,0,0,1,0,0,0,0,0,0,0,
    1,0,0,0,0,0,0,0,0,0,0,0,0,0,0,0,
    0,1,1,0,1,0,0,0,1,0,0,0,0,0,0,0,
    1,0,0,0,0,0,0,0,0,0,0,0,0,0,0,0,
    1,0,0,0,0,0,0,0,0,0,0,0,0,0,0,0,
    0,0,0,0,0,0,0,0,0,0,0,0,0,0,0,0,
    0,1,1,0,1,0,0,0,1,0,0,0,0,0,0,0,
    1,0,0,0,0,0,0,0,0,0,0,0,0,0,0,0,
    1,0,0,0,0,0,0,0,0,0,0,0,0,0,0,0,
    0,0,0,0,0,0,0,0,0,0,0,0,0,0,0,0,
    1,0,0,0,0,0,0,0,0,0,0,0,0,0,0,0,
    0,0,0,0,0,0,0,0,0,0,0,0,0,0,0,0,
    0,0,0,0,0,0,0,0,0,0,0,0,0,0,0,0,
    0,0,0,0,0,0,0,0,0,0,0,0,0,0,0,0
};


//===========================
// Methods
//===========================

public CellChange rule
    (int state,int nbrs)
{
    if (state == 0)
    {
        if (Table[nbrs] == 1)
            return new CellChange(1);
    }
    else
    {
        if (state == 1)
            return new CellChange(2);
        else
            return new CellChange(0);
    }

    return null;
}

}
```

The *CustomAutomata* class generates a look-up table based on values provided via the *setParameters* method. *CustomAutomata* implements the Life rule by default; a call to *setParameters*, with a grid of boolean values, will generate a new table. Note that the value of the echo states should be between one and seven, where one represents an automaton like Life that has only one nondead state.

```java
package coyote.automata;

//
//
// CustomAutomata
//
//
public class CustomAutomata
    implements AutomataRule
{
    private final int [][] LIFE_TABLE =
    {
        // Look-up m_table for dead cells
        {
        0,0,0,0,0,0,0,1,0,0,0,1,0,1,1,0,
        0,0,0,1,0,1,1,0,0,1,1,0,1,0,0,0,
        0,0,0,1,0,1,1,0,0,1,1,0,1,0,0,0,
        0,1,1,0,1,0,0,0,1,0,0,0,0,0,0,0,
        0,0,0,1,0,1,1,0,0,1,1,0,1,0,0,0,
        0,1,1,0,1,0,0,0,1,0,0,0,0,0,0,0,
        0,1,1,0,1,0,0,0,1,0,0,0,0,0,0,0,
        1,0,0,0,0,0,0,0,0,0,0,0,0,0,0,0,
        0,0,0,1,0,1,1,0,0,1,1,0,1,0,0,0,
        0,1,1,0,1,0,0,0,1,0,0,0,0,0,0,0,
        0,1,1,0,1,0,0,0,1,0,0,0,0,0,0,0,
        1,0,0,0,0,0,0,0,0,0,0,0,0,0,0,0,
        0,1,1,0,1,0,0,0,1,0,0,0,0,0,0,0,
        1,0,0,0,0,0,0,0,0,0,0,0,0,0,0,0,
        1,0,0,0,0,0,0,0,0,0,0,0,0,0,0,0,
        0,0,0,0,0,0,0,0,0,0,0,0,0,0,0,0
        },
        // Look-up m_table for live cells
        {
        0,0,0,1,0,1,1,1,0,1,1,1,1,1,1,0,
        0,1,1,1,1,1,1,0,1,1,1,0,1,0,0,0,
        0,1,1,1,1,1,1,0,1,1,1,0,1,0,0,0,
        1,1,1,0,1,0,0,0,1,0,0,0,0,0,0,0,
        0,1,1,1,1,1,1,0,1,1,1,0,1,0,0,0,
        1,1,1,0,1,0,0,0,1,0,0,0,0,0,0,0,
        1,1,1,0,1,0,0,0,1,0,0,0,0,0,0,0,
        1,0,0,0,0,0,0,0,0,0,0,0,0,0,0,0,
        0,1,1,1,1,1,1,0,1,1,1,0,1,0,0,0,
        1,1,1,0,1,0,0,0,1,0,0,0,0,0,0,0,
        1,1,1,0,1,0,0,0,1,0,0,0,0,0,0,0,
        1,0,0,0,0,0,0,0,0,0,0,0,0,0,0,0,
        1,1,1,0,1,0,0,0,1,0,0,0,0,0,0,0,
```

```
        1,0,0,0,0,0,0,0,0,0,0,0,0,0,0,0,
        1,0,0,0,0,0,0,0,0,0,0,0,0,0,0,0,
        0,0,0,0,0,0,0,0,0,0,0,0,0,0,0,0
        },
};

public static final int MAX_ECHO = 7;

//=========================
// Fields
//=========================

private int [][] m_table;
private int m_echo;

//=========================
// Constructors
//=========================

public CustomAutomata()
{
    m_table = LIFE_TABLE;
    m_echo   = 1;
}

//=========================
// Methods
//=========================

public void setParameters
    (boolean [][] checks,
    int max)
{
    if (max >= MAX_ECHO)
        m_echo = 7;
    else
        m_echo = max;

    if (m_echo < 1)
        m_echo = 1;

    m_table = new int [m_echo + 1][256];

    // Generate m_table data
    for (int j = 0; j <= 255; ++j)
    {
        // Count the bits in j
        int x =  (j & 1) +
                 ((j >> 1) & 1) +
                 ((j >> 2) & 1) +
```

(continued)

```
                                  ((j >> 3) & 1) +
                                  ((j >> 4) & 1) +
                                  ((j >> 5) & 1) +
                                  ((j >> 6) & 1) +
                                  ((j >> 7) & 1);

            // Load table for dead cells
            if (checks[0][x])
                m_table[0][j] = 1;
            else
                m_table[0][j] = 0;

            // Load table for live cells
            if (checks[1][x])
                m_table[1][j] = 1;
            else
            {
                if (m_echo > 1)
                    m_table[1][j] = 2;
                else
                    m_table[1][j] = 0;
            }

            // Load table for "echo" cells
            if (m_echo >= 3)
            {
                for (int i = 2; i < m_echo; ++i)
                    m_table[i][j] = i + 1;
            }

            // Load final state table with automatic 0 state
            if (m_echo >= 2)
                m_table[m_echo][j] = 0;
        }
    }

    public CellChange rule
        (int state,int nbrs)
    {
        int s = m_table[state][nbrs];

        if (s != state)
            return new CellChange(s);
        else
            return null;
    }
}
```

LifeBox

Finally, it's time to look at the applet class, *LifeBox*. Here is where all the pieces of code above come together to create a complex application or applet. In fact, *LifeBox* is both. It can be run as part of an HTML document, as shown in Figure 13-9, or as a standalone application, as shown in Figure 13-10.

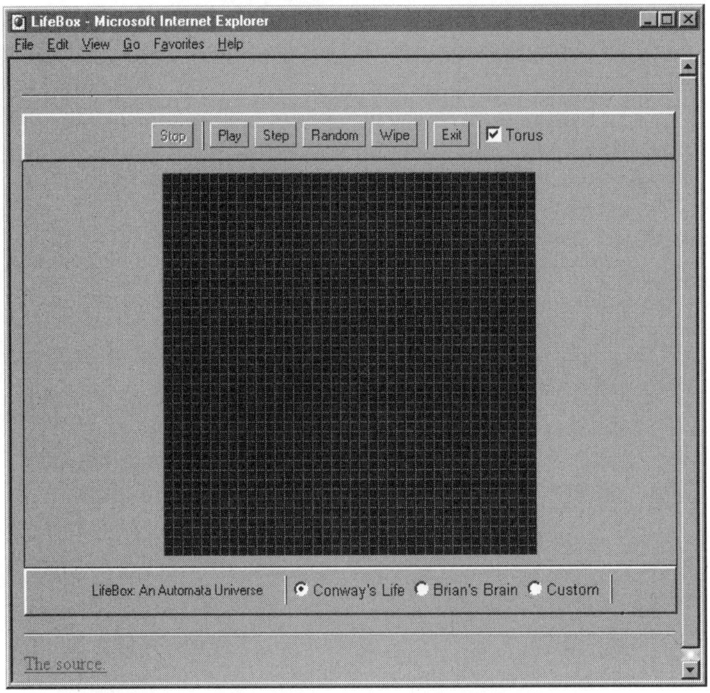

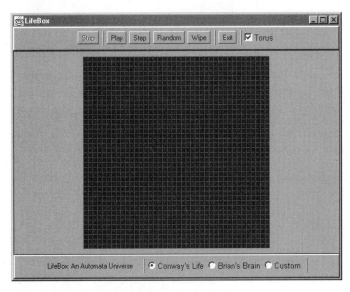

Figure 13-9. *LifeBox as an applet.*

Figure 13-10. *LifeBox as an application.*

The *LifeBox* class itself, a subclass of *Applet*, follows.

```
//------------------------------------------------------------------
//  LifeBox -- A Java Application (or Applet)
//
//  Copyright 1997 Scott Robert Ladd. All rights reserved.
//------------------------------------------------------------------

import java.applet.*;
import java.awt.*;
import java.awt.event.*;
import coyote.ui.*;
import coyote.automata.*;
import coyote.math.*;
import LifeBoxFrame;

public class LifeBox
    extends Applet
{
    //-------------------------
    // Constants
    //-------------------------
    private final String FILE_SPLASH =
        "image/lbsplash.gif";

    private final int BTN_STOP = 0;
    private final int BTN_PLAY = 1;
    private final int BTN_STEP = 2;
    private final int BTN_RAND = 3;
    private final int BTN_WIPE = 4;
    private final int BTN_EXIT = 5;

    private final int TYPE_LIFE   = 0;
    private final int TYPE_BRAIN  = 1;
    private final int TYPE_CUSTOM = 2;

    private final ActionListener [] BTN_LISTENERS =
    {
        new listenerStop(),
        new listenerPlay(),
        new listenerStep(),
        new listenerRand(),
        new listenerWipe(),
        new listenerExit()
    };

    private final String [] TEXT_BTN =
    {
```

```
        "Stop",
        "Play",
        "Step",
        "Random",
        "Wipe",
        "Exit"
};

private final String WORLD_NAME [] =
{
    "Conway's Life",
    "Brian's Brain",
    "Custom"
};

private final String CHECKNO [] =
{
    "0: ",
    "1: ",
    "2: ",
    "3: ",
    "4: ",
    "5: ",
    "6: ",
    "7: ",
    "8: ",
    "9: "
};

private final String CHECKHD [] = { "B", "S" };

// Map of colors
private Color [] m_colorMap =
{
    Color.darkGray,
    new Color(  0, 255, 255), // Cyan
    new Color(  0, 192, 255),
    new Color(  0, 160, 255),
    new Color(  0, 128, 255),
    new Color(  0,  96, 255),
    new Color(  0,  64, 255),
    new Color(  0,   0, 255)  // Bright blue
};

//-------------------------
// Fields
//-------------------------
private Button []       m_btn;
private Checkbox        m_chkTorus;
```

(continued)

```
        private Label            m_status;
        private EdgedPanel       m_toolbar;
        private EdgedPanel       m_autoPanel;
        private EdgedPanel       m_custPanel;
        private Checkbox []       m_worldType;
        private CheckboxGroup    m_worldGroup;
        private CheckGrid        m_custChecks;
        private TextField        m_custEcho;
        private Image [][]        m_img;
        private Automata         m_automata;
        private AutomataRule []  m_autoRule;
        private int              m_currentRule;
        private int              m_nGridW = 40;
        private int              m_nGridH = 40;
        private int              m_nCellX =  8;
        private boolean          m_isApplication;

        private BetterUniformDeviate randNo =
            new BetterUniformDeviate();

        //-------------------------
        // Initialization
        //-------------------------
        private Image getSplashImage
            (Frame app)
        {
            // Create a media tracker for loading images
            MediaTracker tracker = new MediaTracker(this);

            // Image reference to be returned
            Image splash;

            if (app == null) // Running as app
            {
                // Get splash Image
                splash = getImage(getDocumentBase(),
                    FILE_SPLASH);
            }
            else
            {
                // Get a toolkit for frame
                Toolkit tools = app.getToolkit();

                // Get splash Image
                splash = tools.getImage(FILE_SPLASH);
            }

            tracker.addImage(splash,0);

            try
            {
```

```
            tracker.waitForAll();
        }
    catch (InterruptedException e) { }

    return splash;
}

private void addSeparator
    (Container cont)
{
    SeparatorBar sb = new SeparatorBar();
    cont.add(sb);
    sb.setForeground(Color.gray);
    sb.setSize(4,24);
}

private void initHelper()
{
    // Preparation
    setLayout(new BorderLayout());
    setSize(560, 420);

    setBackground(Color.lightGray);
    setForeground(Color.black);

    // Set format and colors for applet panel
    repaint();

    // Create a tool bar via a band object
    m_toolbar = new EdgedPanel();
    m_toolbar.setBackground(Color.lightGray);
    m_toolbar.setLayout(new FlowLayout());

    // Create and add buttons
    m_btn = new Button [6];

    int b; // Button index

    for (b = 0; b < 6; ++b)
    {
        // Add button to applet toolbar
        if ((b == BTN_PLAY) || (b == BTN_EXIT))
            addSeparator(m_toolbar);

        m_btn[b] = new Button(TEXT_BTN[b]);
        m_toolbar.add(m_btn[b]);
        m_btn[b].setBackground(Color.lightGray);
        m_btn[b].setForeground(Color.black);
        m_btn[b].addActionListener(BTN_LISTENERS[b]);
    }
```

(continued)

```
        addSeparator(m_toolbar);

        // Add check buttons
        m_chkTorus = new Checkbox("Torus", true);
        m_chkTorus.setBackground(Color.lightGray);
        m_chkTorus.setForeground(Color.black);
        m_chkTorus.setState(true);
        m_chkTorus.addItemListener(new listenerTorus());

        m_toolbar.add(m_chkTorus);

        // Create a panel to hold southern items
        EdgedPanel psouth = new EdgedPanel();
        psouth.setBackground(Color.lightGray);
        psouth.setForeground(Color.blue);
        psouth.setLayout(new FlowLayout());

        // Create a status bar
        m_status = new Label(
            "LifeBox: An Automata Universe");
        psouth.add(m_status);
        m_status.setBackground(Color.lightGray);
        m_status.setForeground(Color.blue);

        addSeparator(psouth);

        // Add radio buttons
        m_worldGroup = new CheckboxGroup();
        m_worldType  = new Checkbox[3];

        listenerType lt = new listenerType();

        for (b = 0; b < 3; ++b)
        {
            m_worldType[b] =
                new Checkbox(WORLD_NAME[b], false,
                m_worldGroup);
            m_worldType[b].addItemListener(lt);
            psouth.add(m_worldType[b]);
        }

        // We start with "Life" selected
        m_worldType[0].setState(true);

        addSeparator(psouth);

        // Add toolbar and world panel to applet window
        add("North",m_toolbar);
        add("South",psouth);
```

```
// Create a center panel to hold the Automata
m_autoPanel = new EdgedPanel(EdgedPanel.FLAT,
    1);

m_autoPanel.setBackground(Color.lightGray);
m_autoPanel.setForeground(Color.black);
m_autoPanel.setLayout(null);

add("Center",m_autoPanel);
validate();

Rectangle prect = m_autoPanel.getBounds();

// Create and add Automata
m_automata = new Automata
                (this,
                 m_nGridW, m_nGridH,
                 m_nCellX, true,
                 m_colorMap, true);

m_autoPanel.add(m_automata);

// Put automata grid in center of panel
m_automata.setLocation(
    (prect.width  -
        m_automata.getWidth())  / 2,
    (prect.height -
        m_automata.getHeight()) / 2);

m_automata.fill(0);
m_automata.redraw();

// Create rule
m_autoRule    = new AutomataRule [3];
m_autoRule[0] = new GameOfLife();
m_autoRule[1] = new Brain();
m_autoRule[2] = new CustomAutomata();
m_currentRule = 0;

// Create panel of check columns
m_custChecks = new CheckGrid(10, 2,
    CHECKNO, CHECKHD);

m_custChecks.setBackground(Color.lightGray);
m_custChecks.setForeground(Color.black);

// Create echo edit control
m_custEcho = new TextField("1");
```

(continued)

```
        // Create panel to hold custom
        // automata parameters
        m_custPanel = new EdgedPanel();
        m_custPanel.setLayout(new FlowLayout());
        m_custPanel.setBackground(Color.lightGray);
        m_custPanel.setForeground(Color.black);

        m_custPanel.add(m_custChecks);
        m_custPanel.add(new Label("Echo:"));
        m_custPanel.add(m_custEcho);

        // Set button status
        setButtonsStopped();
    }

    public void init()
    {
        // Create Splash screen
        SplashFrame sframe =
            new SplashFrame(null,
                getSplashImage(null));

        m_isApplication = false;
        initHelper();

        // Hide splash frame
        sframe.dispose();
    }

    public void init
        (LifeBoxFrame frame)
    {
        // Create Splash screen
        SplashFrame sframe =
            new SplashFrame(frame,
            getSplashImage(frame));

        m_isApplication = true;
        initHelper();

        // Hide splash frame
        sframe.dispose();
    }

    public LifeBox()
    {
        // Everything handled in init
    }
```

```
//-------------------------
// Methods
//-------------------------

protected synchronized void randomizeGrid()
{
    m_automata.fill(0);

    for (int n = 0; n < (m_nGridW *
        m_nGridH / 10); ++n)
    {
        int r = randNo.nextValue(0,m_nGridW);
        int c = randNo.nextValue(0,m_nGridH);

        m_automata.setCellState(r,c,1);
    }

    m_automata.redraw();
}

protected void setButtonsStopped()
{
    m_btn[BTN_STOP].setEnabled(false);
    m_btn[BTN_STOP].repaint();
    m_btn[BTN_PLAY].setEnabled(true);
    m_btn[BTN_PLAY].repaint();
    m_btn[BTN_STEP].setEnabled(true);
    m_btn[BTN_STEP].repaint();
    m_btn[BTN_RAND].setEnabled(true);
    m_btn[BTN_RAND].repaint();
    m_btn[BTN_WIPE].setEnabled(true);
    m_btn[BTN_WIPE].repaint();
    m_chkTorus.setEnabled(true);
    m_chkTorus.repaint();
    m_worldType[0].setEnabled(true);
    m_worldType[1].setEnabled(true);
    m_worldType[2].setEnabled(true);
    m_custChecks.setEnabled(true);
    m_custEcho.setEnabled(true);
}

protected void setButtonsRunning()
{
    m_btn[BTN_STOP].setEnabled(true);
    m_btn[BTN_STOP].repaint();
    m_btn[BTN_PLAY].setEnabled(false);
    m_btn[BTN_PLAY].repaint();
    m_btn[BTN_STEP].setEnabled(false);
    m_btn[BTN_STEP].repaint();
```

(continued)

```
        m_btn[BTN_RAND].setEnabled(false);
        m_btn[BTN_RAND].repaint();
        m_btn[BTN_WIPE].setEnabled(false);
        m_btn[BTN_WIPE].repaint();
        m_chkTorus.setEnabled(false);
        m_chkTorus.repaint();
        m_worldType[0].setEnabled(false);
        m_worldType[1].setEnabled(false);
        m_worldType[2].setEnabled(false);
        m_custChecks.setEnabled(false);
        m_custEcho.setEnabled(false);
    }

    private synchronized void setCustom()
    {
        // Construct array of booleans
        boolean [][] checks = new boolean [2][10];

        for (int r = 0; r < 10; ++r)
        {
            checks[0][r] = m_custChecks.isChecked(r,
                0);
            checks[1][r] = m_custChecks.isChecked(r,
                1);
        }

        int echo = Integer.parseInt(
            m_custEcho.getText());

        if (echo > CustomAutomata.MAX_ECHO)
        {
            echo = CustomAutomata.MAX_ECHO;
            m_custEcho.setText(String.valueOf(echo));
        }

        if (echo < 1)
        {
            echo = 1;
            m_custEcho.setText("1");
        }

        ((CustomAutomata)m_autoRule[2]).setParameters(
            checks, echo);
    }

    //-------------------------
    // Application methods
    //-------------------------
    public String getAppletInfo()
    {
```

```java
        return "Name: LifeBox\r\n" +
               "Author: Scott Robert Ladd\r\n" +
               "Copyright 1997 Scott Robert Ladd, " +
               "All Rights Reserved.";
    }

    public static void main(String args[])
    {
        // Create window to contain applet GATest
        LifeBoxFrame frame =
            new LifeBoxFrame("LifeBox");

        // Show Frame to get insets
        frame.show();
        frame.hide();

        // Resize frame
        Insets i = frame.getInsets();

        frame.setSize(i.left + i.right  + 560,
                      i.top  + i.bottom + 420);

        // Start the applet running
        // in the frame window
        LifeBox applet_LifeBox = new LifeBox();

        frame.add("Center", applet_LifeBox);
        applet_LifeBox.init(frame);
        applet_LifeBox.start();
        frame.show();
    }

    public void start()
    {
    }

    public void stop()
    {
    }

    //------------------------
    // Event listeners
    //------------------------

    private class listenerStop
        implements ActionListener
    {
        public synchronized void actionPerformed
            (ActionEvent event)
```

(continued)

```
        {
            if (m_automata.isBusy() == false)
            {
                m_automata.stop();
                setButtonsStopped();
            }
        }
    }

    class listenerPlay
        implements ActionListener
    {
        public synchronized void actionPerformed
            (ActionEvent event)
        {
            if (m_currentRule == TYPE_CUSTOM)
                setCustom();

            setButtonsRunning();
            m_automata.start();
        }

    }

    class listenerStep
        implements ActionListener
    {
        public synchronized void actionPerformed
            (ActionEvent event)
        {
            if (m_currentRule == TYPE_CUSTOM)
                setCustom();

            m_automata.update();
        }
    }

    class listenerRand
        implements ActionListener
    {
        public synchronized void actionPerformed
            (ActionEvent event)
        {
            randomizeGrid();
        }
    }

    class listenerWipe
        implements ActionListener
    {
```

```
        public synchronized void actionPerformed
            (ActionEvent event)
        {
            m_automata.fill(0);
            m_automata.redraw();
        }
    }

class listenerExit
    implements ActionListener
{
    public synchronized void actionPerformed
        (ActionEvent event)
    {
        System.exit(0);
    }
}

class listenerTorus
    implements ItemListener
{
    public synchronized void itemStateChanged
        (ItemEvent event)
    {
        m_automata.setTorus(m_chkTorus.getState());
    }
}

class listenerType
    implements ItemListener
{
    public synchronized void itemStateChanged
        (ItemEvent event)
    {
        if (event.getStateChange() ==
            ItemEvent.SELECTED)
        {
            if (event.getSource() ==
                m_worldType[TYPE_CUSTOM])
            {
                m_currentRule = TYPE_CUSTOM;

                // Display the custom
                // parameters panel
                m_autoPanel.add(m_custPanel);

                Rectangle r =
                    m_automata.getBounds();
```

(continued)

```
                    m_custPanel.setBounds
                        (r.x + r.width + 10,
                        r.y + 10,
                        80, r.height - 20);
                }
                else // Remove custom parameters panel
                {
                    m_autoPanel.remove(m_custPanel);

                    if (event.getSource() ==
                        m_worldType[TYPE_LIFE])
                        m_currentRule = TYPE_LIFE;
                    else
                        m_currentRule = TYPE_BRAIN;
                }

                m_automata.setRule(
                    m_autoRule[m_currentRule]);

                m_autoPanel.validate();
                m_custPanel.repaint();
            }
        }
    }
}
```

The *LifeBoxFrame* class, used when LifeBox runs as an application, has the following definition.

```
import java.awt.*;

//
//
// LifeBoxFrame
//
//
public class LifeBoxFrame extends Frame
{

    public LifeBoxFrame(String str)
    {
        super(str);
    }

    public boolean handleEvent(Event evt)
    {
        switch (evt.id)
        {
            case Event.WINDOW_DESTROY:
                // TODO: Place additional clean up code here
                dispose();
```

```
                    System.exit(0);
                    return true;

                default:
                    return super.handleEvent(evt);
            }
        }


    }
```

LifeBox implements a pair of *init* methods, one for applet operation and the other for use with an application frame. The bulk of the initialization code is located in the *initHelper* method, which creates controls, panels, and layouts for the program display. I placed it there to handle the loading of images. When an *Applet* object is running as part of an HTML page, it can determine the document that contains the applet with the *getDocumentBase* method. For an application, *getDocumentBase* fails; therefore, I created a *Toolkit* for the application frame and used its methods in loading my images. Loading the splash picture is handled by the *getSplashImage* utility method. The *addSeparator* method creates standardized *SeparatorBar* objects, adding them to the given container.

The applet window uses the *BorderLayout* method to organize its constituent components. Those components include the LifeBox toolbar, a simple panel containing buttons and controls, placed at the top of the display. The bottom of the window contains a set of grouped radio buttons and a label describing the application. In the middle, a panel shows the automaton display and an optional pop-up panel of settings for customizing the automaton rule. I've used separator bars and edged panels to give the application a sculptured look. All buttons are initialized from arrays of labels and event listener objects; a set of constants give names to indexes for specific controls.

The program routes all button and checkbox events to component-specific inner classes, with names like *listenerStop* and *listenerTorus*. I designed them this way to encapsulate the functions of each control, maintaining a clean separation between application and component code. Instead of a single *actionPerformed* method in LifeBox, I created eight inner classes implementing from either *ActionListener* or *ItemListener*. The most complex of these is the *listenerType* class, which handles changes in the type of automaton rule being displayed. Based on a user's selection, *listenerType* will show or hide the panel of custom automaton parameters.

LifeBox maintains an array of *AutomataRule* objects, with an entry for *GameOfLife*, *Brain*, and *CustomAutomata*. When the user clicks the Play button, the program reads the selected automaton type from the *RadioPanel m_worldType*; if the user chooses a custom automata, the application constructs an array of boolean values by reading the state of checkboxes located in the *CheckboxColumns* object *m_custChecks*. This array and the value of *m_custEcho* become arguments in a call to *CustomAutomata.setParameters*. The *listenerPlay.actionPerformed* method then starts the *Automata* thread.

Figures 13-11 and 13-12 on the following page provide a set of interesting patterns to use with the Life automaton. The oscillators show a variety of repetitious patterns; the spaceships are a set of three patterns that move orthogonally across the automaton universe. You might also try creating a few gliders, as described earlier in this chapter.

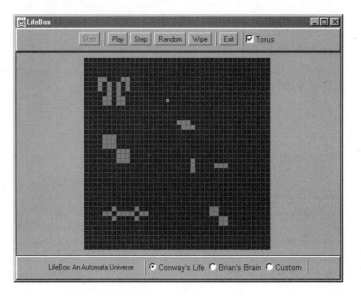

Figure 13-11. Life oscillators.

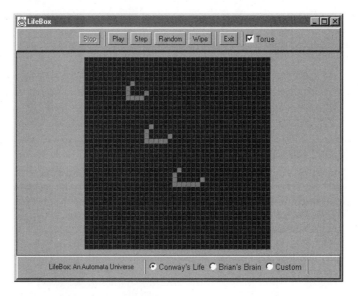

Figure 13-12. Life spaceships.

The Brain universe consists only of gliders. Figure 13-13 shows a Brain automaton begun from a random start with several sprites moving about. The small pattern in the lower-right corner is a butterfly, the only common Brain pattern that moves on a diagonal. If you let the pattern run, collisions will evolve it into a single butterfly.

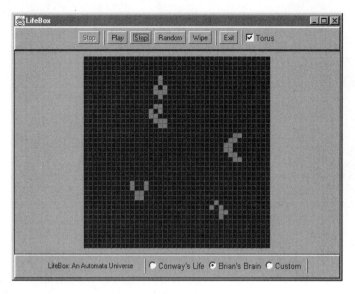

Figure 13-13. Brain sprites.

For custom automata, I recommend that you try the patterns and settings given in Figures 13-14 and 13-15. The settings in Figure 13-14 belong to Frogs, an automaton I discovered a few years ago; in Figure 13-15 on the following page, you'll see what are known as Belousov-Zhabotinsky patterns, which often appear in bacterial colonies. On Figure 13-15, change the parameters to remove the check for birth with three neighbors. Then, with just two checkmarks, the automaton shows a Brain-like mass of gliders that collide in spectacular fashion.

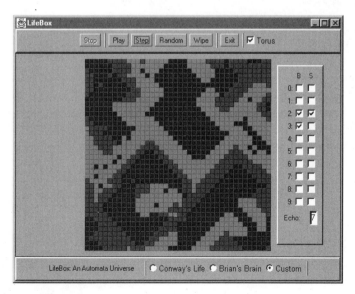

Figure 13-14. Frogs automaton.

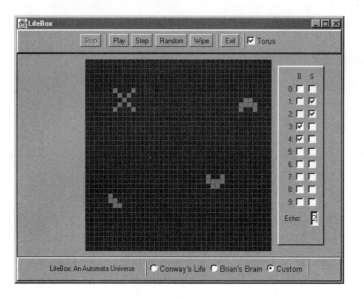

Figure 13-15. *Belousov-Zhabotinsky automaton.*

Feel free to experiment with the custom automata. You'll find an amazing array of behavior types, and you might just discover something remarkable.

Onward

As with all learning processes, understanding Java and Visual J++ will be easiest if you pick a project and just begin coding. Wander the Internet and discover what other people have done with Java. Buy books like this one and examine the code for working applications. In the end, you'll be a Java guru, building powerful applets that impress friends and coworkers.

A

Deprecated Methods in Java 1.1

Deprecated Method	Class	New Method in Java 1.1
action	*Component*	See Chapter 8
allowsMultipleSelections	*List*	*isMultipleMode*
appendText	*TextArea*	*append*
bounds	*Component*	*getBounds*
clear	*List*	*removeAll*
countComponents	*Container*	*getComponentCount*
countItems	*Choice, List, Menu*	*getItemCount*
countMenus	*MenuBar*	*getMenuCount*
delItems	*List*	No replacement
deliverEvent	*Component, Container*	*dispatchEvent*
disable()	*Component, MenuItem*	*setEnabled(false)*
enable()	*Component, MenuItem*	*setEnabled(true)*
enable(expression)	*Component*	*setEnabled(expression)*
getBoundingBox	*Polygon*	*getBounds*
getClipRect	*Graphics*	*getClipBounds*
getCurrent	*CheckboxGroup*	*getSelectedCheckbox*
getCursorType	*Frame*	*getCursor* method in *Component*
getLineIncrement	*Scrollbar*	*getUnitIncrement*
getPageIncrement	*Scrollbar*	*getBlockIncrement*
getPeer	*Component*	No replacement.
getVisible	*Scrollbar*	*getVisibleAmount*
gotFocus	*Component*	*processFocusEvent*
handleEvent	*Component*	*processEvent*
hide	*Component*	*setVisible(false)*
insertText	*TextArea*	*insert*
insets	*Container*	*getInsets*

Deprecated Method	Class	New Method in Java 1.1
inside	Component, Polygon, Rectangle	contains
isSelected	List	isIndexSelected
keyDown	Component	processKeyEvent
keyUp	Component	processKeyEvent
layout	Component, Container, ScrollPane	doLayout
locate	Component, Container	getComponentAt
location	Component	getLocation
lostFocus	Component	processFocusEvent
minimumSize	Component, Container, TextArea, TextField	getMinimumSize
mouseDown	Component	processMouseEvent
mouseDrag	Component	processMouseMotionEvent
mouseEnter	Component	processMouseEvent
mouseExit	Component	processMouseEvent
mouseMove	Component	processMouseMotionEvent
mouseUp	Component	processMouseEvent
move	Component, Rectangle	setLocation
nextFocus	Component, Container, Window	transferFocus
postEvent	Component, Window	dispatchEvent
preferredSize	Component, Container, List, TextArea, TextField	getPreferredSize
replaceText	TextArea	replaceRange
reshape	Component, Rectangle	setBounds
resize	Component, Rectangle	setSize
setCurrent	CheckboxGroup	setSelectedCheckbox

Deprecated Method	Class	New Method in Java 1.1
setCursor	Frame	setCursor method in Component
setEchoCharacter	TextField	setEchoChar
setLineIncrement	Scrollbar	setUnitIncrement
setMultipleSelections	List	setMultipleMode
setPageIncrement	Scrollbar	setBlockIncrement
show()	Component	setVisible(true)
show(expression)	Component	setVisible(expression)
size	Component	getSize

B

Using Microsoft
Visual J++ 1.1 with the
Microsoft Java SDK 2.0

As shipped, Microsoft Visual J++ 1.1 does not include the AFC libraries or the Java 1.1–compatible compiler. These are features of Microsoft's Java SDK version 2.0, which is included on this book's CD-ROM. Installing the SDK will put the Java 1.1 and AFC class files onto your system, ready for use, but you need to take a few extra steps to install the Java 1.1 version of the compiler.

By default, the SDK will install itself into C:\SDK-Java.20; you'll find the Java 1.1 compiler in the bin subdirectory. You'll need to copy two files, *jvc.exe* and *msjvc.dll*, from the SDK into your Visual J++ installation. If you've used the default installation, copy those files into the C:\Program Files\DevStudio\SharedIDE\ bin directory.

Visual J++ comes with a version of *jvc.exe* that is implemented as a single file, without a DLL. Before you copy the new compiler from the SDK, you might want to save the old compiler under a new name; I renamed mine *jvc10.exe*. Although I haven't had any trouble compiling code with the SDK compiler, you would still be wise to save the Java 1.0 compiler in case you do run into problems or want to test code with both versions of the language.

References

Cormen, Thomas H., Charles E. Leiserson, and Ronald L. Rivest. *Introduction to Algorithms.* Cambridge, MA: McGraw-Hill, 1990.

Davis, Lawrence. *Handbook of Genetic Algorithms.* New York: Van Nostrand-Reinhold, 1991.

Eigen, Manfred, and Ruthild Winkler. *Laws of the Game: How Principles of Nature Govern Chance.* Princeton, NJ: Princeton University Press, 1981.

Ellis, Margaret A., and Bjarne Stroustrup. *The Annotated C++ Reference Manual.* Reading, MA: Addison-Wesley, 1990.

Emmeche, Claus. *The Garden in the Machine.* Princeton, NJ: Princeton University Press, 1994.

Fogel, David B. *Evolutionary Computing: Toward a New Philosophy of Machine Intelligence.* Washington, DC: IEEE Computer Society Press, 1995.

Goldberg, David E. *Genetic Algorithms in Search, Optimization, and Machine Learning.* Reading, MA: Addison-Wesley, 1989.

Gosling, James, Bill Joy, and Guy Steele. *The Java Language Specification.* Mountain View, CA: Sun Microsystems, 1996.

Gosling, James and Frank Yellin. *The Java Application Programming Interface.* Mountain View, CA: Sun Microsystems, 1996.

JavaBeans 1.0 API Specification. Mountain View, CA: Sun Microsystems, 1996.

Knuth, Donald E. *Fundamental Algorithms*, 2nd ed., Vol. 1, *The Art of Computer Programming*. Reading, MA: Addison-Wesley, 1981.

———. *Seminumerical Algorithms*, 2nd ed., Vol. 2, *The Art of Computer Programming*. Reading, MA: Addison-Wesley, 1981.

———. *Sorting and Searching*, 2nd ed., Vol. 3, *The Art of Computer Programming*. Reading, MA: Addison-Wesley, 1981.

Koza, John R. *Genetic Programming II: Automatic Discovery of Reusable Programs*. Cambridge, MA: MIT Press, 1994.

Ladd, Scott Robert. *Genetic Algorithms*. Redwood City, CA: M&T Books, 1996.

———. *Simulations and Cellular Automata*. Redwood City, CA: M&T Books, 1995.

Langton, Christopher G., ed. *Artificial Life II*. Reading, MA: Addison-Wesley, 1992.

———. *Artificial Life III*. Reading, MA: Addison-Wesley, 1994.

Press, William A., Brian P. Flannery, Saul A. Teukolsky, and William T. Vetterling. *Numerical Recipes in C: The Art of Scientific Computing*. 2nd ed. New York: Cambridge Univ. Press, 1992.

Sedgewick, Robert. *Algorithms in C*. Reading, MA: Addison-Wesley, 1990.

Index

String objects, 64–67, 110
  checkbox column control and, 263
stringWidth method, 224
subclasses, 31
subinterfaces, 40
superclass, 31
superclass methods, overriding, 35–37
superinterfaces, 40
super keyword, 35
Super Label control, 129, 133
System properties, security restrictions, 247

T

Temperature class (sample code)
  access modifiers, 30–31
  class and instance members, 27–29
  constants, 29–30
  inheritance qualifiers, 32–37
  syntax for fields and methods, 21
testFitness method, 90, 92
TextArea constructors, 215
TextArea subclass, 215–16
TextDoc class, 9
Ticker class, 151, 157–59
Timer control, 133, 135, 136
Title property, 229
toBack method, 228
toFront method, 228
Toolkit object, 209
topography, 281
torus topology, 281, 288
toString method, 65, 67
translate method, 227
two-point crossover, 98, 100, 102
TwoPointCrossover class, 100
type libraries (TLBs), 126, 149
types (data types), 8, 54, 55
  C++/Java differences, 60–62
  IDL-Java correspondences, 151–52
  numeric, sizes and ranges of, 61
  primitive, 60–62
  reference, 60
  translation of, 151, 159

U

Unicode character set, 61
UniformDeviate class, 47–50
uniform deviates, 45–53
  BetterUniformDeviate class, 51–53
  SimpleUniformDeviate class, 50–51
  UniformDeviate class, 47–50
unsigned shift operator ($>>$), 101
unsigned types, 61
update method, 208, 282
updateNeighbors method, 288
user interface, 206. *See also* Abstract
      Window Toolkit (AWT)
utility classes, 221–24
uuid entries, in IDL files, 151

V

validate method, 212
VARIANT class, 151
VBScript, 247, 249
Vector class, 102
verbs, genetic algorithms and, 88
VeriSign, 251
virtual key codes, 234–35
virtual keyword (C++), 36
virtual machines, 5–6, 59
Visual Basic, Scripting Edition, 127
Visual J++, 5. *See also* Developer Studio
Void class, 54

W

web pages, 124
Window class, 227, 234
Window constructor, 227
window events, 235
WindowListener interface, 236, 237
window_onLoad subroutine, 135, 138
windows, 227–28
World Wide Web, 4–5

Scott Robert Ladd

In the past decade, Scott Robert Ladd has published hundreds of articles and more than a dozen books about computer programming. He began programming in the mid-1970s and has worked with systems ranging from PDP-8s and IBM mainframes to the latest in PC technology. When he isn't absorbed in compilers and software, Scott enjoys astronomy and backcountry hiking. With his wife and three daughters, Scott lives in Silverton, Colorado, a historic mining town set high in the mountains of southwestern Colorado.

The manuscript for this book was prepared and submitted to Microsoft Press in electronic form. Text files were prepared using Microsoft Word 7 for Windows. Pages were composed by Microsoft Press using Adobe PageMaker 6.5 for Windows, with text in Stone Serif and display type in Univers. Composed pages were delivered to the printer as electronic prepress files.

Cover Graphic Designer
Greg Hickman

Interior Graphic Designer
Pam Hidaka

Illustrator
Joel Panchot

Desktop Publishers
Abby Hall
Steven Hopster

Principal Proofreaders
Patricia Masserman
Shawn Peck

Copy Editor
Katherine Krause

Indexer
Maro Riofrancos

Strategic thinking

about applications for

Windows®

and the Internet.

U.S.A.   **$22.95**
U.K.   £20.99
Canada $30.95
ISBN 1-57231-216-5

It's your job to make strategic development and design decisions about new applications, Windows, the Internet, and how they all interact. To do your job even better, get UNDERSTANDING ACTIVEX™ AND OLE. It's a conceptual, language-independent technical introduction to all of the powerful ActiveX technologies—the Component Object Model (COM), ActiveX Controls, OLE technology, Internet applications, and more. With UNDERSTANDING ACTIVEX AND OLE, you'll gain a firm conceptual grounding without extraneous details or implementation specifics. You'll see the strategic significance of COM as the foundation for Microsoft's object technology. And you'll get a clear introduction to subjects such as the relationship among OLE, ActiveX, and COM; sharing files among objects with Structured Storage; using monikers to identify objects; and far more. This book is for every professional, whether you work in C++, Java™, Visual Basic®, Visual Basic Script, or other environments. And it's equally useful for managers. In short, UNDERSTANDING ACTIVEX AND OLE is the efficient way to quickly get up to speed on a fundamental business technology.

Microsoft®Press

Blueprint for excellence.

This classic from Steve McConnell is a practical guide to the art and science of constructing software. Examples are provided in C, Pascal, Basic, Fortran, and Ada, but the focus is on successful programming techniques. CODE COMPLETE provides a larger perspective on the role of construction in the software development process that will inform and stimulate your thinking about your own projects—enabling you to take strategic action rather than fight the same battles again and again.

CODE COMPLETE

A Practical Handbook of Software Construction

STEVE McCONNELL

U.S.A.	**$35.00**
U.K.	£29.95
Canada	$44.95
ISBN 1-55615-484-4	

Winner—
Software Development
Jolt Excellence
Award, 1994!

Get all of the *Best Practices* books.

Rapid Development
Steve McConnell
U.S.A.   **$35.00** ($46.95 Canada; £32.49 U.K.)
ISBN 1-55615-900-5

"Very few books I have encountered in the last few years have given me as much pleasure to read as this one."
—**Ray Duncan**

Writing Solid Code
Steve Maguire
U.S.A.   **$24.95** ($32.95 Canada; £21.95 U.K.)
ISBN 1-55615-551-4

"Every working programmer should own this book."
—**IEEE Spectrum**

Debugging the Development Process
Steve Maguire
U.S.A.   **$24.95** ($32.95 Canada; £21.95 U.K.)
ISBN 1-55615-650-2

"A milestone in the game of hitting milestones."
—**ACM Computing Reviews**

Dynamics of Software Development
Jim McCarthy
U.S.A.   **$24.95** ($33.95 Canada; £22.99 U.K.)
ISBN 1-55615-823-8

"I recommend it without reservation to every developer."
—Jesse Berst, editorial director, **Windows Watcher Newsletter**

he definitive book on software construction. This is a book that belongs on every ftware developer's bookshelf."

—Warren Keuffel,
Software Development

cannot adequately express how good this book really is...a work of brilliance."
—Jeff Duntemann,
PC Techniques

you are or aspire to be a professional programmer, this may be the wisest $35 estment you'll ever make."

—IEEE Micro

crosoft Press® products are available worldwide wherever quality nputer books are sold. For more information, contact your book or nputer retailer, software reseller, or local Microsoft Sales Office, or visit Web site at mspress.microsoft.com. To locate your nearest source for crosoft Press products, or to order directly, call 1-800-MSPRESS in the . (in Canada, call 1-800-268-2222).

ces and availability dates are subject to change.

Build
great programs
for 32-bit Windows® platforms with
Visual C++®!

Inside Visual C++
Fourth Edition
David Kruglinski

Covers:
- MFC 4.0
- 32-bit programming in Windows
- OLE, ODBC, and ActiveX topics
- Components Gallery
- Visual C++ programming for the Internet
- Other advanced tools and techniques

Microsoft Press

Building on the solid achievements of three previous editions, INSIDE VISUAL C++, Fourth Edition, presents detailed and comprehensive coverage of Visual C++ and the intricacies of 32-bit programming in Windows. This book is loaded with inside information and real-world examples to help you fully exploit the capabilities of Microsoft's powerful and complex development tool.

U.S.A.	$49.99
U.K.	£46.99 [V.A.T. included]
Canada	$66.99
ISBN 1-57231-565-2	

Microsoft®Press

Register Today!

Return this
Active Visual J++
registration card for
a Microsoft Press® catalog

U.S. and Canada addresses only. Fill in information below and mail postage-free. Please mail only the bottom half of this page.

1-57231-609-8A   *ACTIVE VISUAL J++*   *Owner Registration Card*

_____

NAME

_____

INSTITUTION OR COMPANY NAME

_____

ADDRESS

_____

CITY   STATE   ZIP

Microsoft®Press
Quality Computer Books

For a free catalog of
Microsoft Press® products, call
1-800-MSPRESS

MICROSOFT PRESS REGISTRATION
ACTIVE VISUAL J++
PO BOX 3019
BOTHELL   WA   98041-9946